WONDERS
of the
WORLD

MASTERPIECES OF ARCHITECTURE FROM 4000 BC TO THE PRESENT

Edited by
ALESSANDRA CAPODIFERRO

BARNES & NOBLE BOOKS
NEW YORK

CONTENTS

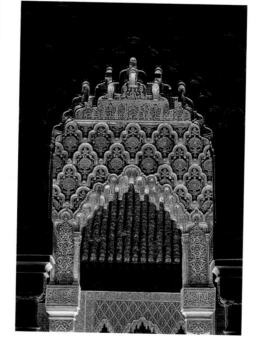

EDITED BY
Alessandra Capodiferro

TEXTS
Flaminia Bartolini
Maria Eloisa Carrozza
Beatrix Herling
Guglielmo Novelli
Miriam Taviani
Maria Laura Vergelli

PROJECT EDITOR
Valeria Manferto De Fabianis

COLLABORATING EDITORS
Maria Valeria Urbani Grecchi
Giada Francia
Enrico Lavagno
Alberto Bertolazzi

GRAPHIC DESIGN
Paola Piacco

© 2004 White Star S.r.l.

This edition published by
Barnes & Noble, Inc.,
by arrangement
with White Star S.r.l.
2004 Barnes & Noble Books

M10987654321
ISBN 0-7607-5793-3

Translation
Timothy Stroud

PREFACE

For anyone wishing to take a journey through time and space visiting architectural wonders there are many possible itineraries. Megalithic constructions, traces of the most ancient historical ages, medieval masterpieces, images of the modern world and contemporary icons all preserve and pass on a universal intellectual and creative vision.

'I have gazed on the walls of impregnable Babylon, along which chariots may race, and on the Zeus by the banks of the Alphaeus. I have seen the Hanging Gardens and the Colossus of Helios, the great man-made mountains of the lofty pyramids, and the gigantic tomb of Mausolos. But when I saw the sacred house of Artemis that towers to the clouds, the others were placed in the shade, for the sun himself has never looked upon its equal outside Olympus' (*The Palatine Anthology*, IX, 58).

Celebrated in the epigram attributed to Antipater of Sidon, the walls and hanging gardens of Babylon, the statue of Zeus at Olympia, the Colossus of Rhodes, the pyramids of Giza, the tomb of Mausolus at Halicarnassus, and the temple of Artemis at Ephesus formed, in the 2nd century BC, the first set of Seven Wonders of the Ancient World. The more recent list, drawn up in the Middle Ages, is very similar but in it the Pharos of Alexandria replaced the Walls of Babylon.

Theamata (things worthy of being seen) and *thaumata* (marvelous things) have always attracted the enquiring mind. In the mid-5th century BC, the splendor of the city of Babylon and the grandeur of the Egyptian pyramids had strongly impressed Herodotus, who considered them surviving symbols of Oriental civilizations. His sense of amazement and deep admiration was such that he classified them as wonders, and the written Classical tradition included them among the Seven for being models of proportion, majesty and beauty.

Besides being recorded individually by Greek and Latin writers, in the Hellenistic epoch those works that roused wonder and amazed admiration began to be put in lists and summaries that were known and variously modified in the Roman and medieval eras. Studying and selecting from these earlier sources, Renaissance scholars drew up their own catalog of wonderful ancient buildings when time – 'the great sculptor' – had effected their delicate and poetic ruination.

Nothing is eternal, not even the 'Seven famous Wonders, and if human ambition should ever erect anything more marvelous in the centuries to come, one day or other they will all be razed to the ground' (Seneca, *Ad Polybium de Consolatione*, I, 1).

Of those ancient wonders only the Pyramids remain.

The compilation of catalogs that include both millennia-old constructions and contemporary buildings has continued from antiquity to the present. They include buildings and monuments, constructed in various historical and cultural contexts, whose conceptual power is such that they have acquired symbolic values.

Man exists at the center of this cognitive and organizing system, 'continually contemplating the world in which he lives and considering, in addition to the marvels of nature, the works that other men have set in the natural landscape' (P. A. Clayton and M. J. Price, *The Seven Wonders of the World*). In that landscape marked by man, the buildings that have survived from the past appear immortal; whether the models they follow have been assimilated or repudiated, they assert themselves over their modern equivalents – and the longer they last the more influential they become.

The point of departure is the character and capacity of man to intervene in his environment and – using his power of observation and his intellectual and creative faculties – to relate reality and the goal he wishes to achieve, the search for resources and the need he wishes to satisfy.

'In the long period of the Paleolithic, man adapted his life to his environment and thus spread across the globe. From the Neolithic onwards, man adapted his environment to his life, undertaking long- and very long-term projects, and beginning to transform the Earth' (L. Benevolo and B. Albrecht, *The Origins of Architecture*).

It was a fundamental transition. 'One of the most significant turning points in human history was

unquestionably the one that transformed prehistoric society to that of the fully historical era, … the original cradle … was the Near East: first in Egypt, later in Mesopotamia, as archaeological discoveries inform us. Today it is believed that evolution was polycentric and that in any case it should be studied that way, without preconceived classifications' (M. Liverani, *Uruk, the First City*).

Man produced architecture in his natural environment from the earliest days and, 'at the end of the Neolithic' the basis of coherent, complex and differentiated development began to be laid that was to determine 'the unity and plurality of man's architectural heritage' (Benevolo and Albrecht). Closely linked to man's activities, architecture arouses an infinite number of emotions through its relationship with the external space and by including us in the internal space that it generates.

Exploring the three old continents (Africa, Asia and Europe), the new continent (America) and the very new (Australasia), the route taken in this book among the architectural wonders ranges in time from prehistory to the modern day, lighting upon moments of essential importance in various cultural contexts. Images of images, the photographs bring the past to the present and endow our association of the buildings with a sense of reality.

Here we are, two thousand years on, once again renewing the theme, but this time needing to multiply tenfold the works to be included, though without any fixed number, prompted by admiration of unquestioned masterpieces and astonishment at strongly innovative and controversial architectural forms.

The buildings presented in this book are either embedded in the public awareness with connotations of the eternal, or are recent wonders that we feel will be exposed to an uncertain future. It conveys a sense that the limitations of the present should be overcome. Built for the future, the works of man are the realization of an idea and represent the aspiration to survive through the illusive power of physical symbols.

The pleasure to be had from this book lies in the impression we receive of making a journey. Not that we experience the physical or emotional sensations stimulated by a place, or sense the atmosphere that pervades it, but photographs are capable of providing an awareness of reality; we may therefore experience the pleasure of a country we already know or a place we like, perhaps catching a detail of which we were unaware, or we may enjoy the feeling of discovery of a new site, knowing that one day we will visit it.

This book is the result of several hands. In addition to the contributions of the authors, the prologues to the sections on North America, Australia and Oceania were the work of a poetic and imaginative spirit that prefers to remain anonymous. To the books I used in my studies and interests, I must add the extensive research I carried out at the American Academy in Rome, particularly in the library. The effort and commitment required have on many occasions been lightened by the pleasure I take in the subject, by the willingness of the publisher to accept the inevitable extensions required to do the job properly, by the people with whom I work in my capacity as an archaeologist, and of course by those people who are always close to me. To all of them, and most of all to Paolo, thank you.

Alessandra Capodiferro

EUROPE

An understanding of the long period during which European civilizations developed and matured can be gained from a variety of archaeological sources. The Greek and Roman past, which is a fundamental and constituent element of the intellectual formation and culture of Europe that goes beyond temporal and geographical boundaries, is part of a wider cultural horizon that includes earlier and coeval civilizations.

As architecture interacts with the natural environment, the permanence of man's constructions, whether they have survived or been worn down by time and events, provides us with a means of knowing the past and a better understanding of the present, and also helps us to plan the future.

Stonehenge on Salisbury Plain in southern England is the first setting. The Sarsen Stones, spectacular megaliths, are evidence of man's capacity to build on a grand scale and to take possession and transform a piece of land. This newfound ability was developed in the Neolithic but Stonehenge did not reach its current form until the Bronze Age when, in the second millennium BC, Europe was approaching the historical era with the development, in Greece, of the first European forms of writing.

The strides taken by the Greeks conditioned the development of Western architecture for more than two thousand years. Characteristics of Greek architecture were its careful insertion in the natural environment, symbolism, representational power, visual delicacy and construction techniques. These were developed during a unique process of intellectual creation deeply rooted in the development of the various historical epochs of ancient Greece.

Naturally, the temple was the most important type of building. The tiny cella inside, which was closed and reserved for the statue of the god being worshipped, has led to its definition as a 'typical example of non-architecture,' as the italian critic Bruno Zevi stated, as the emphasis was placed on the quality of the sculpture. On the other hand, the careful study of its dimensions, appreciation of its details as being more than mere differentiation of style, and the recognizability of its function set the Greek temple

in a meaningful spatial relationship with its physical setting. Man relates to his environment through a natural order and interprets the 'character' of the individual places where he decides to build.

In Roman architecture the multiplicity and innovation of types of building, combined with new construction techniques that enabled large walls, arches and vaults to be built resulted in making the interior of a building the most important feature of structures. The decision to build on a monumental scale, the integration of buildings in the urban context and the endowment of a city with monuments can be taken as indicators of the interest in outdoor space; this the Romans dominated by laying down a network of roads and building large public works. And construction came to include social themes in which buildings were erected for functional reasons and the public good, where the people could live and interact.

The spread of Christianity strengthened by the freedom of worship granted by the Edict of Milan in AD 313 made churches the main place for communities to meet, and for centuries these buildings were the most important form of construction in European architecture.

Reflecting less the religious dimension of Roman temples than the public dimension, early Christian basilicas were the place where worshipers gathered and prayed. The spiritual aspect was incorporated in these buildings through the treatment of surfaces and natural light to produce an effect in which the interior seemed 'dematerialized.' The original plan of the basilica was longitudinal and directional, but this came to be varied with the circular plan of Byzantine and paleo-Christian basilicas in which space was dilated, making movement within the building more dynamic and varied. Byzantine architecture evolved towards spatial unification, crystallizing in circular spaces and the dome, and its influence echoed throughout the East.

Heralded in part in smaller buildings, Romanesque architecture was strongly innovative. It produced complex churches, monasteries and castles in which the concatenation of structural elements determined and proportioned the size, distribution and volume of the construction.

The vertical dimension was emphasized by the widespread inclusion of a tower as a symbol of protection and transcendence, and could be either integral to or independent of the main building. Even though it differed from country to country, and evolved in local schools of thought, the architecture of the Romanesque period was common to all European culture.

Its paths of development were taken to their logical end by Gothic architecture. From the twelfth to fifteenth centuries in France, England and Germany, architectural buildings were strengthened by buttresses and rampant arches, lightened by the thrust created by pointed arches, defined by dynamic transversal and upward lines, and tapered as they reached up to the sky in an attempt to establish a spatial continuity between the interior and exterior. The two contrasting directions – longitudinal and vertical – were measured in terms of width (a nave with either two or four aisles) and the overall dimensions were related to the human scale. A 'mirror of the world,' through their decorations and ornamentation, Gothic cathedrals illustrated the stories of the Bible and the Gospels for the benefit of the congregation.

Architectural historians have now blurred over the presumed breach between the Gothic and Renaissance, yet it has been accepted that the Renaissance building represented a radical renewal in the relationship between man and building, and laid the foundation for the modern premise that man is the owner of his architectural space. Reduction of this space to a single unit, like a round space, facilitates its control, whereas completeness of a design ensures that nothing can be removed, added or modified without detracting from its quality.

In the fifteenth century the idea of absolute and canonical beauty began to gain ground, and the following century this concept was used as the basis for Classicist culture; the result was the increasing relevance in both religious and non-religious architecture of symmetry, plasticity, and eurhythmic proportion.

The notion of divine perfection being reflected in the natural and human spheres fostered the perception of a harmonious cosmic order in Renaissance man, which was also transferred into architectural works. Initiating the crisis on the intellectual and moral order on the centrality of man in the universe, architecture moved towards an 'emotional' involvement of man in its spaces that was to culminate in the extremes of the Baroque.

Europe's great Baroque period came to an end around the mid-eighteenth century when, turning against the old, established order, the revolutionary surge, the shift in emphasis from the grand or religious to social themes in construction (primarily residential or work-related), the advent of the Industrial Revolution, the arbitrary and formal return to architectonic styles, and the eclecticism of the various architectural revivals eventually produced modern architecture.

All the possibilities tested in architecture over the centuries can now be made use of as 'existential' forms: free to move in space, modern man is able to create his own place wherever he wishes to live.

As one means of expression of European cultural development, the importance of architecture has been summed up by Christian Norberg-Schulz as follows: 'Architecture is a tangible phenomenon.

It consists of landscapes and settlements, buildings and developments, it is therefore a living reality. Since remote times architecture has helped man give meaning to his existence.

Through architecture he has created a balance in space and time. Therefore architecture deals with concepts that lie beyond practical necessity and economics. It deals with existential meanings, and these are derived from natural, human and spiritual phenomena. Architecture translates them into spatial forms.... Architecture must be understood in terms of meaningful forms.

The history of architecture is the history of meaningful forms.' (*Meaning in Western Architecture*, 1974).

Alessandra Capodiferro

17 left Built by Pericles, the Parthenon was begun in 447 BC under the direction of Phidias, who was also responsible for the decorative work.

17 center Dating to the thirteenth century, the Duomo in Siena is one of the most luminous examples of Italian Gothic architecture.

17 right The Pompidou Center occupies more than 1 million square feet in the Beaubourg area, in Paris.

Stonehenge
SALISBURY,
GREAT BRITAIN

by Miriam Taviani

The megalithic remains known as Stonehenge on Salisbury Plain are the best known and most dramatic in Europe. However, despite their size and extent, they are no more than a small part of the original complex. The gigantic cromlech was only the central ring of a series built in different phases and with different functions. (The word 'cromlech' means 'a circle of menhirs'; both terms, and also 'dolmen' are derived from the Breton language of northwest of France, and have entered common usage.)

At the end of the 3rd millennium BC, the Stonehenge area was bounded by only an earthwork and dike approximately 300 feet in diameter; inside were fifty or so pits, used presumably for burial purposes following the ritual of cremation.

In the late-3rd and early-2nd millennia BC, a megalithic structure was erected composed of two concentric rings of menhirs made from a type of bluish volcanic rock that came from a zone 190 or so miles away. The menhirs were transported to the site specifically for use in the ring. However, only a small section remains, and it is probable that the structure was never completed.

At the start of the 2nd millennium BC, a circle of thirty or so menhirs connected by stone architraves was erected inside the pre-existing cromlechs. Within this circle a further five triliths were erected in a horseshoe; at the center was a flat block called the 'Altar Stone.' In this last building phase the sandstone blocks used were local in origin or taken from earlier cromlechs. The earthworks and dike had an access avenue running through them along which stand the Heel Stone and the Slaughter Stone.

The eternal appeal of Stonehenge is linked to the mystery of the construction techniques used – it is inexplicable how blocks weighing over 50 tons were transported so far or raised to such a height – and the purpose of the site. The direction the stones face seems to suggest an astronomical function as part of a religious ceremony. Certainly, when the sun rises over the Heel Stone on the day of the summer solstice, Stonehenge exerts an overwhelming primitive fascination.

The Parthenon
ATHENS, GREECE

by Flaminia Bartolini

The Parthenon, the most famous monument on the Acropolis of Athens, is dedicated to Athena Parthénos. The glory of Athenian supremacy, the myth of Athena, democracy and the civilizing of the barbarians are symbolized in its decorations. Construction of the temple was begun on the orders of Pericles in 447 BC and ended in 432. The architects in charge were Ictinus and Callicrates, and the sculptor Phidias supervised the architectural and decorative work. The structure is an enormous Doric temple built entirely from Pentelic marble. It has 8 columns on its short sides and 17 on the long ones. Inside the colonnade lay the cella, divided into the two sections of the *naos* (the holy of holies) and the *opisthodomos* (the portico behind the *naos*). The *naos* once held the gold and ivory statue of Athena by Phidias, of which only small copies exist today. The statue stood in an aisle formed by two rows of 9 columns on the long sides and 3 columns along the back wall. The *opisthodomos* was divided into two by a double row of 2 columns the same size as those on the temple façade, whereas the columns in the *naos* were smaller. Both rooms were preceded by a 6-column portico with a decorated wooden ceiling.

The temple decoration was composed of metopes on the architrave, sculptures on the pediment, and a frieze on the cella walls. The metopes on the west side of the temple depict an amazonomachy (assaults against the Amazons) and on the south side a centauromachy (fighting between Lapiths and Centaurs). On the east side is a gigantomachy (a battle between gods and giants), and to the north, the war between the Greeks and Trojans. By representing themselves in the mythical battles of the gods, the Greeks were expressing the awareness that they had begun a new era. The full-relief sculptures in the pediment on the west side of the Parthenon depict the contest between Poseidon and Athena; those on the east side, the birth of Athena from the head of Zeus. The famous frieze by Phidias runs along the four outer sides of the cella wall, and shows the long ritual procession that ends in the presence of the gods on the east side. Interpretations of the frieze by art historians disagree: it might represent the first Panathenaic procession, or the procession marking the inauguration of the temple.

20 A view at sunset accentuates the evocative power of the Parthenon – the most famous monument on the Acropolis in Athens and, more generally, from ancient Greece.

21 top The Parthenon has retained its original grandeur. It was a large, octastyle, peripteral Doric temple 230 feet long and 100 wide that encapsulated harmony according to the canons of Classical aesthetics.

21 center The west side of the Parthenon still has part of Phidias' sculptural decoration. The original pediment represented the contest between Poseidon and Athena for the possession of Attica.

21 bottom The friezes that embellished the east pediment of the Parthenon have been almost entirely lost. They depicted the birth of Athena from Zeus' head in the presence of a group of gods.

The Parthenon was first damaged in 295 BC when Demetrius Poliorcetes besieged the Acropolis. In the 6th century AD the temple was transformed into a Christian church, and the decorations on the east side sacrificed to build an apse and a bell-tower. When the church was turned into a mosque in 1460, following the Turkish conquest of Greece, the bell-tower was turned into a minaret. During the Greek war of independence from the Turks, the citadel was turned into a small fortress, then into a munitions store. In 1687 the building underwent two days of bombardment from Venetian mortars, which knocked down 14 columns of the peristyle, the walls of the cella and many of the metopes and parts of the frieze on the north and south sides. Between 1802 and 1804 thirty-three ships carried many of the statues and slabs of the frieze to London; authorization to do so, conceded by the Turkish government to Lord Elgin, opened an argument on the lawful ownership of the marbles that has continued to this day. In 1834 the ancient monuments on the Acropolis were freed of the modern buildings and structures that surrounded them, and, with restoration work in 1930, the fallen columns were re-erected.

22 top Of those marbles that have survived to the present day in good condition is this personification of a river in Attica – the Ilissos or Cephissos – which adorned the west pediment.

22 bottom The quadriga of the moon – to which this horse's head belonged – accompanied the birth of Athena on the east pediment.

22-23 top This graphical reconstruction shows the west pediment of the Parthenon. The upper drawing shows gods and characters symbolic of Attica; the Doric frieze has fourteen metopes illustrating an amazonomachy.

22-23 center The east pediment of the Parthenon was decorated with the birth of Athena. The fourteen metopes on the Doric frieze centered on the theme of a gigantomachy.

23 bottom This splendid example of Phidias' sculptural aesthetic includes the goddesses Hestia, Dion and Aphrodite and decorated the east pediment.

The Pantheon
ROME, ITALY

by Flaminia Bartolini

24 top *The facade of the Pantheon has a deep pronaos and a colonnade crowned by a pediment.*

24 bottom *The basic cylinder of the cella, visible in the photograph, culminates in a ringed dome.*

24-25 *The surfaces inside the Pantheon create plays of light and shade in the curves and rectangular and circular niches. Also contributing to the effect are the concentric rings of caissons that circle the oculus, through which the light enters the building.*

The Pantheon was constructed during the reign of Hadrian, and at that time, on the frieze of the architrave, an inscription was attached that had originally belonged to the temple built by Marcus Vipsanius Agrippa in 27-25 BC. Agrippa was a leading figure in the urban and architectural renewal of Rome under Augustus, as well as being responsible for the design and realization of the monumental transformation of the central Campus Martius. A second inscription beneath the first records the restoration work carried out on the Pantheon at the order of Emperor Septimius Severus and his son Caracalla in AD 202.

The 'Pantheon' (with the prefix 'so-called') is the name the historian Cassius Dio passed down to us. He explained it as meaning literally dedicated 'to all the gods' or, he also conjectured, as deriving from the similarity of the constructed vault to the heavenly vault. It is possible, though, that Agrippa's building was dedicated to Mars and that 'Pantheon' was simply the name commonly in use and conserved by Hadrian. This emperor turned the building into an imperial hall in which he could hold audiences with the senators.

The earliest temple was rectangular, faced south, and was built of travertine. Restored by Domitian after the fire of AD 80, it was completely rebuilt following destruction in a second fire during Trajan's reign. Hadrian's reconstruction in AD 125 radically transformed the earlier building: the façade was turned through 180° to face north, and the rotunda was built in the empty space that lay in front of the first temple.

The current version – made distinctive by its embedded colonnaded portico that faces the piazza, and the high, isolated and visible drum over which the dome rises – is

completely different from the Pantheon of Hadrian's time. The round body used to be surrounded by other buildings, and the imposing façade raised on steps was preceded by a long piazza with porticoes on three sides. The famous rotunda was not visible from the outside as it was hidden by arcades, and was better appreciated from the interior. The building was a single large circular space 143 feet in diameter, topped by a hemisphere.

The outer row of columns in the portico is formed by eight monoliths of gray granite, set on bases of white marble and topped with Corinthian capitals. The columns on the inner rows are cut from pink granite and form three aisles: the central aisle that leads to the doors of the Pantheon is wider than the two lateral ones, where large niches once held statues of Augustus and Agrippa. This huge porch is connected to the rotunda by a massive brick avant-corps lined with marble. The bronze door is ancient

but has been extensively restored; it may not be the original one.

To discharge the loads, the wall of the rotunda (71 feet 3 inches high and 20 feet 4 inches thick) is built with particular architectural features and made from increasingly lighter materials as it rises, until arriving at small, volcanic stones around the oculus. An arrangement of massive arches supports the structure, strengthened by radial buttresses. These distribute the weight onto eight massive but partially hollow piers. Inside, these feature eight large niches (the exedras and the entrance) in the masonry. The semi-circular or rectangular exedras, which alternate with eight kiosks on pillars, each contain three niches, and stand behind two grooved, monolithic blue or ancient yellow Corinthian columns.

Most of the floor is original; it is made of multicolored marbles and stones arranged in diagonal rows of squares and circles inscribed within squares. The perfectly hemispherical dome is made from a single section 142 feet in diameter: it is the largest ever to have been built using masonry. The inner face of the dome is divided into five orders of tapering, concentric caissons (28 per row) that culminate in a smooth band. The oculus has a diameter of 29 feet 3 inches. The outer face of the dome is decorated by seven rings of steps but only the highest part is visible. The proportions of the building are exemplary: the cylinder and the dome have the same diameter, in keeping with Archimedes' symmetry.

The perfect preservation of the Pantheon has survived several lootings, modifications and restorations, and is due in part to the Byzantine Emperor Phocas making a gift of the building to Pope Boniface VIII in AD 608, who had it transformed into a church with the name Santa Maria ad Martyres.

26-27 and 27 center The underground rooms of the Amphitheater were completely excavated in 1938–39. Three concentric ring corridors enclose three more symmetrical corridors parallel to the central passage which, extending outward, led to the Ludus Magnus (gladiators' barracks).

26 bottom Seen from the Palatine, the Colosseum (or Flavian Amphiteater) emerges between the gray granite columns of the double colonnade that encircled the Temple of Venus and Roma.

27 top In the valley that lies between the Palatine, Esquiline and Celian hills, Colosseum stands on the site first occupied by a vast man-made lake, the Stagnum Neronis.

27 bottom In the axonometric reconstruction of the interior of the Colosseum we see the underground level and the four external orders that corresponded in the cavea to the five sectors of seats.

28-29 Construction of the Colosseum was completed in AD 80 but it was only in the 8th century that the building was called the Colosseum. This name was probably derived from the presence in the area of a gigantic statue of Emperor Nero that was known as Colossus.

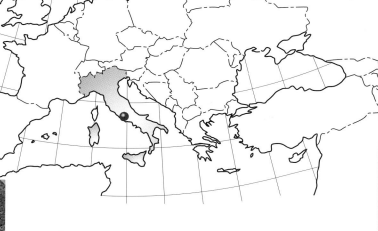

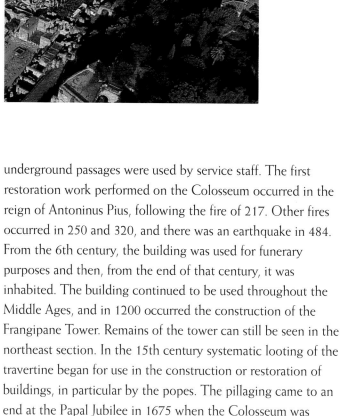

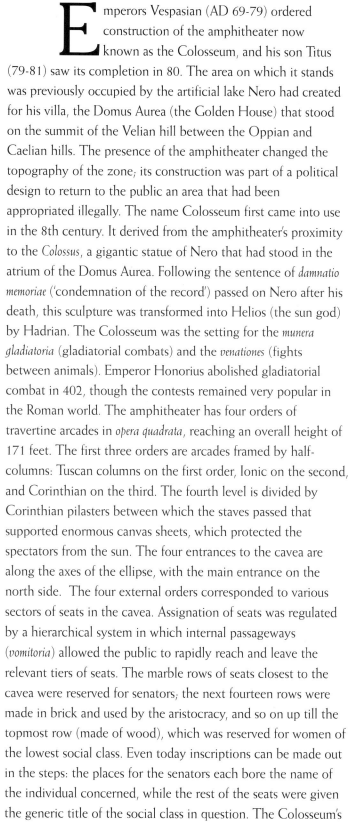

The Colosseum
ROME, ITALY

by Flaminia Bartolini

Emperors Vespasian (AD 69-79) ordered construction of the amphitheater now known as the Colosseum, and his son Titus (79-81) saw its completion in 80. The area on which it stands was previously occupied by the artificial lake Nero had created for his villa, the Domus Aurea (the Golden House) that stood on the summit of the Velian hill between the Oppian and Caelian hills. The presence of the amphitheater changed the topography of the zone; its construction was part of a political design to return to the public an area that had been appropriated illegally. The name Colosseum first came into use in the 8th century. It derived from the amphitheater's proximity to the *Colossus*, a gigantic statue of Nero that had stood in the atrium of the Domus Aurea. Following the sentence of *damnatio memoriae* ('condemnation of the record') passed on Nero after his death, this sculpture was transformed into Helios (the sun god) by Hadrian. The Colosseum was the setting for the *munera gladiatoria* (gladiatorial combats) and the *venationes* (fights between animals). Emperor Honorius abolished gladiatorial combat in 402, though the contests remained very popular in the Roman world. The amphitheater has four orders of travertine arcades in *opera quadrata*, reaching an overall height of 171 feet. The first three orders are arcades framed by half-columns: Tuscan columns on the first order, Ionic on the second, and Corinthian on the third. The fourth level is divided by Corinthian pilasters between which the staves passed that supported enormous canvas sheets, which protected the spectators from the sun. The four entrances to the cavea are along the axes of the ellipse, with the main entrance on the north side. The four external orders corresponded to various sectors of seats in the cavea. Assignation of seats was regulated by a hierarchical system in which internal passageways (*vomitoria*) allowed the public to rapidly reach and leave the relevant tiers of seats. The marble rows of seats closest to the cavea were reserved for senators; the next fourteen rows were made in brick and used by the aristocracy, and so on up till the topmost row (made of wood), which was reserved for women of the lowest social class. Even today inscriptions can be made out in the steps: the places for the senators each bore the name of the individual concerned, while the rest of the seats were given the generic title of the social class in question. The Colosseum's underground passages were used by service staff. The first restoration work performed on the Colosseum occurred in the reign of Antoninus Pius, following the fire of 217. Other fires occurred in 250 and 320, and there was an earthquake in 484. From the 6th century, the building was used for funerary purposes and then, from the end of that century, it was inhabited. The building continued to be used throughout the Middle Ages, and in 1200 occurred the construction of the Frangipane Tower. Remains of the tower can still be seen in the northeast section. In the 15th century systematic looting of the travertine began for use in the construction or restoration of buildings, in particular by the popes. The pillaging came to an end at the Papal Jubilee in 1675 when the Colosseum was deemed a sacred place and 15 shrines were built along the Via Crucis. In 1807 the architect Robert Stern built a triangular buttress in brick to support the southeast corner of the outer wall, which showed worrying signs of yielding. Giuseppe Valadier adopted a similar plan in 1827.

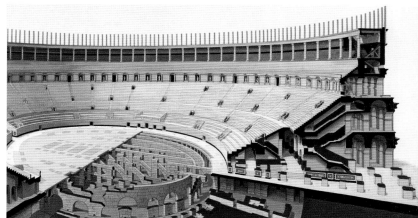

30-31 *The façade of Saint Mark's reflects the diversity of the contributions made to it over the centuries. At the top of the building there are the hemispherical domes crowned by bulb-shaped lanterns, which are a clear reference to Islamic culture. Also of Fatimid inspiration are the six tympana with inwardly curved arches that crown the upper order of the facade. The alternating spires and statues of saints are Gothic.*

30 bottom *The aerial view of the basilica gives a good idea of the proportions between the height and breadth of the domes, which follow Byzantine canons.*

St. Mark's Basilica
VENICE, ITALY

by Flaminia Bartolini

According to the *Life of Saint Mark*, the
evangelist had a vision at the moment he
disembarked at Rialto during a voyage
from Aquileia to Rome. In his vision, an archangel told him
that he would be buried in that place. In AD 828, when
two merchants brought the saint's body to Venice from
Alexandria in Egypt, the doge Giustiniano Particiaco had a
church built. The building was completed in 832 but during
the revolt against Doge Pietro Cardinaio IV in 976, the
church was seriously damaged. During reconstruction work
under Doge Domenico Contarini, the remains of the saint
were lost, but they were refound by Doge Vitale Falier in
1094.

The façade of the basilica has two orders of five arches.
On the lower order, columns of different materials alternate
with low reliefs: some of the materials were taken from
Roman monuments in Ravenna, and the rest was brought from
Constantinople following the Fourth Crusade in 1204. The
first door from the left in the basilica (St. Alipius' door) is
crowned by the building's earliest mosaic, the *Deposition of the
body of Saint Mark*, laid out in 1260.

A 14th-century lunette above the mosaic contains a low
relief of the symbols of the Four Evangelists. On the second
door there is a mosaic taken from a cartoon by Sebastiano
Ricci in which the remains of St. Mark are being worshipped.
The central and largest door is crowned by a mosaic of the
Apocalypse and the extrados above it is decorated with
columns, eight of which are in red porphyry. The Byzantine
bronze doors date to the 6th century AD, and the fourth and

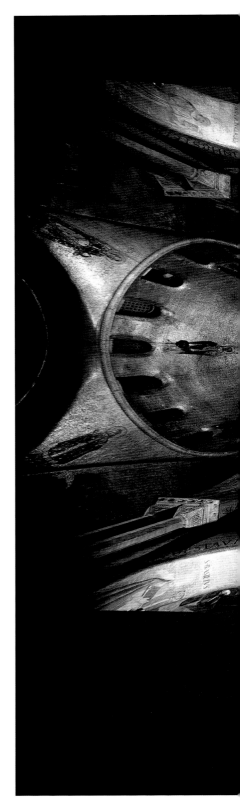

fifth doors have two mosaics by Leopoldo dal Pozzo from a cartoon by Sebastiano Ricci depicting *Venus receiving the body of the saint and the removal of the relics from Alexandria*.

The upper part of the façade has a large central glass window surrounded by mosaics; it is crowned by copies that in 1980 replaced the original famous set of four bronze horses from Constantinople. A number of Gothic sculptures complete the façade: the gold lion that symbolizes St. Mark and, in the south corner, a sculptural group known as the *Tetrarchs*; this 4th-century porphyry work represents Emperor Diocletian and his three co-rulers.

The five doors all lead into the narthex, which also runs down the long sides of the basilica. Crowned by six small domes, it has columns from the original church interspersed with marbles and mosaics that illustrate the Old Testament. Five large roof domes stand above the nave and aisles of the basilica and their intersection.

The most outstanding feature of all the decoration inside basilica is the mosaics in the apses and domes. These magnificent mosaic cycles transform the individual's perception of the interior, dazzling the observer with their glinting gold grounds. The earliest are those in the largest apse and they are probably the only ones to date from the dogate of Domenico Contarini; the most recent (first half of the 13th century) are those in the *Ascension* in the central cupola, but the style of all of them is indebted to the Orient, as Venice was the most dynamic center of Byzantine culture in the West.

The richness of the materials, the splendor of the works of art, and the abundance of the decoration together symbolize the power of the Republic of Venice and the refined culture of the aristocracy that ruled it.

32 top The high altar can be seen at the back of the nave. According to Byzantine imperial ceremony, the private entrance and throne of the Doge were in the right transept, next to the Ducal Palace.

32 center The atrium is seen here from the south. The narthex is crowned by several domes completely lined with mosaics. The stories illustrated are taken from the Old Testament.

32 bottom The dome with the stories from the Book of Genesis is in the basilica's atrium. The scenes narrated there are inspired by a late-ancient codex believed at the time to have been coeval with the Apostles.

32-33 The mosaics in the five domes are complex. Generally speaking, the three domes over the nave represent divine or Christological apotheoses, the Pentecost, the Ascension and the apparition of the Messiah, and are accompanied by evangelical episodes in the large arches. The

dome in the north transept is dedicated to St. John and the arches to the life of the Virgin, and the dome in the south transept has figures of saints while the arch has scenes from the life of St. Mark.

33 bottom The dome of the Pentecost is seen here from the left aisle. The interior is lined with mosaics on a gold ground. The iconography of the Twelve Apostles seated while receiving a flicker of flame has close stylistic parallels with Byzantine manuscripts from the first half of the 12th century.

34 The plan of St. Mark's basilica is taken here from a plate by Antonio Visentini. It shows the reconstruction of the mosaics and polychrome marble inlays that cover the entire floor.

34-35 The presbytery, where the remains of St. Mark are held, is divided from the nave by two ambons with fine polychrome marbles and the marble iconostasis that stands on a row of statues.

35 bottom left Light enters through the rose window in the south transept and refracts on the gilding of the mosaic tiles to create intense reflections and glow. This surreal atmosphere was probably designed to encourage prayer.

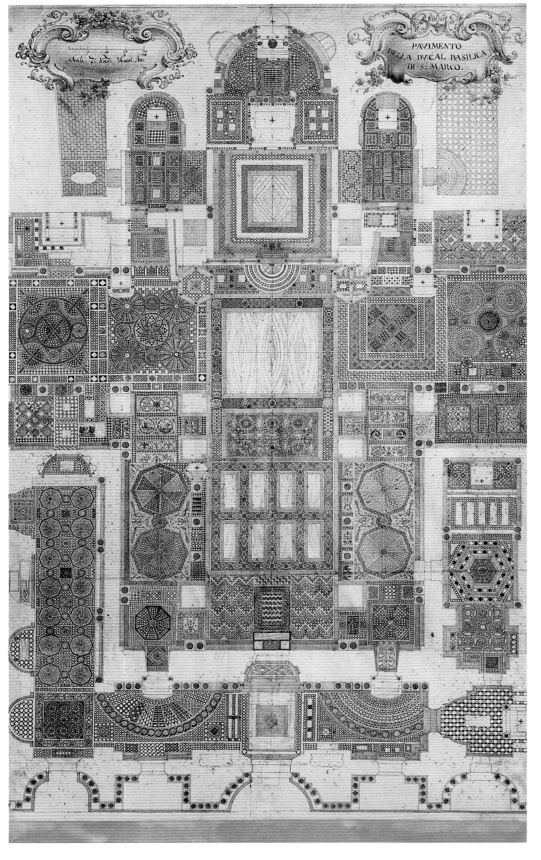

St. Mark's Basilica

35 bottom right The Baptistery stands to the south of the nave. The font at the center was carved by Jacopo Sansovino in 1545 and round it, against the walls, there are tombs of several doges. The walls and vault are completely covered by 14th-century mosaics, and the floors is lined with elegant geometric patterns made from polychrome marble inlays.

36 The positions of the buildings in the Piazza dei Miracoli reflect medieval beliefs. They represent a sort of symbolic route that takes man toward the community of the Church, and then, to Paradise.

37 The inclination of the Leaning Tower is brought out strongly when seen with the right transept of the cathedral. The lean is caused by sinking of the water table beneath.

The Leaning Tower

PISA, ITALY

by Flaminia Bartolini

In 1173 Bonanno Pisano began construction of the Tower of Pisa, one of the architectural masterpieces in the Piazza dei Miracoli, along with the Duomo, Baptistery and Camposanto. However, work was suspended in 1178 because the tower, built on alluvial soil, had begun to show its earliest sign of inclination. The first three levels built by Bonanno leaned 0.5 degrees to the north and the level of the inner service chamber had not been built in axis. Work restarted about a century later under Giovanni di Simone, who built a further three levels between 1272 and 1278. From the third to sixth levels, there was a change in lean, this time 0.5 degrees to the south.

Construction was further slowed by the city's political vicissitudes, which resulted in the battle of Meloria, and in the early 14th century the tower was still missing the topmost section that housed the bells. This section was completed between 1360 and 1370 by Tommaso Pisano, the third and last architect to work on the building of the Leaning Tower. The tower respects the original cylindrical design with a colonnade of six floors and bell-section, but from when the bell-tower began to be used, the lean increased considerably. Consequently, in 1838 the architect Alessandro della Gherardesca had a walkway excavated at the base to examine the foundations and stability of the columns, but this move allowed water to infiltrate the ground even more, thereby worsening the situation. Recent studies have shown that had the tower been slightly taller, it would have collapsed immediately. Last century, during excavation of the foundations, the remains of the sarcophagus of Bonanno Pisano were found. He had been buried by the city of Pisa beneath what was considered to be his monument.

38 top left The Church of the
Archangel Michael was designed
by Alvise il Nuovo in the early
years of the 16th century. In the
picture we see the bell-tower of
Ivan the Great, which was
completed in 1600.

38 top right The Great Palace in
the Kremlin was for decades the
center of political life in the USSR.
The imposing but elegant main
facade looks onto the River
Moscova, that runs through the
Russian capital.

38 bottom The Tower of the
Savior, or Spasskaia, is one of the
symbols of the Kremlin and, more
generally, of Moscow. The clock
and bells date from 1625.

38-39 Fortification of the Kremlin,
seen today in the defense towers and
the perimeter walls that entirely
ring the site, began at the start of
the 15th century.

The Kremlin
MOSCOW, RUSSIA

by Flaminia Bartolini

S ince its foundation in 1147, the Kremlin ('fortified city') has been Moscow's political and administrative center. The fortress' walls are 2,444 yards long, and during restoration work under Ivan III, 20 towers were built to replace the original ones. This task was carried out between 1486 and 1516 by Italian engineers who specialized in fortifications; the Italian crenellation is an indication of their work.

The most famous tower in the Kremlin is the Vasily Ermolin tower with its imaginative decoration; it was built in 1466 but rebuilt in 1491 by Pietro Solari. The Beklemishev Tower in the fort's south corner was designed by the Milanese architect Marco Friazin, one of Solari's fellow builders. In the years 1490-1493 Solari built a further five towers: the Borovitsky, Constantine and Helen, Frolov, Nikolosky, and Arsenal towers. In 1487, collaborating once more with Friazin, Solari began work on the Granovitaia Palata

39 *Trinity Gate Tower looks down on one of the busiest entrances in the Kremlin. The fortification works, of which this tower is an example, were mostly carried out by Italian engineers in the late-15th and early-16th centuries. The work of Italian builders has left a permanent trace in the Kremlin, mitigating the severity of the buildings with imaginative decoration typical of the Mediterranean. One of the masters of the new style was Pietro Solari from Milan, who built and rebuilt seven of the Kremlin's most famous towers.*

40 top left Ivan the Great's Bell-tower has been one of the symbols of czarist Moscow since its completion in 1600.

40 center left The Church of the Annunciation faces onto Cathedral Square. The Great Palace can be seen behind.

40 bottom left The Cathedral of the Dormition was for centuries where the Russian sovereigns were crowned, right up to Nicholas II, the last royal ruler.

40 top right The Church of the Archangel Michael was also built in the early years of the 16th century by an Italian architect, Alvise il Nuovo, who fused Renaissance elements with the traditional five-dome Russian model of building.

41 The golden domes of the Cathedral of the Annunciation shine under the clear Moscow sun. Built between 1484 and 1489, the cathedral was designed as the private chapel of the czar.

('Banqueting Palace'), where all official ceremonies were held.

In 1470, when restoration work on the cathedral was to begin, Muscovite architects were called in, but they were so inexpert that they caused one of the building's walls to collapse. Once again an Italian architect was invited to head the works, this time Aristotele Fioravanti, who arrived in Moscow in 1475. In making use of Russo-Byzantine motifs, such as a large central dome ringed by four smaller ones, Fioravanti also made important innovations: he had metal retaining hooks inserted in the vaults and stone slabs between the vault and the dome. During the same period, small churches in Muscovite tradition were built inside the Kremlin, such as the Church of the Deposition of the Body and the Cathedral of the Annunciation. The Italian period in the Kremlin came to an end with the Cathedral of the Archangel Michael, which was built between 1505 and 1508. The exterior has a series of cornices, pillars and arches reminiscent of Venetian motifs. The last works during the reign of Ivan III were the bell-tower of Ivan the Great and the Cathedral of the Archangel, both of which were completed between 1505 and 1508. The architect Bon Friazin built the bell-tower on two levels to a height of 197 feet; its extraordinary solidity is evident from the fact that it survived the fires started inside the Kremlin and the bombardment of the city by the French in 1812. In 1598, Boris Godunov had the height of the bell-tower increased by 69 feet, in preparation for which the walls at the base were strengthened with iron pillars inserted in the masonry. The most significant addition to the Kremlin in the 17th century was the Church of the Twelve Apostles, which was commissioned by the patriarch, Nikon. An integral part of the Patriarch's Palace, the church was originally dedicated to the Apostle Philip in tribute to the martyr of the same name who opposed Ivan IV and his reign of terror. The typology of the building follows the motifs of the Church of Vladimir in its intent to take the architecture of sacred sites back to its ancient purity. During the reign of Catherine the Great, the Neoclassical Senate Palace was built by Matvei Kazakov. Rectangular in shape, it has a large dome, inside which the high magistrates' court used to meet. Between 1839 and 1849 the Great Palace was constructed in an eclectic Gothic-cum-Neoclassical style; the previous building had been heavily damaged during the Napoleonic occupation. More recently, the Congress Palace, a product of the Soviet era, was finished in 1961, completely lined with marble.

42-43 The interior of the Terem
Palace reflects the original meaning
of the term terem ('private house'). It
is warm and snug, unlike the
public, overblown residences.

43 top left A monumental entrance
leads into the salon on the second
floor of the Palace of Facets. This
building is an example of the Byzantine
style of the Russia school of decoration.

43 top right Typical stoves
lined with ceramic tiles warm
Terem Palace. The one in
the picture stands in the corner
of the hall.

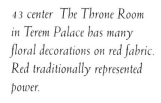

The Kremlin

43 center The Throne Room in Terem Palace has many floral decorations on red fabric. Red traditionally represented power.

43 bottom The walls and columns that separate the rooms in the majestic interior of the Cathedral of the Archangel Michael are literally lined with frescoes and icons.

44-45 The salon in the Palace of Facets was built between 1487 and 1491 by the architects Ruffo and Solari. The paintings were completed in 1668 by Simon Ushakov.

46-47 A masterpiece of French Gothic architecture, Chartres stands on the site of a sacred wood that had a miraculous spring, which was venerated by the indigenous Celts in the Romano Gallic era.

46 bottom Outside the apse, the flying buttresses have series of semi-arches among intermediate orders of small rounded arches.

47 top Differently designed bell-towers stand on either side of the facade of Notre Dame. The taller is in Flamboyant Gothic style and the other based on Romanesque.

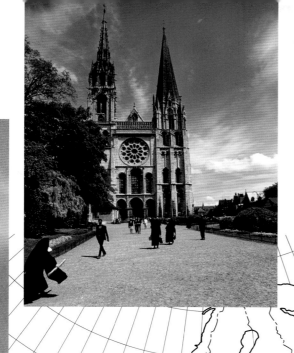

47 center Above the Kings' Gallery at the top of the façade, a trilobate shrine contains a statue of the Madonna and Child, and a smaller angel on either side.

47 bottom A series of small Gothic arches on the north side of the cathedral frames a procession of figures of very different appearance and posture.

The Cathedral of Notre Dame

CHARTRES, FRANCE

by Flaminia Bartolini

The Cathedral of Notre Dame in Chartres has been called the Acropolis of France. The original church was built in the 4th century at the request of the first bishop, Adventus, but it was destroyed by a fire. Five other churches followed on the same site, but all were lost to the flames. It was only after the fifth burned down in 1194 that Bishop Regnault de Mouçon decided a new cathedral required a new design. The sixth and final building was constructed in pure French Gothic in the brief period between 1194 and 1225, thereby maintaining a rare unity of style. The lower section of the façade (built in the last years of the 12th century) is characterized by the three-door entrance, the three-part window above it, then the 13th-century rose window, and, crowning all, the Kings' Gallery. Standing on either side of the façade are the cathedral's two differently sized bell-towers. The *clocher Neuf* on the left is from 1134, to which a flowered spire was added in 1506, and on the right the *clocher Vieux* of 1145, with a simple spire. As happened with the cathedrals in Paris and Bourges, the towers of a previous church

48 top *Figures are carved on the columns that decorate the embrasures of the three portals on the main facade. Of the 24 originals only 19 remain. Some figures wear crowns and are probably saints or benefactors of the church.*

48 center *The ornamentation of the portals is clearly symbolic: the various statues represent the 'pillars' on which the Christian doctrine and Church are founded. Above, on the continuous strip of capitals, episodes from the lives of Christ and the Virgin are shown.*

were reused by the local stonemasons. At Chartres, the east façade was also so used; the architect-restorer Viollet-le-Duc decided to remove this façade and to alter the proportions between the nave, aisles and enormous twin-apse choir. The three-door entrance, called the King's Portal, is one of the masterpieces of Romanesque art. Built between 1145 and 1455, it is embellished with elongated statue-columns that narrate the stories of Christ the Savior. To the south, another portal is preceded by a three-arch portico and step, and its decoration dates to 1220; the portal on the opposite side, the north, is symmetrical to the south one and also an addition. It was built following completion of the flying buttresses, but required their partial removal, thus putting the solidity of the transept at risk. To compensate, metal hooks were inserted to hold the portico and rest of the church together. The west façade is the most elegant and most complex. With a three-door entrance built between 1134 and 1150, the entire façade is lined with ornamentation and sculptures that make it one of the loveliest examples of early Gothic. The most spectacular feature of the exterior is the majestic flying buttresses, each formed by two superimposed arches. The lower arches are rounded and the upper ones are each perforated with a series of four small arches. Unfortunately the harmony of the series of flying buttresses was spoiled by the construction in 1416 of the Chapelle Flamboyante, which was heavily restored in 1872. The church has two aisles, a wide transept, and a deep presbytery ringed by a dual ambulatory with radial chapels. The triforium gallery runs above the arches in the nave, transept and presbytery, with large windows above it. The windows are the most valuable feature of the entire building. Completed in the 12th and 13th centuries, there are 176 in all, illustrating scenes from the Bible and the Lives of the Saints.

48 bottom *Yves, the bishop of the city from 1090 to 1116, commissioned the decoration of the triple portal of the main facade (the Royal Portal). The tympana are carved with theophanies: Christ on the Day of Judgment, the Nativity, the revelation of Christ to the shepherds, the Pentecost, and Christ's appearing before to the apostles.*

49 *The north portal of the cathedral is decorated with biblical characters known as the 'precursors' of Christ. One of these is John the Baptist, who can be recognized by his humble camel-skin tunic (as worn by desert hermits) and his characteristic attribute of the lamb he holds in his arms.*

The Cathedral of Notre Dame

50-51 The choir has a stone enclosure carved with scenes from the lives of Christ and the Virgin. A historiated wall on the south facade – between the large clock and the scene of the Visitation with Saint Elizabeth greeting the Virgin – hides the steps that led to the clock's mechanism. The quadrant of the clock remains but the mechanism has been destroyed.

50 left The Baptism of Christ is shown in one of the panels in the choir. The Baptist stands on the bank of the Jordan and pours water onto the head of Christ on the left, who is shown lower as he is standing in the waters of the river. The carving is by Nicholas Guybert (c. 1543).

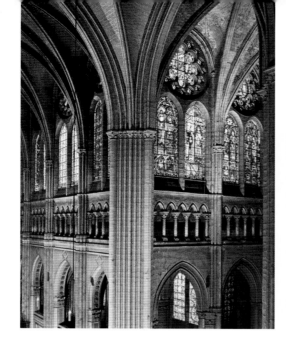

51 top left and right The interior of Notre Dame has three orders: the lowest has arches with pillars which branch out at the height of the abacus; the triforium has an order of small arches; and, at the top, the clerestory is lined with windows.

51 bottom Pillars rise right up to the ceilings of the nave and transepts. The hexapartite cross-vaults are created by the meeting points of the round arches which increase the vertical thrust of the building.

52 Known as the 'Rose of Francs,' the rose window in the north transept is dedicated to the Glorification of the Virgin and was commissioned by Louis IX and Blanche de Castile. The decorative themes are symbols of the two royal houses: the gilded lilies of France on a blue ground and the castles of Castile. In the central tondo, the Virgin is enthroned with the Child. In the five pointed windows, St. Anne holds the Virgin in the center, and biblical figures appear on either side.

53 top left, bottom left and right The Crucifixion, Visitation and Nativity of Jesus, and the Madonna enthroned with the Child are some of the scenes in the windows over the Royal Portal.

53 center left This detail from the south side of the nave shows the Expulsion from Eden. The window is dedicated to the parable of the Good Samaritan and was donated by the 'Sutores' (Shoemakers) in the 13th century.

55 The facade of the Duomo is elegantly decorated despite the rich ornamentation provided by niches, statues and symbolic motifs. It was designed by Nicola and Giovanni Pisano.

The Duomo
SIENA, ITALY

by Flaminia Bartolini

54 top The view from above reveals the harmony and grandeur of the Latin-cross plan of Siena Duomo, which was completed in 1382.

54 bottom left The Duomo's facade is made from white, red and black marble and was completed in the 14th century.

54 center and bottom right The statuary that embellishes the church has mostly been replaced by high-quality copies. As a tribute to Italian Gothic decoration, the recurring elements are symbolic animals such as horses and lions, but they also anticipated the Renaissance in the patterns and combinations of colored materials.

A magnificent example of Italian Gothic architecture, the Duomo in Siena was begun in 1229 and completed at the end of the next century. Between 1258 and 1285 the works were under the direction of the Cistercian monks of San Galgano who called Nicola and Giovanni Pisano to Siena to work on the project. Father and son were responsible for the sumptuous white, red and black marble façade that was eventually finished at the end of the 14th century. The statues that are seen today are mostly copies of the originals, and even these have been all heavily restored. The mosaic on the spire is a modern Venetian work by Mussini and Franchi.

The growing political importance of the city at the start of the 14th century led to the decision to build a magnificent, enlarged version of the cathedral, but defects were found in the construction completed between 1317 and 1321, which were pointed out by Lorenzo Maitani to the Consiglio Generale della Campana. The design – of which the current church has only the transept – was assigned to Lando di Pietro in 1339 but wars with neighboring states and the Black Death in 1348 sank the entire project with the exception of the right side.

The bell-tower, designed by Agostino and Agnolo di Ventura, was erected in 1313. It has a square plan and is lined with black and white marble fillets. The number of lights in the windows increase from one to six, and the building culminates in an octagonal spire surrounded by four small pyramids. In 1376 work was restarted on the rear façade under the direction of Giovanni di Cecco but it was only in 1382, with the raising of the vaults in the nave and reconstruction of the apse, that the cathedral could be called complete.

56-57 The dome and its twelve-sided base stand over the transept. Its five concentric rows of caissons culminate in a central eye.

56 bottom The Latin cross plan of the church has a nave, two aisles and a transept. The nave was raised in 1382 when the original design for a larger building was abandoned and the then transept was transformed into the main body. The choice of a vaulted roof decorated with a starry ceiling lightens the prevalently Romanesque forms of the nave.

57 top The Piccolomini Library at the end of the left aisle has many precious illuminated manuscripts. Built for Cardinal Francesco Tedeschini Piccolomini, it was decorated by Pinturicchio.

57 bottom The interior of the Duomo has many interesting and beautiful motifs, in particular the floor with its square inlays. Other features are the Chigi Chapel designed by Bernini in 1661 and the high altar (in the photograph) by Baldassare Peruzzi. In the choir is one of the oldest windows in Italy, designed by Duccio di Buoninsegna.

The Duomo

The peculiarity of the Duomo is the perfect fusion of Gothic architecture and the decoration, which anticipated the style of the Renaissance. The plan is a Latin cross with a wide nave and two aisles. The twin-nave transept has a hexagonal cross beneath a twelve-sided dome. The terracotta busts of the popes that look over the nave and choir were executed in the late 15th and early 16th centuries.

The superb floor with inlaid marble was laid down in various phases between 1370 and 1550 and illustrates the history of Man and his salvation. Traditionally, this masterpiece was thought to be by Duccio and to have inspired Dante to write the *Purgatorio*, but ancient documents have revealed that it was by Giovanni da Spoleto and was not begun before 1369.

The left transept contains the pulpit sculpted by Nicola Pisano. It is a masterpiece of Italian Gothic that was completed by his pupils in 1268. At the end of the left aisle there is the entrance to the Piccolomini Library. This Renaissance creation was commissioned by Cardinal Francesco Tedeschini Piccolomini to hold the books of his uncle Pope Pius II.

58 center *The Lions' Court is named for the Lion Fountain; this has a channel at each of the four compass points that all continue inside the rooms in the palace.*

58 bottom *The Lions' Court is surrounded by a set of splendidly carved portals that resembles filigree or the most delicate lace: in fact the materials used are marble, ivory and cedarwood.*

58 top *The sober and traditional palace of Charles V was built in 1526–27 inside the Alhambra. The inner courtyard is considered a masterpiece of Spanish Renaissance architecture.*

The Alhambra
GRANADA, SPAIN

by Flaminia Bartolini

The last stronghold of the Islamic dominion in Spain, Granada remained the seat of the caliphate until 1492, when it was captured by the Catholic monarchs, Ferdinand of Aragon and Isabella of Castile. The long-drawn-out Reconquest of the country began with the battle of Las Navas de Tolosa in 1212, when the Christians won back that territory of the Nasrid sultans. Cordoba was retaken in 1236 and Seville in 1248, but Granada maintained its autonomy for another 250 years as Sultan Muhammad I declared himself a vassal of the kingdom of Castile. The Alhambra, the magnificent palace of the Nasrids, was built on a hill overlooking the city of Granada and was a symbol of the refinement of Islamic art. Its name is derived from the Arabic *al-Qalat al Hamra* (the 'Red Castle') after the color of the bricks with which the first fort was built. The ancient complex (11th-12th centuries) was surrounded by walls. The new residence was built on the orders of Muhammad I and construction, which began in 1238, surprisingly was completed the following year. The first sultan to effectively take his seat in the Alhambra was Muhammad IV (1325-33), but the magnificence of the decorations is attributed to his successor Yusuf I (1333-54). It was during Yusuf's reign that decoration of the Torre de Comares and Torre de la Cautiva was carried out, as are evidenced by the epigraphic poems of Ibn al-Yayyab (1274-1349).

The Alhambra's period of greatest splendor was during the reign of Muhammad V, who governed from 1354 to 1359 and again from 1362 to 1391. He was responsible for the construction of the Lion Palace and the Myrtle Court, but no information has survived to tell us about the building of the Nasrid palace, its architects or its costs. Nor is much known

58-59 *The portico of the Lion Palace has slender columns that exalt the lightness of the entire structure, which is elegant and delicate like most Moorish architecture.*

59 bottom *The Alcazaba, seen here from the gardens of the Generalife, is one of the three sectors into which the Alhambra is divided. As is clear from its fortifications, it was part of the section used for military purposes.*

about the life that went on inside the Alhambra or about its rooms. The buildings were constructed in brick with marble used in the columns and their capitals and to line the floors. Decoration of the walls and ceilings was made using inlaid wood, ceramics, and stucco. A masterpiece of the carpenter's art is represented by the ceiling in the Hall of the Ambassadors, through which the light that illuminates the entire room is filtered. Both the interior and exterior of the palace are lined with brightly colored ceramics arranged in geometric patterns, but the most outstanding decorations are the works in stucco that represent inscriptions and plant motifs. The most beautiful examples are seen in the *muqarna* ('stalactite') ceilings in the Hall of the Two Sisters and Hall of the Abencerrajes. The Alhambra is divided into three sections: the Alcazaba, which was built purely for military purposes, the Medina and the palaces. The

rectangular court of the Comares Palace is divided north-south by a long fountain enlivened by jets of water. The portico of the Lion Palace is the most refined and famous in the Alhambra: at the center is the Lion Fountain surrounded by four long canals that run into rooms in the palace lined by 124 columns.

Built for Muhammad II outside the walls is the Palace of the General, a sort of country house surrounded by Islamic gardens. The last phase of construction was the palace built in 1527 for Charles V, who was elected Holy Roman Emperor and as such ruled Austria and Hungary. He was also king of Spain, though he never stayed in the country for long until his final retirement. The difference between the Christian and Islamic cultures is emphasized by the contrast in the classical layout and somber decoration of Charles' palace with the lightness and elegance of that of the Moors.

60-61 *One of the many collection pools lies in the garden vegetation. Pools like these, called* acequias, *were important for the regular operation of the Alhambra, which depended on the presence of water for everyday functioning.*

61 top left *The Patio de la Acequia lies in the central section of the old residence among myrtle and orange trees, flowers and fountains.*

61 top right *The Torre de Comares overlooks the north side of the Patio de los Arrayanes. The roofing and side towers were built recently.*

61 center *What was probably the harem faces the south side of the Patio de los Arrayanes. The windows are protected by grates.*

61 bottom *Like the other courts in the Alhambra, the Cypress Patio is filled with water, plants and a cool porticoed building.*

The Alhambra

62 top Sometimes a detail gives a better idea of the decorative richness of a room. This is the case with this stucco tile, in which we see stylized motifs and an almost perfect use of relief.

62 bottom In addition to its rich decoration of floral and geometric elements, the Mirador de Daraxa provides a view onto the internal gardens through the large windows on three sides of the terrace.

62-63 An explosion of decorative effects, the Sala de las dos Hermanas is a masterpiece of muqarnas architecture. Another feature of the room is the verses of the poet Ibn Zamrak, which are inscribed along the walls.

63 bottom The entire Alhambra has decorative effects carefully designed to lighten the structures while retaining their richness, and to dissolve the transition between rooms with effects of light and shadow.

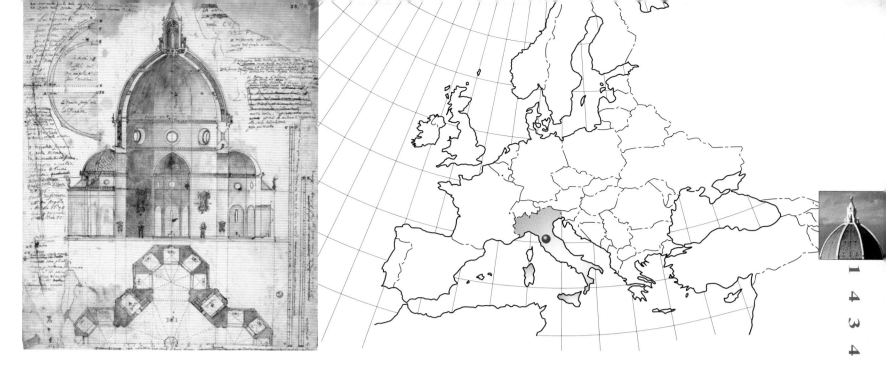

The Dome of Santa Maria del Fiore

FLORENCE, ITALY

by Flaminia Bartolini

64 Santa Maria del Fiore is a masterpiece of Italian Renaissance art. The profile of the dome and bell-tower has defined the city skyline for six centuries.

65 top This 16th-century drawing by Ludovico Cigoli reproduces the principal architectural lines of the basilica.

65 bottom The dome designed by Filippo Brunelleschi is undoubtedly the focal point of the cathedral. This aerial view shows the disproportion between the dome and the rest of the structure. What gives the complex balance vertically is Giotto's bell-tower and, in plan, the Baptistery.

The initial plans for the new cathedral in Florence, to replace the old church of Santa Reparata, were commissioned from Arnolfo di Cambio in 1296. On the death of the architect in 1302, the works were continued under the direction of Giotto. In 1412 the new church was named Santa Maria del Fiore in allusion to the lily, the emblem of the Florentine republic.

Santa Maria del Fiore (the Duomo) is the third largest church in the world after St. Peter's in Rome and St. Paul's in London. It has a Latin-cross plan with two aisles, and the interior is embellished with frescoes by Paolo Uccello, Andrea del Castagno, Giorgio Vasari, and Federico Zuccai. The bell-tower, which was begun by Giotto in 1334, was continued by Andrea Pisano, who built the first two levels, and was finished by Talenti in 1359. The Duomo's current façade, which was executed by Emilio de Fabris, is a 19th-century version of the Florentine Gothic original.

A symbol of Florence, the dome of Santa Maria del Fiore was designed by Filippo Brunelleschi to complete the cathedral's original design by Arnolfo di Cambio, which had no such element. The colossal size and internal diameter of 147 feet created many problems during construction, so a competition was announced in 1418 for the management of the construction. Brunelleschi was the winner. On the basis of his studies of the rotunda of the Pantheon in Rome, he arranged for construction to be carried out with a system of self-supporting buttresses, without any scaffolding rising from the ground level. The dome has a double shell, with the external one pointed and raised. The reinforcing structures in the space between the shells are the white ribs that are seen on the outside. The dome was completed in 1434, and the lantern that crowns the dome placed upon it two years later.

68-69 For the square in front of St. Peter's, Bernini designed a diamond-shaped space in an oval. The short, slightly convergent sides correct the horizontality of the facade built by Maderno.

68 bottom 'The two hemicycles widen to receive the Catholics with open arms and ... reconciling heretics and infidels to the Church'; so wrote Bernini of the colonnade, which he called the 'theater of the porticoes.'

69 top The colonnaded hemicycle is crowned by 140 statues, in this case Sts. Vitale and Petronilla, and by large coats of arms of Pope Alexander VI (1656–67).

69 bottom The obelisk (84 feet tall) was transported from Egypt to Rome for Caligula in AD 37 and erected in Nero's circus. Originally standing at the side of the square, in 1586 Pope Sixtus V had it moved to the center.

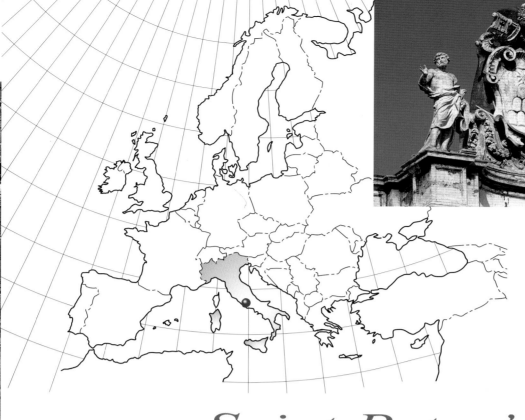

70-71 *The dome (140 feet in diameter) rests on four sets of arches on top of four pylons. Inscribed on a gold ground on the band that acts as the springer of the dome are the words with which Jesus instituted the Church, 'Tu es Petrus et super hanc petram aedificabo ecclesiam meam,' 'Thou art Peter and on this Rock I will build my Church.'*

Saint Peter's Basilica

VATICAN CITY,

ITALY

by Flaminia Bartolini

Saint Peter's Basilica in Vatican City is the largest house of worship in the Christian world. The origin of the building goes back to the tomb of the Apostle Peter, which lay in the necropolis on Mons Vaticanus: the first version of the basilica, consecrated in 326 for Emperor Constantine, stood over the grave of the saint. In 1300 Giotto and the artists in his workshop produced the mosaic *Bust of an angel* and the polyptych on the high altar. In 1452, Pope Nicholas V decided to have the church remodeled by Bernardo Rossellino, but when Nicholas died three years later the work remained substantially at a halt until the papacy of Julius II, who had many ambitious new plans. As a symbol of the power of the papacy, he wished the basilica to be rebuilt on a massive scale and with unequalled beauty. Donato Bramante, the new architect, produced a radically new design that required the demolition of all of the old church as well as the new apse built by Rossellino.

First, a small building with spiral columns was erected to protect Peter's tomb, then, on April 18, 1506, work on the new church began. The plan was a Greek cross with a huge central dome and apses at the end of each side. Each aisle was given its own additional apses in the remaining spaces, and two tall towers were built to adorn the façade. However, on Julius II's death in 1503, only the four central pillars had been built with the connecting arches that would support the future dome. Leo X invited Raphael to work in collaboration with Antonio da Sangallo and together they produced a design based on a Latin cross. Raphael was an unusual choice

as architect as he was primarily a painter, and consequently he was obliged to rely on Sangallo's experience. The design was prepared with a mountain of preliminary drawings, but actual construction was set back once more, this time by the death of Raphael in 1520 and the dramatic Sack of Rome by Emperor Charles V's troops in 1527.

In 1547 Pius III invited Michelangelo Buonarroti to oversee the works, which he did until his death in 1564. He returned to Bramante's conception of a Greek cross plan but added a more magnificent dome. On the death of the master, construction of the drum and three principal apses had almost been completed, but Michelangelo's design of the double dome had to be carried out by Giacomo della Porta.

72-73 The Vatican's Second Ecumenical Council began in 1962, having been called by John XXIII, and was concluded by Paul VI in 1965. The Council of more than 2,000 priests was held in the nave of the basilica.

72 bottom left Designed by Bernini (1624–33), the canopy over the high altar was commissioned by Pope Urban VIII. The spiral columns topped by angels support a cornice adorned with pendants.

72 bottom right The magnificent Baroque throne of St. Peter made by Bernini (1656–65) at the back of the apse contains the ancient wooden throne inside the bronze version. Above it there is a stucco sculpture of radiating glory framed by clouds and putti, and in the background a large window featuring the dove of the Holy Spirit.

73 top *The chapel of the Madonna of the Column is named for the painting that was part of the 15th-century basilica. The dome, with an oculus at the center, is divided into segments by stucco ribs. The drum is circled by alternating windows and pilasters.*

73 bottom *The ceremony held to open the Synod in 1983 was attended by clergy and worshippers. The papal altar faces the Confession, which is permanently lit by 99 lamps on the balustrade.*

Saint Peter's Basilica

From 1607, Carlo Maderno became responsible for the official completion of the basilica when he transformed the Greek cross plan into a Latin cross for Paul V.

Three bays and the entrance portico were added to the three apses designed by Michelangelo. The current façade is the result of confusion over Michelangelo's design, which was based on the tradition of a Roman temple: the overly long dimensions and absence of the two lateral towers effectively deprive the dome of an impression of majestic grandeur.

Having been substantially completed in 1612, the basilica was finally consecrated by Urban VIII in 1626. One more great architect contributed to St. Peter's: Gianlorenzo Bernini, who provided the building with its magnificent curving colonnade, completed in 1666, to which the square owes its splendor. The superb bronze canopy over the high altar was executed in 1663, taking its cue from St. Peter's tomb.

The basilica contains many of the greatest works in the history of art, including the *Pietà* by Michelangelo, the huge tomb monuments in the aisles, the tomb of Innocent III by Antonio del Pollaiolo, the funerary monuments of Urban VIII and Alexander VIII by Bernini, and the tomb of Clement XIII by Canova.

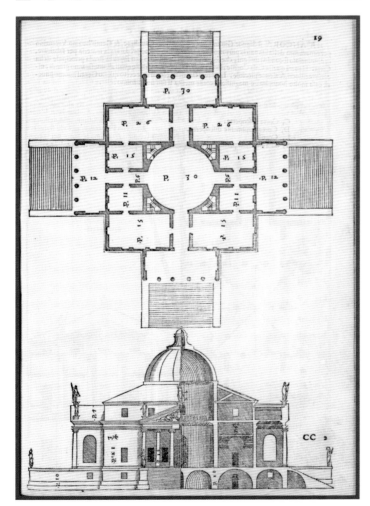

La Rotonda

VICENZA, ITALY

by Flaminia Bartolini

Villa Almerico, called 'La Rotonda', is the best known of Andrea Palladio's works.

Conceived as the country house of the papal prelate Paolo Almerico, the villa was begun in 1566 and completed three years later.

Vincenzo Scamozzi supervised the construction of the dome and the external steps, and was also responsible for the design of the annex built in 1620.

The place seems to have inspired Palladio in his design: this is the only example of a pavilion with a square base in his series of villas. Situated close to a hill, the villa is ringed on three sides by the valleys of Monte Berico, and the main entrance is on the fourth side.

The entrances are each preceded by a hexastyle pronaos topped by triangular tympani and acroters. Palladio himself likened the building to a theater, an interpretation that justified his use of steps on each side of the building.

The circular central room beneath the dome is unusual in that it does not have direct access to the secondary rooms: this motif is reminiscent of religious buildings, which in turn reflected Paolo Almerico's relationship with the Vatican.

Design of the dome drew on that of the Pantheon, including the central oculus. This was originally open (at the center of the room a drainage channel conveyed rainwater into an underground well) but Scamozzi modified the design, making the oculus smaller. Today the dome is similar to the design of the Roman theater in Verona.

The stuccoes were by Lorenzo Rubini, Ruggero Bascape and Domenico Fontana, while the frescoes were painted by Alessandro Maganza and Louis Dorigny.

74 top The sculptures in the villa (this is a male figure with a monster) are attributed to Lorenzo Rubini on account of a note written in Palladio's hand on the view of the villa published in 1570.

74 bottom This plan with an axonometric elevation of the Rotonda is taken from the second of the Four Books of Architecture written by Andrea Palladio and published in Venice in 1570.

74-75 The countryside onto which the four sides of the Rotonda face is one of the focal points on which the design was based.

75 bottom A superb example of Palladian architecture, the structural and design elements of the Rotonda form a perfect and harmonious unity. The identical pronaos on each side of the building and long flights of steps are almost surprising in their repetition.

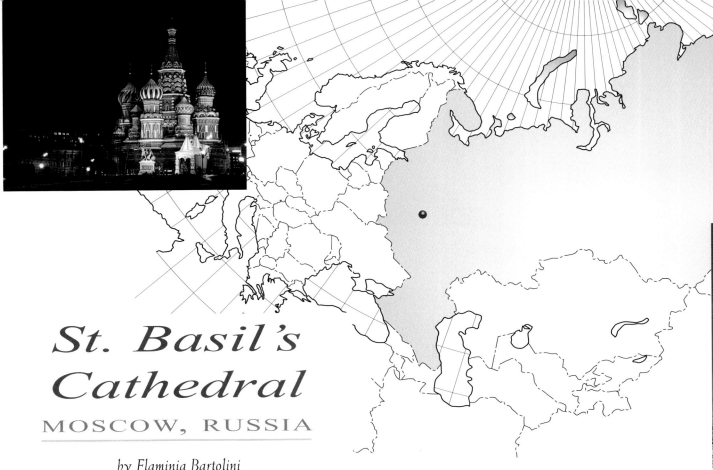

St. Basil's Cathedral

MOSCOW, RUSSIA

by Flaminia Bartolini

St. Basil's Cathedral was built in Red Square in Moscow between 1555 and 1561. Ivan IV, popularly known as Ivan the Terrible, wanted a new cathedral to be built to commemorate the defeat of the Mongols in 1552 and the conquest of their city of Kazan. The names of the cathedral's architects – Posnik and Barma – only became known in 1896, following the discovery of ancient manuscripts, but further finds have revealed that the two names belong to just one person: Posnik Yakovlev, known as Barma. Originally named the Church of the Intercession of the Virgin, it was dedicated to St. Basil after Basil the Blessed (1468-1552) was sanctified. The central chapel lies over his tomb. The cathedral was built over the site of the Church of the Holy Trinity. Ivan IV decided that it was to have eight separate chapels, one of which would lie at the center and seven would radiate out from it, in memory of the eight raids that preceded the taking of Kazan. On the architect's advice, eight chapels were built around a central one to which they were connected by a gallery. The eight are divided into four large and four small chapels and are of different heights and dimensions. Each of the smaller chapels is linked to

an event in the conquest of Kazan. The north chapel was first dedicated to Sts. Cyprian and Faustina, but in 1786, under pressure from the powerful Natalia Hrusheva, the dedication was reassigned to Sts. Adrian and Natalia. The south chapel is consecrated to Nicola Velikoretsky, the general of the Russian troops, while the west chapel is named for the Entry into Jerusalem, to which event the return of the victorious army to Russia was likened. To the south is the Chapel of the Trinity, commemorating the first church. The four other chapels lie along the diagonals: the one to the northeast is named after the saint commemorated on the day Kazan was captured, St. Grigory Armyansky, and the one to the southeast is dedicated to Alexander Svirsky, the commander who routed the Tartar army. The chapel of the Three Patriarchs of Alexandra is still named after the saints of the day Kazan surrendered. And finally, the southwest chapel dedicated to Varlaam Hutynsky is the only one whose naming is not related to the defeat of the Mongols. Two porticoes were added in the 17th century, when pyramidal towers were placed on either side of the entrances. There is a series of round arches that stand on octagonal bases. The largest chapel, the Pokrov ('Protective Veil'), is decorated with frescoes painted in 1784 and others added in the 19th century. Its height (187 feet) is greater than that of the surrounding eight domes. The gallery is decorated with 17th-century frescoes while inside one of the chapels there is a precious 16th-century icon depicting the Entry into Jerusalem. The Chapel of the Trinity has one of the oldest iconostases in Moscow. After Napoleon took Moscow in 1812, the cathedral was damaged by the French troops. Later, in 1817, the graveyard that surrounded it was removed. At the start of the 20th century, the cathedral became a target for the atheistic Bolsheviks. In 1918 the Soviet authorities killed the priest, Ioann Vostogov, and confiscated the cathedral. The bells were removed and the building closed. In 1930 Lazar Kaganovich, one of Stalin's collaborators, declared that it was necessary to demolish the church to provide greater space for military parades, but the architect Pyotr Baranovsky, who was charged with the task, refused to carry out the order and threatened to cut his throat. It was only as a result of this gesture that the cathedral was saved.

76 top St. Basil's was built for Ivan the Terrible in 1555–61 and is one of the main attractions in Red Square.

76 bottom The cathedral has nine domes, one for each chapel.

76-77 The cathedral was dedicated to Saint Basil after Basil the Blessed was sanctified. The building has a central chapel surrounded by eight smaller ones, and was ordered by Ivan to commemorate the eight attacks that were held before final victory over the Mongols was achieved at Kazan.

77 bottom The chapels that form the body of the cathedral are of different heights and sizes, and each has a different dome. The result gives the building an unreal, unconventional but surprisingly elegant appearance.

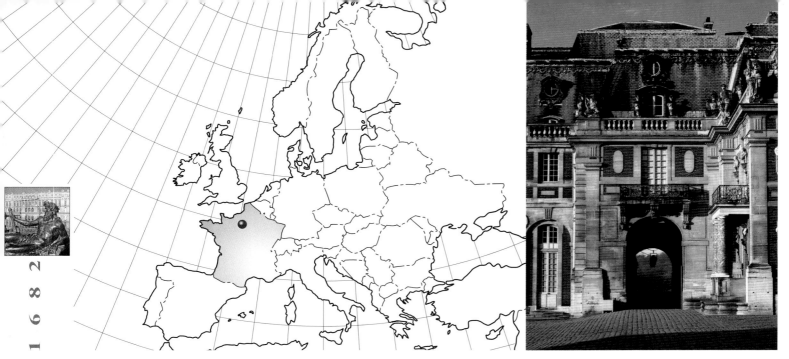

The Palace of Versailles

PARIS, FRANCE

by Miriam Taviani

The fate of what was then a modest village at the gates of Paris was the result of the passion of the future king of France, Louis XIII, for hunting. Once he had been crowned, in 1623 he purchased Versailles and charged Philibert le Roy with building a hunting lodge there. However, it was Louis XIV, the Sun King, who in 1661 began the transformation of the lodge (still called the 'Vieux Château') shortly after his marriage to the Infanta of Spain, Maria Teresa. He had it turned into a palace, or perhaps a royal citadel, where the court and government resided from 1682 until the French Revolution. Under the direction first of Louis Le Vau and later Jules Ardouin-Mansart, and with André Le Nôtre as the designer of the gardens and park, the king created what was to be the model for all the European courts until the end of the eighteenth century. The palace that Le Vau enlarged with two wings parallel to the sides of the court and a broad facade that overlooked the gardens, and which Mansart expanded

yet further in 1667 to accommodate the court with two large blocks to the north and south, was right from the start conceived as the center of the entire architectural and landscape project. Mansart designed the Grandes and Petites Écuries, which close the hemicycle of the Place d'Armes on the east side in front of the Palais, and, in the park, the Orangerie and the Grand Trianon. The latter is a small private villa belonging to the king that is used today as the residence of the President of France and for holding state receptions.

Mansart's most brilliant creation was the transformation of Le Vau's terrace, which faces the park, into the spectacular Hall of Mirrors; this was a very refined metaphor for the absolutism of the French monarchy. The palace is universally acknowledged to be the most eloquent expression of the power, magnificence and refinement of the French monarchy at its height, and the approach to it still creates a feeling of awe in the visitor. Once passed the main gate, one crosses three courtyards: the first, the Cour des Ministres, is bounded

78 top This door on the north side of the Cour de Marble leads to Versailles' gardens.

78 bottom The palace is viewed here from Avenue de Paris, which forms the continuation of the building's central axis.

78-79 The west face of the palace (the one that faces the gardens) is reflected in two Parterres d'Eau.

79 bottom The Cour de Marble is five steps higher than the Cour Royale, and was the center of the set of buildings laid out by Louis XIII.

80 *The Bassin d'Apollon by Jean-Baptiste Tuby centers on Apollo's chariot. It lies at the end of the Tapis Vert, a wide avenue that continues from the main axis, also known as the 'Axis of the Sun' as it joins the statue of Leto with that of her son Apollo.*

81 *top The Grand Dragon by the Marsy brothers stands at the center of the Bassin du Dragon, a fountain 130 feet in diameter at the end of the Allée d'Eau.*

81 *center The sun god emerges from the waters in the Bassin d'Apollon at dawn on his chariot drawn by wild horses, and begins his daily route across the sky. He is heralded by a Triton blowing a shell.*

81 *bottom The Bassin de Latone has several pools crowned by the marble group of Leto with Apollo and Diana as children. It was carved by the Marsy brothers.*

The Palace of Versailles

by the wings built by Le Vau and the equestrian statue of Louis XIV. It is the largest of the three and in 1783–84 was the setting for the first attempts at aerostatic flight by Montgolfier and Pilâtre de Rozier. Just behind this courtyard is the Cour Royale, which could only be entered by the carriages of the courtiers. Finally there is the Cour de Marbre, which marked the heart of Louis XIII's original residence.

Behind the palace, the approximately 250 acres of parkland and fountains stretch out of view. For the first time Le Nôtre tried out his ideas on 'French' gardens. Starting from the symmetrical layout characteristic of Italian gardens, he laid down new radiating axial avenues and paths interposed by pavilions, arboreal structures and unexpected clearings that stimulate the perception of space, all embellished with flights of steps, terraces, enormous pools of water and fountains that were added over the decades. Focusing on the central axis of the park only, there are two parallel pools called the Parterre d'Eau, surrounded by 24 bronze statues; the Bassin de Latone adorned by the marble sculpture of Leto, with Apollo and Diana; the Bassin d'Apollon, showing Apollo the sun god in his chariot; and the Grand Canal, a pool of water intersected by the Petit Canal to form a vast cross-shaped tank that has a perimeter of over 3 miles, and which was the setting of the palace's most magnificent court parties. The only exception to the axial nature of the gardens is the English garden in the Petit Trianon, laid out by architect Jacques-Ange Gabriel for Louis XV between 1762 and 1768. It features magnificent exotic trees, is studded with pavilions and small temples, and crossed by deliberately winding paths. Looted and smashed during the Revolution, the palace was abandoned for almost fifty years but returned to its lost dignity by another king: in 1837 Louis Philippe began restoration of the palace, turning the south wing into a museum to celebrate 'all the glories of France', and thereby laying the foundations for the modern history of the palace.

82 top The Salon de Guerre (War Room) lies between the King's Apartment and the Hall of Mirrors.

82 center (above) In the Salon de Diana (one of the six rooms that formed the King's Apartment) there is a bust of Louis XIV by Gian Lorenzo Bernini.

82 center (below) The Salon de la Paix is at the other end of the Hall of Mirrors.

82 bottom The salons of the King's Apartment (this is the Salon de Venus) are named after the deities painted on the ceilings: Abundance, Venus, Diana, Mars, Mercury and Apollo.

82-83 The Hall of Mirrors has 17 large windows that face the park and, on the other side of the gallery, 17 large mirrors. On grand occasions 3,000 lights would be reflected in the mirrors to create a scintillating effect. This was the room in which the German empire was proclaimed in 1871 and the Treaty of Versailles was signed in 1919.

84 left After his marriage to Marie-Louise of Austria, Napoleon I considered moving to Versailles to occupy the Queen's Apartment (shown). His wife would have had the floor below and his sister Pauline the Petit Trianon.

84 bottom The Opéra Royal is an oval room decorated with carved and gilded wood. It was built in less than two years by Ange-Jacques Gabriel for the marriage of Louis XVI to Marie-Antoinette of Austria.

84-85 The pictorial decoration of the Chapelle Royale by Antoine Coypel, Charles de la Fosse and Jean Jouvenet in the style of Le Brun was based on the theme of the Holy Trinity.

85 top The Grand Trianon was built by Mansart for Louis XIV for the court to relax in. At the back of the court, a peristyle with pink marble pillars and columns acts as the entrance to the park.

85 bottom Designed by Mansart and completed by his brother-in-law Robert de Cotte, the Chapelle Royale was dedicated to St. Louis. The gallery upstairs was reserved for the royal family and ladies-in-waiting, and the nave was for use by courtiers.

86-87 Lying in front of the façade of the Great Palace of Peterhof is the Great Cascade, designed by the architect Bartolomeo Francesco Rastrelli. The water flows into a semi-circular pool featuring a statue of Samson defeating a lion, and from there continues down the Maritime Canal to the Gulf of Finland.

86 bottom At the center of the Upper Park, over which the south face of the palace presides, stands the Fountain of Neptune surrounded by sea-horses, dolphins and allegories of rivers.

Peterhof

ST. PETERSBURG, RUSSIA

by Miriam Taviani

During one of his trips to western Europe, Czar Peter I, called 'the Great' because of his height, his achievements, and the extent of his building works, had been highly impressed by the palace of Versailles. After he defeated Charles XII of Sweden at the battle of Poltava in 1709, the czar who opened Russia to the Western world decided to celebrate his winning of an outlet onto the Baltic Sea by building a summer residence inspired by Versailles, but one that would be even more splendid. Thus construction of Peterhof ('Peter's house'), 18th-century Russia's most important and extraordinary palace, was begun in 1714.

Peterhof is situated 18 miles from St. Petersburg, the new capital to which the czar had transferred his court and government in 1712. The palace was designed by the German Johan Friederich Braunstein and built by the Frenchman, Jean-Baptiste Alexandre Leblond, a pupil of Le Nôtre, the man who laid out the gardens at Versailles. In 1717, Leblond also worked on the planning of the new city of St. Petersburg, under Peter the Great's supervision and with contributions from the czar himself, as is confirmed by several autograph sketches.

The French prototype was remodeled for a different environment: Peterhof stands on a strip of land over a mile long parallel to the Gulf of Finland. It is composed of the Lower Park, grounds that slope down to the sea, and the Upper Park, a rectangular garden measuring 350 x 450 yards. Between the two is the Great Palace (Bolshoi Dvorets), 335 yards long, gains architectural interest by the series of recesses and projections represented by sections of the building. The palace was originally built on two floors, but in the mid-18th century Bartolomeo Rastrelli (the architect of the Winter Palace) heightened it and gave it Baroque enhancements at Czarina Elisabeth I's request. What makes the Great Palace unique among all the great dynastic houses is the Great Cascade (Bolshoi Kaskad) on the north side of the palace. The water from the Great Cascade flows into the broad Maritime Canal, lined on

87 top The huge park at Peterhof (called 'Versailles by the Sea') features a large number of fountains, pools and pavilions.

87 bottom The facade is enclosed between the golden domes of the Royal Chapel (in the photograph) and the Eagle Pavilion.

88 top   The statue of Samson forcing open the mouth of the lion is an allegory of the victory of Peter the Great over the Swedes at the battle of Poltava, on Saint Samson's day.

88 center   The central axis of the palace is marked by the Maritime Canal on the north side and the three fountains in the Upper Park on the south side.

88 bottom   The Triton Fountain stands near the Orangery. In addition to being decorative, it is also the focal point of the walkway.

89   This pair of tritons is ringed by fountains. The statue stands at the center of the terrace that looks down onto the Great Cascade.

Peterhof

either side by fountains, and then out into the Gulf.

The Cascade features an abundance of gilded statues, vases, and water spouts shooting up to 66 feet, and the pool into which the water flows is dominated by a statue of Samson defeating a lion: an allegory of Russia and Sweden.

The water that feeds the Peterhof park's more than 170 fountains comes from the Rospin hills some 14 miles south via a specially-built series of natural and man-made basins, canals and locks.

The Upper Park is a French-style garden was laid out symmetrically and features a series of Mesheumny fountains of Neptune and Dubowy, while the Lower Park is open and more structured. Fanning out from the Great Cascade are the Maritime Canal at the center, the avenue that leads to the Hermitage Pavilion on the right, and the avenue that leads to Monplaisir on the left. The main fountains are linked by winding and straight paths: for example, between the Chessboard, Monplaisir, the Roman Fountains, Pyramid Fountain, Umbrella Fountain and Oak and Sun Fountains; and between Monplaisir, the Palace of Marly, the Fountain of Adam, and the Fountain of Eve. Other important fountains are the Triton Fountain, to the east of the Great Palace, and, near the Palace of Marly, the Fountain of the Lions and Fountain of the Golden Mountain, with its gilded bronze steps. To the east of the palace lies Alexander Park where in the early 19th century Nicholas I built a more modest private house.

Badly damaged during World War II during the 900-day siege of Leningrad, Peterhof was immediately restored where possible and rebuilt where destroyed. Today it continues to reflect a sense of the grandeur of its enlightened founder.

90-91 The Throne Room is lit
through two orders of windows and
has a relatively unadorned
decoration of gilded stuccoes and
portraits in medallions and panels.
The use of large mirrors provides
attractive effects of light and color.

91 top The main staircase,
embellished with fancy banisters,
leads to the Throne Room.

91 center (above) Windows, doors
and mirrors in the Audience Hall
are framed by composite pilasters.

91 center (below) Some rooms
contain fine china manufactured
by the Imperial Porcelain Factory.

91 bottom The Portrait Room has
368 portraits of women by Pietro
Rotari from Verona.

Esterházy Palace

FERTOD, HUNGARY

by Maria Eloisa Carrozza

92 top Esterházy courtyard, surrounded by the architecture of the castle, has a large round fountain at its center ringed by shrubs and flowerbeds.

92 center Commissioned by Prince Miklós Esterházy, in 1764 the Austrian architect, Melchior Hefele, designed the central block of the facade of the palace to overlook a French garden, but the garden no longer exists.

This sumptuous Rococo palace was built at Fertod, in the region of Györ-Sopron in western Hungary for Prince Miklós Esterházy, and for decades he lived an extravagant life there, in rivalry with the Austrian court, following the behavioral trends, magnificence, and elegance of the European royal families.

The original building was constructed in 1721 by the architect Anton Erhard Martinelli as a plain country house, but in 1764 Prince Miklós, bolstered by his experience of culture and worldly life on his Grand Tour of Europe, important posts at the court of Vienna, and even more so by his family inheritance, had the house – which he named Esterháza – rebuilt on a grand scale under his personal supervision.

Following the advice of the Italian architect Girolamo Bon, he chose a designed based on the models of Versailles and Schonbrunn. Of the many architects involved in the project, Melchior Hefele was probably responsible for the elegant wrought-iron gates and the façade that looks onto the garden, and Miklós Jacoby for the main façade, which was slightly lengthened in 1766 and given a greater amount of decoration in taste with the Rococo fashion of the age. When the works were completed in 1784, the palace was equally worthy of the description 'Hungarian Versailles' as Prince Miklós was of his own epithet 'the Magnificent,' with which he gained himself a position of prestige in his own dynasty.

The building was built in the shape of a horseshoe. The central block has three floors with eleven rows of balconied windows, and a fourth, central floor with just three windows, all of which alternate with huge pilasters. The two curved wings form a *cour d'honneur* with a fountain at the center featuring a cherub and dolphin. The outermost sections of the arms are single-story buildings featuring large arcades, vases and wrought-iron decoration. The palace lawns, French garden (no longer existent), and park

92 bottom and 93 bottom Esterházy Palace is an example of Rococo architecture strongly influenced by Italian style. The palace is U-shaped, with the two wings built to house the winter garden and the picture gallery.

92-93 Elegant wrought-iron patterns of volutes, Greek keys and plant motifs designed by Melchior Hefele adorn the stone balustrade of the main staircase to the second floor and the railings on the balconies of the residence.

Esterházy Palace

were often the setting for concerts and parties.

Inside are 126 rooms, all situated in the central section of the palace, which is the only part to have remained almost intact. Many features in the wings of the palace have been destroyed: the puppet theater, the Chinese rooms, the art gallery, the winter garden and, not least, the room in which Franz Joseph Haydn played his compositions. Haydn was the musical director employed by the Esterházy family, who were patrons of art and aware of the prestige that good music brought to the social life of the palace.

There still remain the attractive frescoes by Josef Ignaz Mildorfer, one of the many academic artists called from Vienna. He decorated the chapel, the *Sala Terrena* and the Banquet Room, where sculptures by Johann Joseph Rossler can be admired.

At the end of the 19th century, a long period of abandonment was followed with restoration by Zsismond Babics and again, more recently, with repair the damage suffered during World War II, with the result that Esterházy Palace has recovered much of its original splendor.

94 top *The second floor of Esterházy Palace is filled with a succession of reception rooms and private apartments decorated luxuriously and imaginatively. A series of passages brings out the spatiality of the building.*

94 bottom *Many of the rooms were furnished with Chinese-style wall panels. In 1773 the Esterházy princes hosted an Oriental ball in costume in one such room in honor of Maria-Theresa, queen of Hungary and Bohemia.*

94-95 *The banqueting room is an example of late Hungarian Baroque. The marble, mirror and boiserie decorations are magnificent; passages, frescoes and furnishings are lined with elegant white-and-gold stucco festoons.*

95 bottom *The polychrome statues of the Four Seasons in the corners of the banqueting room are by Johann Joseph Rossler.*

The Sagrada Familia

BARCELONA, SPAIN

by Beatrix Herling and Maria Laura Vergelli

96 top The sculptures under the porch of the facade of the Passion of the Sagrada Familia represent the last moments in Christ's life.

96 bottom and 97 The slender building has a Gothic flavor and features three densely carved portals and four bell-towers.

In 1883 the task of completing the construction of the Templo Expiatorio de la Sagrada Familia in Barcelona was assigned to the young Catalan architect Antoni Gaudì y Cornet, a representative of Catalan Modernism. Gaudì radically modified the original Neogothic design (1882) by Francisco del Villar, and was to spend 43 years of intense work creating his own highly innovative plans. The towering mass, extraordinary modeling and naturalistic plasticity, combined with an original use of color, are fused with parabolas, hyperbolas and helicoids to create unusual and brilliant solutions that produce a perfect correspondence between the building's structure, form and color.

The design is typified by the prevalence of vertical lines that rush upward toward the sky. With a nave, four aisles, a Latin cross plan and three-aisle transept, the building was uncompleted on Gaudì's death in 1926 and has not yet been finished. The three façades are named to celebrate the Nativity, Passion and Glory. Their every decorative and architectural element makes reference to the individual themes. The façade of the Nativity, which faces east toward the rising sun, expresses the idea of strength and vitality through the plastic power of its individual decorative stones. The over-abundant ornamentation, in itself a metaphor for the richness and joy of life, is based on the flora and fauna of the Mediterranean; this was an unceasing source of inspiration for the Catalan architect, whose naturalistic and symbolic architectural language was derived from his cultural roots. Turtles, snails, geese, cocks, birds and, above all, spring flowers are seen everywhere on the sinuous modern structure. The three doors symbolize Faith, Hope and Charity, the fundamental aspects of Jesus' teachings.

98-99 The central door of the facade of the Nativity culminates in a tall spire. The abundance and richness of the ornamentation symbolize the fullness of life. Behind the portal stand the four bell-towers dedicated to the apostles Matthew, Judas, Simon, and Barnabas.

99 A distinctive feature of Gaudì's style is the cladding in majolica tiles, which is also seen in Parque Güell.

100-101 *This detail is taken from the facade of the Passion; its restrained, austere decoration is in line with the symbolism of Christ's death. The faces of all the figures are sad.*

100 top *The facade of the Passion expresses the sense of loss and desolation even in its six slender, tensed flying buttresses that support a porch with square, cutting stone sculptures.*

101 center *The light passes through the perforated walls. Following the example of the great Gothic cathedrals from which Gaudí drew inspiration, light is a fundamental element in the building as a symbol of the presence of the divine.*

101 bottom *The central door is dedicated to Faith and culminates in the representation of the Coronation of the Virgin, while the door of Hope is decorated with episodes from Jesus' infancy.*

The Sagrada Familia

Unlike the façade of the Nativity, the westward-facing Passion tends to represent the feeling of irreversible loss created by death. The building is no longer soft and sinuous but square and rigid. Six stylized flying buttresses, which seem more like flesh-stripped bones than buttresses, support a structure almost bare of ornamentation that represents the misery and desolation of the death of the Son of God. The fruits seen on the façade are of autumn and winter: chestnuts, pomegranates and oranges. It is only at the top of four of the eight bell-towers that the hope of life reappears: with their flowers and crosses covered with brightly colored tiles, the tips of the spires herald the miracle of the Resurrection and the Glory.

The Glory is the theme of the third and uncompleted south-facing façade. Eight bell-towers, between 290 and 360 feet tall, crown the east and west façades, four on each. The set of twelve (a further four are yet to be built on the south side) symbolize the apostles. The tallest tower, dedicated to Jesus, is 556 feet high, and will be crowned by a shining cross and surrounded by five smaller towers dedicated to the Virgin and the Four Evangelists. The Neogothic apse, transept, crypt (in which Gaudì is buried in the chapel dedicated to the Virgin) and the external cloister are the sum total of the finished sections of the cathedral, but they are as yet isolated. As the various missing sections are concluded, the unity of the building will become apparent.

It has been written that the rich decorative program of the Templo Expiatorio de la Sagrada Familia represents faith: on the exterior the life of Jesus is narrated from birth to death, and inside the Heavenly Jerusalem is depicted.

The religious inspiration is fundamental: elements of Catholic doctrine and popular tradition, mythological references and pagan iconography are brought together in an exuberance of decoration and architectural symbolism of powerful and expressive visibility.

102-103 The Eiffel Tower was the tallest building in the world from 1889 to 1930, the year in which the Chrysler Building was completed in New York.

102 bottom The tower focused attention on iron as a new construction material. Its tapering profile dominates the flat land of Paris and can be seen from every corner of the city.

103 *The Eiffel Tower is one of the symbols of Paris. It is lined with 20,000 lights which are switched on for the first ten minutes of every hour.*

The Eiffel Tower

PARIS, FRANCE

by Guglielmo Novelli and Maria Laura Vergelli

Designed by Alexandre Gustave Eiffel for the Exposition Universelle that commemorated the centenary of the French Revolution, the Eiffel Tower has become one of the greatest attractions and the symbol of the city of Paris.

The first studies for the tower were made in 1884, but because of the many problems encountered construction only began in 1887. It was completed 26 months later. Many protests appeared in *Le Temps*, a leading newspaper of the time, against M. Eiffel's tower, even though plans called for it to be dismantled at the end of the World Fair. Voices of dissent were heard also from the cultural world, from such figures as Charles Gounod, Guy de Maupassant, Alexandre Dumas *fils*, Guillaume Bouguereau, Ernest Meissonier, Charles Garnier, as well as from many others. It is easy to imagine the astonishment and in some cases affront aroused in an era in which construction was almost exclusively in stone and brick; after all, an iron tower so light, a thousand feet high, and built in the middle of the city could not go unobserved. The purpose of the tower was to demonstrate the technical capacity, flexibility, and resistance of a material that during that period (thanks to the Industrial Revolution) was beginning its increase in popularity. To construct this 'experiment' required 6,300 tons of metal in prefabricated parts assembled on the spot.

What brought an end to the question of the dismantlement of the tower was the first radio transmissions made in January 1908 by the French army. Shown to enable a very powerful form of communication to be made, and to be indispensable to a modern and dynamic Paris, the Eiffel Tower received official approval to remain indefinitely.

From 1920 the tower became a symbol of the city, emphasizing the capital's forward-thinking spirit. Many poets, directors, photographers and painters were inspired by its shape. The first was Georges Seurat, the originator of Pointillism (a style of painting similar to Divisionism), who chose it as a subject in 1888 before construction had been completed. Following Seurat came many famous names: Rousseau, Signac, Bonnard, Utrillo, Gromaire, Vuillard, Dufy and Chagall. The series of canvases entitled *Le Tour Eiffel* that Robert Delaunay painted in 1910 is very famous for its translation of the tower's modern shape into Cubist terms.

In 1889 the tower was roughly 1,023 feet high and the tallest construction in the world; and in 1957, when a television antenna was added, its height was increased to 1,063 feet. The base is formed by four huge curved pillars that come together to support the structure. Tapering as it rises, the tower is divided into sections by three observation

The Eiffel Tower

104-105 *The photograph, taken from the base of the tower, shows its iron skeleton. Gustave Eiffel was prevalently a bridge designer and built many throughout Europe.*

104 bottom *This series of photographs illustrates the tower's construction from base to top between 1887 and 1889.*

105 *The top of the tower is crowned by a large television antenna that was positioned in 1957, approximately seventy years after construction. Today the tower is a tourist attraction, and visitors can ascend in an elevator or walk up the steps to the observation terrace and enjoy the view of the city.*

1887-1889

decks. The overall design of the tower was the result of studies of the loads and the strain caused by wind. The extent of the great empty spaces derived from the decision not to include large surfaces that would create resistance to the wind.

The tower has steps and elevators to the three observation decks. On the first level there is a restaurant and at the top a weather station, a radio station and a television relay, and at one time it was also the location of Eiffel's office.

Leaving aside its formal aspect, the tower's revolutionary characteristic is the way it was perceived: whereas previously the relationship of a building with its urban context was normally viewed from one direction only, the Eiffel Tower is visible from every corner of Paris.

The Tower Bridge
LONDON, GREAT BRITAIN

by Maria Laura Vergelli

Until the early 19th century London Bridge was the only bridge spanning the Thames. Following the city's economic growth, when London began to establish itself as the capital of Europe, its population grew enormously. A series of modifications and new additions to the city became necessary, particularly with regard to the means of crossing between the two banks of the river. A series of bridges was built in the city's western half, but toward the middle of the 19th century, when the population of the East End (already a busy river port) increased, a new connection between the two banks became essential, but one that would not interrupt the continuous river traffic. For this reason the 'Special Bridge or Subway Committee' was set up in 1876 to approve and construct the new means to cross the river. More than fifty plans were put forward, but in October

106 top At one time the only means of crossing the Thames near the Tower of London was by boat or London Bridge, and the authorities were urged to build another connection. In 1885 an Act of Parliament commissioned the construction of Tower Bridge.

106 bottom The arms took about a minute to achieve the fully open position of 86°. The energy created by the steam-powered pumps was stored in six massive accumulators and released to the motors.

106-107 A symbol of London, Tower Bridge was designed by Sir Horace Jones and Sir John Wolfe-Barry between 1886 and 1894. Two platforms in the Thames provide the foundations to support the symmetrical rectangular towers. Connected by a dual walkway at a height of 143 feet above the water, the Gothic Revival towers still hold the original gearing that raised the bridge.

107 bottom The pride of British engineering, Tower Bridge was opened on 30 June 1984 by the Prince of Wales, later Edward VII, accompanied by his wife Alexandra of Denmark. To mark the occasion, the bridge was opened to allow the royal ship to pass through. At that time Tower Bridge opened and shut around 6,000 times a year, but today the event is rare.

1884, Sir Horace Jones (a city architect) and the engineer John Wolfe Barry were announced to be the winners with their plan for a bridge.

Over 11,000 tons of iron were required to build the bridge's massive framework, which was then lined with Cornish granite and Portland stone. More than 400 workers were involved in the construction. Sir Horace's initial design gave the bridge a medieval appearance in keeping with the Gothic Revival, at that time very popular in England as a pure English style entirely free from the influences of either the French or Italian academic traditions.

Then next year, however, when the architect died, responsibility for the design passed to Wolfe Barry, who abandoned Sir Horace's archaeological references and introduced a design that was freer and more inventive, typical of Victorian Gothic. The bridge's distinctive element, innovative for the time, was that it is a bascule bridge: as its roadway is just 30 feet above water level, the bridge has to open to allow the river traffic to pass, which it does in just 90 seconds.

Of the 29 bridges that cross the Thames, only Tower Bridge has a moving structure, even though these days it needs to be opened only a few times a week. As the river docks are now concentrated to the east, ships no longer need to steam west and transit Tower Bridge.

Still visible in the North Tower are the hydraulic gears that raised the bascule until 1976, when the obsolete equipment was replaced with an electric system. The South Tower can be visited; it has exhibitions and a collection of drawings that show the history of London's bridges. Toward the end of the 1970s the bridge was repainted to celebrate Queen Elizabeth II's Silver Wedding anniversary, and the original dark tones were changed to the more patriotic red, white and blue.

108 top right and bottom left The original dark colors of the bridge were replaced in 1977 by the more patriotic red, white and blue to mark the Silver Jubilee of Elizabeth II.

108 center left 'Domine, dirige nos' ('Lord, guide us,' the motto of the City of London in Latin) is seen on various parts of the bridge with St. George's cross and the sword of St. Paul.

108-109 The 795-foot span of Tower Bridge joins the two banks of the Thames. The moving arms open like a bascule bridge and are raised and lowered around huge hinges by which they are joined to the foundations.

109 bottom The towers that support the bridge are built in the Gothic Revival style dear to the Victorians. The moving section of the bridge is a bascule design, whilst the side sections are suspended.

The Bauhaus
DESSAU,
GERMANY

by Guglielmo Novelli

The Bauhaus was the 20th century's most influential institution in architecture, design, and the teaching of art. It was founded in Weimar in 1919, with the architect Walter Gropius as its director. The philosophy of this school lay in the fusion of art and crafts, with the transfer of the traditional, noble craft skills into industrial mass production.

The product of an age of rapid change, in which the dominant opinion was that unaesthetic mass-produced objects could be made beautiful by the artist, the

Bauhaus successfully merged industrial products with artistic creativity to produce industrial art.

The name 'Bauhaus' referred to medieval building sites (*Baubütten*), in which theory and practice had to be unified in a total work of art: the construction itself. At the Bauhaus the teachers were referred to as 'masters' and students divided into 'apprentices' and 'workers.' Although the school was perfectly at one with the times, its short history was beset by financial difficulties, the hostility of official institutions and disagreements between the 'masters.'

The Bauhaus went through three main periods – and these coincided with changes in location: 1919-24 Weimar, the late-Expressionist period; 1925-30 Dessau, the period characterized by hope in Rationalism and conflict with the previous phase; and 1930-33 Dessau-Berlin, the Rationalist period.

The Dessau phase was the first in which the 'Bauhaus school' was responsible for its own existence, not just in deciding the courses it taught, but also in the design of its buildings. It was at Dessau that the school building and workshops were constructed. This new center, designed by Gropius, was a multifunctional building for use by everyone who worked in the school. It had a block of classrooms, a second block with glass outer walls in the workshops, and a third, connecting block that contained the offices, library and director's study.

The plasticity of the building, fostered by the clean separation of the individual blocks and by their physical arrangement, reflected the neat definition of the various areas, and the use of particular materials further clarified the separation of the individual functions.

Gropius compared the Bauhaus to the buildings of the Renaissance and Baroque, with their symmetrical façade arranged around a central axis; however, the Dessau building, reflecting the contemporary spirit, had a three-dimensional character that did not favor any one prospect. For this reason, Gropius loved to show aerial photographs of the building.

He also designed houses for the 'masters.' The location plan of the houses formed an 'S' as a result of the pairing of two L-shaped arms turned through 180°. This way Gropius could apply his theories on plasticity.

110 The Bauhaus school made
an enormous impact in
architectural innovation, and its
interior reflects the school's
emphasis on industrial art.

110-111 The school was designed
by Walter Gropius in three
separate blocks to contain the
classrooms, workshops, and offices.
The use of innovative materials like
reinforced concrete, the visible iron

framework, the glass walls and the
organic arrangement of the three
blocks disclose Gropius' real
intention: that of recreating the
flexibility typical of Renaissance
palaces in a modern building.

111 bottom Gropius' original
drawings reveal the underlying
philosophy of the Bauhaus:
that of creating an industrial
building with an aesthetic value.

As in the Bauhaus building, the interiors were furnished
with articles designed and made in the school workshops.
Visitors must have been surprised when, on the
inauguration day, they first saw the innovative building
with its glass curtain, the small balconies with their iron
parapets that stood out clearly in the students' lodgings,
and the juxtaposed walls that seemed to dissolve with their
luminosity.

The Bauhaus building was the fruit of the collaboration of
all the arts, and the realization of new ideas on the culture of
living, or rather, the quality of life.

The Pompidou Center

PARIS, FRANCE

by Guglielmo Novelli

At the request of President Georges Pompidou, an international competition was announced in 1971 for the design of a new and important cultural center that would bring together the various artistic disciplines in the Place Beaubourg in Paris. The winning design was by Renzo Piano and Richard Rogers; construction began in April 1972 and the center was opened on January 31, 1977.

Occasionally referred to as an 'urban machine' owing to its unusual appearance, the building occupies an area of 120,000 square yards in the center of Paris. The winning idea of the Piano-Rogers design was not to occupy the entire site, but to leave half of it empty, like a large square, right up to the entrance. And everyday, tourists, visitors, caricaturists, and street artists fill this space.

The Centre Georges Pompidou hosts a gallery of modern art and rooms dedicated to temporary exhibitions and performances. There is also a library, a collection of graphical works, a vidéothèque, a collection of designs and architectural plans, an industrial creation center, an institute

that specializes in acoustics and music (IRCAM), and the reconstruction of the workshop of the sculptor Constantin Brancusi.

The design attempted to provide the flexibility required for a place where experimentation and cultural interchange could take place. This was made possible by the creation of open spaces in which there were no obstacles, and in which the plants and equipment could be modified as required.

Transparency and clarity are the other features that have

112 Light is a descriptive feature of the interior of the Pompidou Center in Paris, which offers visitors areas as open as possible. The structure of the building and its plants are emphasized rather than hidden and thus create, inside and outside, a curious blend of art and industry summed up in the concept 'urban machine.'

112-113 The design of the cultural center dedicated to the former president of France – Georges Pompidou – was by the architects Richard Rogers and Renzo Piano. The building contains a modern art gallery, a library and a series of interdisciplinary spaces used for temporary exhibitions.

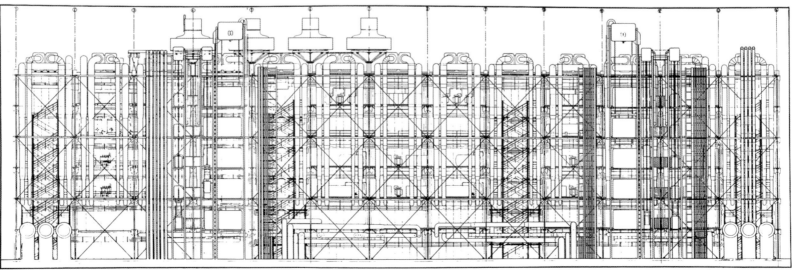

115 top A gargoyle on Notre Dame seems to look down perplexed at the Pompidou Center in the distance. From here it looks like a ship slung between the tubular structures of a shipyard, waiting to be launched.

115 bottom The south face of the Pompidou Center has a certain correspondence with the building constructed later that contains IRCAM, an institute that experiments in the field of acoustics and music.

114-115 The entire structure appears like a giant industrial building made from steel girders and colored tubes. The pipes of the plants are colored differently to signify their different use.

114 bottom Renzo Piano's drawing shows the elevation of the Center and the apparently inextricable tangle of plants.

made this building a unique example of functionality. The structure is formed by vast 'plateaux' measuring 80,000 square feet of surface area, free of internal enclosures or intermediary structures, that allow the building to open itself to the city and thus become an animated meeting place.

Unlike buildings before the Pompidou Center, the steel frame, the walkways and conduits of the various plants are brought out into the open to create a new aesthetic that acclaims the museum's functionality and organic unity.

The large pipes visible outside are painted different colors so that each tint is associated with a different function: blue is used for the air-conditioning pipes, yellow for electrical cables, red for circulation and green for fluids. However, despite its appearance as a piece of machinery made up of rods, trusses and carefully assembled pipes, this gigantic building was designed like a craftwork. According to Renzo Piano, the Beaubourg 'is a large prototype, a gigantic craft object made by hand, piece by piece.'

Construction required great precision and skill, in particular the structure designed with Peter Rice. The collaboration of architects, engineers and builders made it possible – through a process of re-design of an industrial product – to create the characteristic 'gerberettes' (stiffening cantilevers) that support the external walls.

Somewhere between the mechanical and the monumental, Piano and Rogers' building has an image of dynamism typical of the ceaseless activity of a contemporary metropolis.

The Pompidou Center

116 The outside of the Center is lined with walkways, transparent galleries and public terraces that give superb views of the Beaubourg area and Paris.

116-117 An escalator takes visitors from the square up to the lookout terrace and inside. The use of steel and glass (well exemplified in this photograph) allowed aesthetic ideas to be implemented that were innovative in the 1970s, when the building was designed. In particular, the visible load-bearing structure, the external corridors and the colored piping highlight the functionality of the Center, and combine practicality with organic unity.

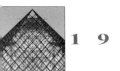

118-119 The pyramid built in 1989 in the Napoleon Courtyard of the Louvre is only the visible part of a much larger underground expansion project to make the museum easier to use by the public.

118 bottom Taking geometry as his starting point, the architect I.M. Pei built this upturned pyramid on another similar solid inside the large glass covering.

119 top Ieoh Ming Pei is a Chinese-American architect who follows Walter Gropius' philosophy. He has designed many innovative buildings, including the new Deutsche Historischen Museum in Berlin.

119 center The photograph shows a moment during construction, which was divided into two phases: the pyramid was built during the first, which began in 1987, and was strongly desired despite much criticism.

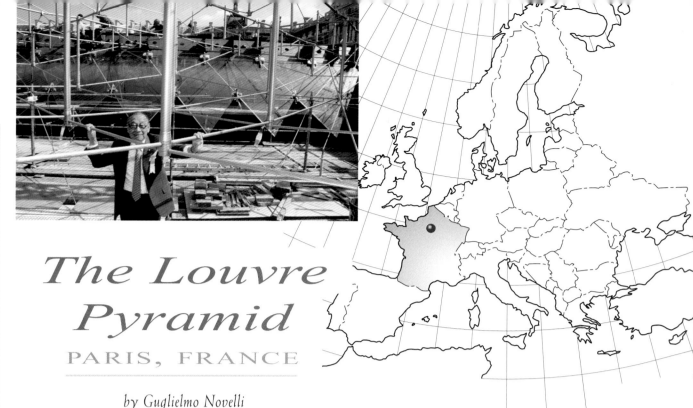

The Louvre Pyramid

PARIS, FRANCE

by Guglielmo Novelli

The Louvre Museum in Paris was founded in 1793 in the magnificent residential palace of the French kings, and it houses an immense art collection. In the 1980s a project was undertaken to enlarge and adapt the Louvre to the growing number of visitors it was receiving.

Two phases of construction work by the architect I. M. Pei (in 1987 and 1993) led to the creation of the 'Grand Louvre.'

The famous pyramid belongs to the first phase; it stands over a basement section built under Napoleon's courtyard. Flanked by smaller pyramids, the pure volume conveys light into the atrium below connected to the wings of the museum.

The expansion of the Louvre has made it easier for the flow of visitors to be distributed to the various destinations in the museum and provided a series of services for their benefit: an information office, differentiated ticket desks, a library, a refreshments area, a coat-check and an auditorium.

With the other smaller skylights, the pyramid is the only section of the large underground spaces visible.

The combination of the glass surface, which reveals the pyramid's structure of slender steel tie-rods, and the fountains creates a dynamic and expressive spectacle.

It would not do the pyramid justice to call it simply the atrium's light-well. It is a point of reference, a visual landmark that connects the historical with the modern.

The choice of a volume of absolute purity was deliberate: the form of a pyramid represents the idea of absoluteness and essentiality that perfectly matches the monumental façades of the Paris museum, thereby obviating any comparison between the two.

119 bottom The interior of the pyramid shows why it was built: the museum needed a more efficient means of distributing the public to the different sections of the building.

120-121 The aesthetics of the main pyramid and the smaller subordinate ones are more clearly seen at night when the glass structures are turned into gigantic skylights.

122 top The basis of the design for the Guggenheim Museum in Bilbao was experimentation into the dramatic nature of form.

122 center The architect Frank Gehry is seen here in his house in Santa Monica (Ca), which was the first example of his deconstructivist approach.

122 bottom In 1999 a sculpture, called Maman, of a gigantic stylized spider by Louise Bourgeois was placed in the square in front of the Guggenheim Museum. Made from bronze and steel, the figure evokes the artist's image of her mother, who was both a parent and a terrible creature with menacing features.

The Guggenheim Museum

BILBAO, SPAIN

by Guglielmo Novelli and Maria Laura Vergelli

The Guggenheim Museum is the architectural and iconographic symbol of the cultural and urban renewal of the city of Bilbao. The building was the successful result of the convergence of interests of the Basque government – which was attempting to rebuild its image and urban identity – and the strategies of the Guggenheim Foundation, which exists to support research and artistic creation.

'Building this museum has been like building Notre Dame. Notre Dame, and all other cathedrals built in the Middle Ages, were created to be the focal point of their cities, which developed around them, almost arranging themselves as a function of the centrality, even symbolically so, of the religious building.' This secular visual and conceptual evocation of a cathedral was made by the museum's architect, Frank O. Gehry.

Completed in 1997, this building with spectacularly sculptural forms dominates the left bank of the Nervión river, standing out against the cityscape like the profile of a ship. Amplified by the reflection in the water and reflecting the different tones of the sky, the unusual soft shapes of the museum, ruffled by the wind, seem to be extraordinarily alive due to the thin titanium sheets that line it. Arranged like fish scales, the titanium sheets intersect in original combinations with glass and steel walls, and smooth curtains of beige-colored stone blocks.

The design of such a complex building, with complexity due to its absolute freedom in its conception of forms and spaces (a feature of much of Gehry's work) and strongly characterized by its extension of curved surfaces, was made possible by the introduction of an advanced system of computerized design used in the aeronautics industry.

122-123 The Guggenheim Museum in Bilbao was conceived as an 'exhibition machine' for contemporary art and as a work of art in itself.

123 bottom left The works exhibited in the 110,000 square-foot museum are enhanced by their unusual and flowing distribution.

123 bottom right Large works of art have plenty of space in the huge exhibition rooms.

124-125 The soft, receding lines of the Guggenheim Museum were created using sophisticated design software in use in the aeronautics industry.

124 bottom The attractive forms of the exterior correspond inside to a more neutral architecture that encourages the contemplation of the works on display.

125 top left The experimental layout of the interior is famous for the huge exhibition spaces.

The Guggenheim Museum

The unexpected volumes and the variety of the profiles reflect the architect's creative genius: 'I thought that a museum building had to submit to the art, but the artists I spoke to said 'no.' They wanted a building that would be admired by the people, not a neutral container.'

Inside, the gaze wanders freely from the colossal central atrium to the wings and huge gallery. Natural light flows down from above and from the glass walls. The display area covers 118,000 square feet distributed between 19 regular and irregularly-shaped galleries that can be recognized from outside by their square stone façades and sinuous metallic sides. The various works of contemporary art, whose dimensions and forms are not always compatible with traditional exhibition spaces, are brought out by the huge gallery, which seems to put large installations back into perspective.

125 top right Bilbao's Guggenheim has an auditorium, a restaurant and various commercial and administrative areas.

125 bottom The Guggenheim marries the distorted and faceted lines of Cubism and Futurism with contemporary design.

126-127 The curved surfaces of the exterior are lined with 33,000 titanium sheets like fish-scales which create attractive chromatic effects in the sunlight.

The Reichstag
BERLIN, GERMANY

by Guglielmo Novelli

128 The old Reichstag was the center of political power in Germany before and during the Nazi era. It was a severe yet elegant 19th century building. The renovation by Norman Foster retained, where possible, the structure of the past and added clearly modern elements, such as the glass and steel dome.

The rebuilding project of this German government structure by Sir Norman Foster carefully followed the social and political changes taking place in reunified Germany. The result is a technologically advanced building that has become the symbol of the new Berlin skyline.

The 19th-century Reichstag was devastated by World War II and successive historical events. During demolition, the structure of the old building was revealed, bearing certain important traces of the past. On this subject Foster commented, 'We found we had before us a building whose changed symbolism had very little significance for contemporary Germans. The simplest approach would have been to gut the Reichstag and insert a modern building in place of the existing framework. But the more we looked into awareness of the building, the more we realized that history still resounded loudly inside it and that we could not simply remove it.' It was therefore decided to allow the original structure to remain and to bring out the various historical layers it represents. The new design creates a dialog between past and present, between the huge original structure and the new transparent dome.

All the activities relevant to government are in view, so the elector or tourist is able to observe the Chamber of Deputies at work. The principal parliamentary level has been returned to the first floor. The second floor is where the rooms of the President and Council of Ministers are housed, and the third floor is the setting for the party meeting rooms and entrance for personnel when Parliament is not in session.

Above these working levels, the public can visit the roof terrace where there is access to a restaurant and the dome. The new 'lantern' dome (77 feet high and 130 feet in diameter), built from a steel structure and glass sheets, quickly became the emblem of the new Berlin. Inside, two

129 bottom right After the war, in 1949, the capital of West Germany was transferred to Bonn. Nonetheless, in 1956, it was decided that the Reichstag would be restored rather than demolished.

128-129 The windows in the dome lantern reflect one of the Reichstag's four towers. Both a Parliament and a tourist attraction, the building has maintained its leading role in modern Berlin.

129 bottom left The large glass dome on the roof is a distant relation of the original one built in 1894 and allows visitors to the Reichstag a splendid all-round view of Berlin.

The Reichstag

spiral ramps allow the visitor to observe the Plenary Chamber from above, a characteristic that has an obvious symbolic value, that of the direct participation of citizens in political life. The dome is a fundamental element in the composition, communicating to the outside world qualities of lightness, transparency and permeability, and the fact that it is also part of the public domain. It is also essential to the use of energy and light in the building: the nucleus of this futuristic structure is the 'light sculptor' – an upturned cone 8 feet in diameter at the bottom and 52 feet at the top – lined with 360 carefully oriented mirrors.

This cone has a highly important technological and structural function and plays a fundamental role in Foster's poetics.

The 'light sculptor' is essentially a 'lighthouse in reverse' because it absorbs the natural light from outside the dome and conveys it down into the Plenary Chamber. Meanwhile, the control and regulation of heat and sunlight entering the dome directly are managed by an automated moving screen

that follows the path of the sun to block heat and direct sunlight from entering.

This process is inverted during the night so that the artificial light in Parliament is reflected outward, illuminating the dome which, like a lighthouse, becomes visible to the Berliners. And besides being crucial to internal illumination, the upturned cone is decisive in the natural ventilation system used in the Chamber of Deputies.

The Reichstag is a model of sustainable architecture designed to use state-of-the-art systems to save energy while maintaining a high standard of comfort. It reflects the great concern by the architect for the improvement in the quality of the internal environment, something that is closely related to the quality of our lives and the many daily activities that take place in public and private spaces.

Sir Norman Foster has paid careful attention to the social dimension of the work, raising architecture to the level of public art, while remaining sensitive to the culture and climate of the setting, and to the needs of the public.

131 bottom left The picture shows the inauguration of the new Parliament building on April 19, 1999. The eye at the top of the building is visible above the guests.

131 bottom right The Chamber of the Deputies is refreshed by a natural ventilation system provided by the light sculptor.

132-133 and 133 bottom The unmistakably modern elliptical shell of the Planetarium is made from metal and sheets of glass, and contains a spherical room built entirely from reinforced concrete.

132 bottom left This is an aerial view of the whole site while still under construction.

132 bottom right Calatrava's model shows the ogival plan of the site.

133 top The gallery of the Planetarium runs right round the spherical room.

133 center The Palace of Arts is in the north section of the site.

The City of Arts and Sciences

VALENCIA, SPAIN

by Guglielmo Novelli

The City of Arts and Sciences designed by the famous architect-engineer Santiago Calatrava stands in an area 3 miles from Valencia's city center.

The site is being built in stages on a long plot of land cut in three sections by two cross roads and flanked on one side by the River Turia and on the other by a motorway.

The Palace of Arts stands in the north section, the Oceanographic Museum in the south, and in the central part there are the Planetarium, Museum of Sciences and an access road. This portico is called 'Umbracle' and contains a pathway covered with vegetation that runs parallel to the main axis of the complex.

Measuring 350 yards long and nearly 70 wide, it is like a winter garden decorated with 55 fixed arches and 54 fluctuating arches 59 feet high. Beneath this extraordinarily light structure is a large parking lot.

Opposite the path is the Planetarium; this is an elliptical structure with a huge shell that can be opened from top to base using a sophisticated mechanized system made of metal and plate glass. The shell is supported by inclined perimetral arches and hosts the spherical planetarium room made from reinforced concrete.

Continuing along the main axis, the visitor arrives at the Palace of Arts. Calatrava's sculptural building offers Valencia a technologically advanced item of infrastructure that is used for performances of classical and contemporary music.

This modern and efficient auditorium, which quickly became a symbol of the urban landscape, brings the avenue to a dynamic end.

Beyond the Planetarium, a rectangular building is home to the Principe Felipe Museum of Natural Sciences, created around the modular repetition of the transversal section. The building has a gallery of 36,000 square yards dedicated to science and technology.

Terraces and mezzanines are dedicated to particular

134 bottom left The photograph shows the access avenue. This is a light portico called the 'Umbracle' that is approximately 350 yards long and 70 wide.

134 bottom right The interior of the Umbracle has more than 100 arches and is rather like a winter garden.

134-135 The Science and Technology Museum is an original terraced gallery with a unique ribbed roof covering and a facade made from glass and steel.

This lightens the structure which is supported by immense white concrete arches. Overall, the building is rectangular in plan.

135 top left The amazing arched structure of the Science Museum is compensated aesthetically by the large glass and steel windows.

135 top right The Science and Technology Museum in Valencia was designed to involve the public, as it is based on interactivity.

135 bottom The use of white concrete and, in general, the decision to paint almost everything that color confers a sense of dazzling modernity and lightness on the museum building. The series of external transversal arches, terraces and mezzanines that connect with the interior further lighten the structure and set it harmoniously among the other buildings.

themes with which the visitors are expected to experiment, rather than just admire. A series of concrete arches 33 feet wide crosses the room. The large ribbed roof has a glass and steel facade that looks onto the gardens, and the south side is protected by a system of white concrete arches.

At the opposite end of the main axis, in the area at the south of the City, a group of buildings houses the Oceanographic Museum.

The pavilions are arranged along the bank of a man-made lake and connected to one another by walkways and paths. On the lowest level there are underwater tunnels and ramps. Of all the various shapes and forms to be seen, those that stand out are the pavilion dedicated to the Mediterranean Sea and the enormous Dolphinarium, hyperbolic structures whose lightness suggests the fluctuating forms of sea creatures.

Calatrava's works are based on lightness and transparency, and on the forces that govern the structure of a building. In the City of Arts and Sciences, the Spanish architect has taken these themes one step further by surrounding his buildings with water. This way, the volumes charged with architectural tension seem to float and the attractive effects of the light are doubled.

136-137 The large concrete sphere that contains the Planetarium is like a shell that holds a pearl. Here it is reflected in one of the pools of water that surround the buildings in the City of Arts and Sciences.

136 bottom Illuminated by a series of small lights, the weave of arches that support the outer structure of the Science Museum allows the last rays of twilight to pass.

137 top The City of Arts and Sciences is the symbol of the new Valencia. This appealing complex was opened in 2003 and has relaunched tourism and the role of the city in the Spain of the new millennium.

137 center The lights and reflections at night turn the Planetarium and Science Museum into surprising prehistoric animals with see-through shells.

137 bottom The shell of the Planetarium was designed to be opened from top to base using a sophisticated metal and glass mechanism.

The City of Arts and Sciences

138 bottom right Libeskind did not give the building a direct entrance. To reach the Jewish section, visitors have to pass through the City of Berlin Museum next door.

139 top The windows are no more than wounds and suggest that, like the Holocaust, the building was designed to be a painful experience from the moment visitors approach it.

138-139 The unmistakably dart-like Jewish Museum in Berlin was designed by Daniel Libeskind.

138 bottom left The deconstructionist museum stands in the center of Baroque Berlin.

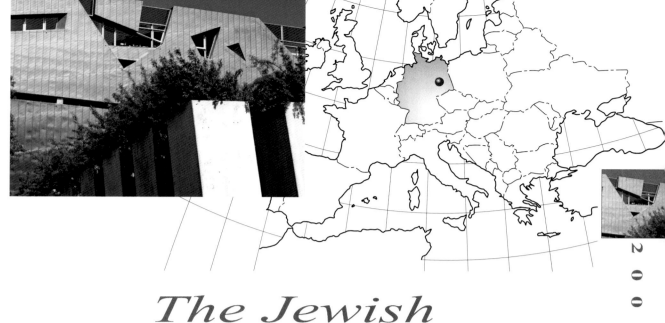

The Jewish Museum

BERLIN, GERMANY

by Guglielmo Novelli

Designed by deconstructionist Daniel Libeskind, the enlargement of the Museum of the City of Berlin to hold the Jewish section of the collections stands in the Baroque heart of the capital. The institution was created to hold the documents and artifacts of the suffering of the Jewish people. Its characteristic dart-like shape, like a distorted Star of David, arose from the intersection on the city map of the places where Jewish intellectuals worked. The inward-looking volume of the building remains isolated from the exterior as there is no direct entrance. To enter the Jewish section of the museum, one has to enter the old building and be swallowed up by a passage.

The soft, indirect light, which helps to dramatize the atmosphere, does not penetrate through windows but through a series of gashes like wounds in the zinc-lined volumes.

Once inside, the visitor is faced by three routes around the museum. The first, following a winding path, displays documents of the history of the German Jews since the Roman era. The second leads to the Tower of the Holocaust, a space 39 feet high that is completely closed with the exception of a narrow slit high up. It is not possible to see out, so that it is not even possible for visitors to know where they are.

The third option leads to the Promised Land, characterized by a sloping floor on which 49 concrete columns support planted olive trees.

The new Jewish Museum immediately became one of the most visited places in Berlin, as much by tourists as the city's inhabitants. The extraordinary museum has enabled the Jewish community to recover its history and the traditions of its culture while also placing itself at the forefront of artistic experimentation.

139 center and bottom The interiors are as dramatic as the exterior. Simple and bare, the rooms follow three routes that together represent the history of the Jews. They lead to the Holocaust and the Promised Land, two points in the museum that are more places of the spirit than cold commemorative monuments.

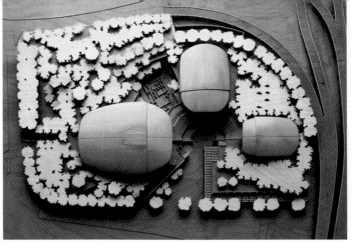

140 *The wooden model of Rome's Music Park clearly shows the three large dome-shaped buildings that contain auditoria dedicated to symphonic, chamber, and contemporary music. The Music Park was designed by Italian architect Renzo Piano.*

140-141 *The Santa Cecilia Hall is the largest in the complex. It can seat 2,700 and was designed for full orchestral music. The materials chosen to line the interior and the shape of the volumes together provide almost perfect acoustics.*

The Auditorium Parco della Musica

ROME, ITALY

by Guglielmo Novelli

The Auditorium Parco della Musica (Music Park) designed by architectural master Renzo Piano is one of the most ambitious projects to be built in Rome in the last few decades and represents an economic, artistic and media triumph.

Composed of three large volumes conceived as musical instruments themselves, the musical complex is another development of the Eternal City. By turning a largely empty area into a perfectly organized space, the city has reabsorbed an urban fracture.

The Music Park has grounds of 7.5 acres now planted with 400 trees, and it has thus become a new urban feature.

The lush vegetation surrounds the amphitheater – the hub of the design – where stage performances and concerts are held to audiences of up to 3,000 people. Around this open space are arranged the three concert halls: the Santa Cecilia Hall (2,700 seats) for orchestral music, the Sinopoli Hall (1,200 seats) for chamber music, and the Settecento Hall (700 seats) for contemporary and experimental music.

The physical separation of the buildings benefits their acoustical qualities.

The three large volumes – which for Renzo Piano represent musical instruments – are designed to suggest the domes of a contemporary cathedral of music, including up through the lead lining on the roof coverings.

The combination of architecture and music has resulted in many technological features, and a careful study of acoustics and the use of suitable materials have produced an almost perfect sound quality.

The roof is made with long laminar wood beams. Each interior has been lined with panels of American cherry wood, the mechanical characteristics of which are ideal to optimize the acoustics.

All the music halls are installed with recording equipment and have different size and spatial attributes.

During excavation of the site, the discovery of the foundations of a Roman villa led to the modification of the initial plans. Renzo Piano decided that the ruins could be used as a feature of the design and were thus incorporated into the foyer of one of the halls.

In addition to the three 'loudspeakers' and the amphitheater, the complex includes a museum of musical instruments, a library, offices and a series of service, commercial, recreational and exhibition rooms.

The flexibility of the halls allows performances of opera, chamber or Baroque music, symphonic music and theatrical productions. Designed from the inside out, these musical buildings have been designed down to the last detail, and with the spirit and care typical of a craftsman.

141 center left and bottom right
The three auditoria are huge shells lined with lead and supported by wood laminar girders. They are of different size but share the quality of being 'sound-boxes', i.e., musical instruments with superb acoustics.

141 bottom left These sketches by Renzo Piano immediately make clear his idea of creating three large volumes, separate so as to achieve the best possible acoustic effect and sound quality. Together they represent a perfect fusion of architecture and music.

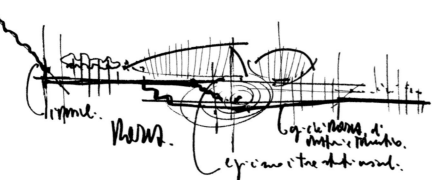

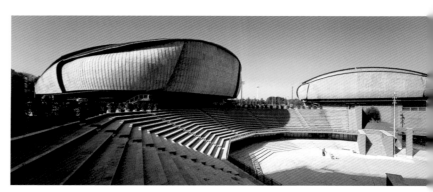

142 top A 41-floor, cigar-shaped tower, the Swiss Re is one of Norman Foster's most inspired designs.

142 bottom The tower has a radiating plan, unlike the other skyscrapers nearby, which are all square or rectangular.

143 Supported by a cross-girder frame, the glass panels follow the curvature of the building, producing a degree of transparency that is especially apparent in full sunlight. The slots that provide a natural ventilation system are distributed around the cladding.

The Swiss-Re Tower

LONDON, GREAT BRITAIN

by Guglielmo Novelli

Situated in London's City (the financial district), the new Swiss-Re Tower designed by Sir Norman Foster is an unusually shaped tower, with 41 floors of offices and a gallery of shops reached from a new square. This aerodynamic skyscraper has an unusual dialog with its surrounding urban landscape, and is made to look slimmer by the rectangular towers of equal size nearby. The reason for this is primarily the curvature of the external surface which reduces reflections and highlights the building's transparency: in turn, this creates a direct relationship between the tower's interior and exterior.

The base, with levels at double the standard height, is for use by the public and is in the form of a covered square with benches, a café and shops. The design is innovative technologically and environmentally, and has a system of natural ventilation. Fresh air enters slots in the cladding and is distributed naturally throughout the building by pressure differentials; the used air can be recycled as a source of heating and then expelled. This efficient system means reduced air conditioning through much of the year, producing energy savings.

The tower has a radial plan with a circular perimeter, but the novelty of this building lies in the fact that it calls into question the structure of a typical vertical building. Each floor is slightly rotated over the one below to create an ascending spiral. The interior of this unusual building has a series of hanging gardens (which also follow the spiral trend) onto which neighboring rooms face.

From the inside, the 'winter gardens' create unusual views over the City, while from the outside they break up the mass of the building and allow observers to see inside.

The important quality of this 'ecologically responsible' building is the optimization of the areas available to users, which encourages use of the common spaces.

144-145 With a height of 590 feet, the Swiss-Re tower dominates the London skyline filled with buildings of medium height. Designed to accommodate offices, the Swiss-Re tower also has a commercial section, a covered plaza and various shops.

145 The photographs show three moments during construction. At top we see the vertical curvature, which allows the maximum diameter of the building to be not at the base, as might be logical, but at the 26th floor. The progressive lightening of the building as it tapers upward, and the use of innovative materials and techniques allowed balances to be achieved that would otherwise have been impossible in a building of this kind.

The Swiss-Re Tower

'More than two thousand years have passed since the end of the Egyptian culture but we still remain profoundly moved by its existential themes: the themes of its place of belonging, and its life, being and time.' When the modern age views the imposing Egyptian constructions, the words of the architectural historian Christian Norberg-Schulz strike home.

Our knowledge of ancient Egypt, the culture of which was ended by the Arab conquest in the 7th century, and the 'many marvelous things that it possesses' is derived from Greek documentation, and the accounts of travelers and learned men of Greek language and culture who visited Egypt before the country was transformed by the spread of Christianity, the domination of the Byzantines, and the neglect permitted by the Arab conquerors. The sand-covered ruins emerge from the diaries of those who followed until the first scholars of antiquity and their fellow scientists arrived in Napoleon's Egyptian expedition of 1799. The expedition's reports stimulated 'sympathy' among Europeans, in which scientific interest and a fascination with the exotic were mixed, aided by the congeniality of Egyptian architecture to the Neoclassical taste of the period. The early archaeological missions gave rise to the nuclei of the first collections of antiquity now be seen in the major European museums. With Jean-François Champollion's triumph in deciphering hieroglyphic writing in 1822, following comparative studies with Greek and demotic writing on the Rosetta Stone found during the Napoleonic expedition, studies of Egyptology and archaeology were able to provide greater understanding of the documentary materials and monumental and archaeological heritage that had been preserved.

Leaving aside the many millennia of life during Egypt's Paleolithic and Neolithic prehistory, early human settlements were concentrated along the Nile and in the oases. Agriculture was developed in the early historical epoch circa 3000 BC. The Egyptians in the Nile delta lived on the zones that lay above the level of the annual flood; they worked the fertile plain and traded with lands to the east. To the south and in Nubia, villages were strung out along the green banks and flanks of the Nile, and made use of the easy means of communication offered by the river. Once villages grew into cities, the territory was organized into districts under the aegis of two kingdoms, the north and the south. These two kingdoms the rulers of the south succeeded in uniting, establishing their political authority, administrative system and, above all, their cultural models. The pharaohs, the Ptolemaic dynasty and then the Roman emperors presented themselves as 'personifications of a god that brought the community together,' as the Egyptologist Silvio Curto noted, for over three thousand years of civilization. The 4th-century BC Egyptian priest and historian Manetho divided pharaonic history into thirty-one dynasties (from c. 2850 to 333 BC), which were followed by the Ptolemies (332–32 BC) and then the Roman era (32 BC–AD 394). In ancient Egyptian architecture, constructions of clean-cut geometrical design predominate, which seem to fit perfectly into the harmonious landscape of the Nile. The country's main axis was formed by the Nile, which runs from south to north, crossed by its secondary axis (east-west) represented by the trajectory of the sun. The river's fertile and cultivated banks were divided orthogonally into fields as far as the edge of the desert, with its mountains and oases. The stereometric shapes of the pyramids, the axial designs of the temples, and the regularity of the rock temples defined and were defined by the natural space, and represented the unit by which the river landscape was measured. In this integrated arrangement, the orthogonal organization of space and the axial basis of construction were used to 'create a constant and eternally valid space' (Norberg-Schulz). This immutability is in part modified by the variety in the distribution of individual elements, such as cornices and moldings, and particularly in the different shaped columns, which were represented as lotus plants, papyruses and palms. In addition, the decorations could give a particular building an individuality through figured reliefs, the interplay of which once again expresses orthogonality. The development of architectural forms was less based on the creation of new ones as on the continual reworking of the same fundamental inspirations.

The aim of giving a work of architecture a fixed, abstract order is admirably exemplified by the pyramid, whose compact mass synthesizes the equilibrium between the vertical and horizontal lines and is highlighted by its clean-cut edges.

The suitability of the pyramid as a form to represent eternity was made manifest by its monumental dimensions and the importance given to funerary architecture, through which the pharaoh's aspiration to become eternal in the afterworld was materialized. Many symbolic meanings have been attributed to temple architecture, including the following: a representation of the cosmos, which is suggested by the structure of the entrance pylon and its relationship with the hieroglyph of the world (the pylon is thought to have represented the 'celestial threshold'); and the representation of the cycle of life, suggested by the route taken toward the center of the building, which becomes progressively more restricted to signify 'eternal return.' Pervading the various aspects of Egyptian civilization, 'all the symbolism is based on the assumption that things are related, and on the relationship that is intuitively felt and seen between the microcosm and macrocosm,' as the cultural historian Manfred Lurker comments. Ancient Egypt's ineffable magnificence underwent transformation following the glory of the Ramessid period owing to the progressive breaking up of the country's political unity under Libyan and Ethiopian dynasties. The arrival of the Greeks under Alexander the Great at the end of the 4th century BC was celebrated by the foundation of the city of Alexandria (332–331 BC), in front of the small island of Pharos. According to Plutarch, Octavian made a speech to the Alexandrians gathered in the city's gymnasium in which he stated that he wished to save the rich city from destruction because he admired its beauty and grandeur. The last of the Hellenistic kingdoms to submit to the power of Rome, Egypt was turned into a Roman province following the battle of Actium and the disappearance of Antony and Cleopatra (31–30 BC) from the political scene.

A silver patera found in Boscoreale, and now in the Louvre, has a relief bust of a woman wearing an elephant-headed headdress in which the trunk and tusks are quite visible. With her left hand the figure holds the symbol of the soil's fertility, a cornucopia; with her right, in the folds of her chiton, fruit and ears of corn. In a fresco in Pompeii (House of Menander) and a mosaic in the villa in Piazza Armerina in Sicily, the use of color allowed the flesh of a similar female figure, who presents the same attributes, to be darkened.

All three females are the personification of Africa which, to Roman writers, signified the southern shores of the Mediterranean, though it did not always include Egypt.

The Romanization of this strip of the continent – characterized by Greek influence to the east and Phoenician-Punic culture to the west – was carried out over a long period of wars and conquests and voluntary annexations. In the latter episodes, individual kingdoms became vassal states of Rome and were organized into provinces.

Africa, which was given the epithet *proconsularis* to indicate the type of administration by which it was run, was the province created following the destruction of Carthage in 146 BC. It incorporated the Punic lands conquered by the Romans. *Africa nova* was the name given to the province constituted by the kingdom of Numidia, which sided with Pompey, following Caesar's victory over Pompey's troops at Tapso in 46 BC. Thus Sabratha, like other important cities, was transformed from a Phoenician-Punic trading center into a Roman city during the reign of Augustus. It obtained the rights of a colony and was laid out on the standard plan of a Roman city in the second half of the 2nd century AD, with buildings dedicated to public, religious and entertainment functions. Sabratha's decline began with the barbarian invasions in the 4th and 5th centuries, and culminated (after a brief resurgence under Justinian in the 6th century) in the abandonment of the city following the Arab invasions of the 7th and 11th centuries.

The destiny of Alexandria changed when the city was conquered in 642 by Amr Ibn al-As, commander of the army of Caliph Omar, following a siege to several months. The city's ruins gave rise to the splendor of the cosmopolitan metropolis as described by ancient writers, who listed the splendid buildings that stood in the royal quarters. And the great library by the sea that was annexed to the Museum 'incarnated the surreal dream that there might be, or may have existed somewhere, of a place where all the books from all over the world were collected.' The library was destroyed by fire, the 'devastating consort of books in all eras,' as the historian Luciano Canfora noted.

Alessandra Capodiferro

147 left *The Sphinx and Menkaure's pyramid, on Giza plateau in Egypt.*

147 center *The amphitheater at Sabratha in Libya, built in the 2nd and 3rd centuries AD.*

147 right *The new Library in Alexandria in Egypt, built on the site of the ancient library.*

149 center and bottom right
Deprived of its lining of 12
layers of stone blocks, the top of
Khufu's pyramid (above) is like
a square platform of 33 feet on
each side. Khafre's pyramid
(below) still has its tip and lining
for almost a quarter of its height.

The Pyramids of Giza
CAIRO, EGYPT

by Miriam Taviani

148 The pyramids built by Khufu,
Khafre, and Menkaure have been
reached by the spreading city of
Cairo. To the south of Menkaure's
monument there are three 'satellite'
pyramids: the last on the right is
attributed to the king's wife
Khamerernebti II.

149 top Its lining gone, the top of
Khufu's pyramid reveals the perfect
construction technique using
continuous triangular faces.

149 bottom left The entrance to
the burial chamber in Khufu's
pyramid is narrow but widens out
into an upward-sloping gallery
155 feet long and 26 feet high. It is
covered by a false vault.

The archaeological complex of El-Giza, a
city of Arab origin on the Nile's west bank,
now swallowed up by Cairo, is ancient
Egypt's most famous site, and one of the most magnificent
and inspiring in the world. Studied since Napoleon's military
and scientific expedition to Egypt in 1798-1800, and
explored in detail in the first half of the 20th century, the site
owes its fame to the wonder of its pyramids and to the
disquieting presence of the Great Sphinx, known in Arabic as
Abu el-Hol ('Father of Terror').

Nothing on Earth projects the sense of immutability as
powerfully as the grandeur of these funerary monuments built
to preserve for eternity the bodies of the pharaohs (however,
their bodies have not been found in the burial chambers, just
their empty, broken sarcophagi).

The pyramids' massive bulk had a dual function: in
addition to their undeniably dramatic effect, their size
allowed them to rise in the immensity of the desert without
being rendered negligible.

The three largest pyramids belonged to Fourth Dynasty
pharaohs – Khufu (often referred to as Cheops), Khafre (or
Chephren), and Menkaure (or Mycerinus) – and were the
central features of three separate burial complexes built
between 2590 and 2506 BC. Each complex also included a
funerary temple to the east of its respective pyramid, a
second temple at the bottom of the slope by the canal that
led from the Nile to the site, smaller pyramids for the
queens, and huge pits in which ships from the royal fleet
were buried.

The pyramids were constructed with blocks of stone
weighing up to 15 tons, and originally had an external lining,
but over the millennia the facing stones were carried off to
and used in other buildings. As a result, the pyramids' overall
heights have been reduced.

The largest and oldest funerary complex is that of
Khufu, whose 'Great Pyramid' was originally 479 feet tall
(today 450) and measures 755 feet along each side. It
dominated a series of other burial and service buildings laid
out on such a regular basis that they seem to be the work

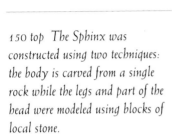

150 top The Sphinx was constructed using two techniques: the body is carved from a single rock while the legs and part of the head were modeled using blocks of local stone.

150 bottom The stele of Thutmosis IV stands between the front legs of the Sphinx. It is called the 'Dream Stele' as it records that restoration work was ordered by the king following a dream in which the enormous sphinx wept that it had been abandoned for so long.

150-151 The face of the Sphinx in Giza is of the pharaoh Khafre wearing the nemes headdress; it still has traces of the red used to decorate it.

The Pyramids of Giza

of a city planner. Deservedly numbered among the Seven Wonders of the World, the pyramids of Giza were the oldest of the Wonders, and the only one to have survived almost intact.

According to Herodotus, who wrote in the 5th century BC, Khufu's pyramid took the Egyptian people thirty years to construct; likewise, the pyramid built by his son Khafre, though it was slightly smaller (448 feet in height, with sides of 691 feet). Menkaure was the best loved of the three rulers, consequently his much smaller pyramid (just 217 feet high with sides of 354 feet) remained unviolated.

The most surprising monument of the entire archaeological site, however, is the Sphinx. Khafre had this monument carved out of a rocky hill (with fill-ins of blocks of stone) just behind his pyramid. Standing 66 feet high and 187 feet long, the Sphinx has the body of a lion and the head of a pharaoh.

This symbolic and enigmatic creation faces east and refers to the sun god Atum, whose cult originated in Heliopolis. Its function was to watch over the eternal abode of Khufu behind it. A temple was built at its feet and called the Temple of the Sphinx.

At the end of the Old Kingdom in the 22nd century BC, the royal tombs were violated for the first time, and during the Middle Kingdom (21st to 18th centuries BC), they were forgotten. In the New Kingdom, which lasted from the 16th to the 8th centuries BC, the Sphinx returned the entire funerary area to popularity, and became an object of popular, spontaneous cult worship.

Later, the cult was made official and identified with the god Har-imkhet, known to the Greeks as Harmakis. With this renewed interest, the first 'maintenance' operations were carried out on the archaeological area (which was continually being swamped with sand), as the stele placed between the Sphinx's front paws commemorating Thutmosis I informs the visitor.

151 top left The Sphinx, at the center of the photograph, lies to the right of the processional way that joined the valley temple to the upper temple.

151 top right Though missing his nose, the uraeus serpent on his forehead, and the false beard, the profile of the Sphinx has retained its fascination.

152-153 *The sanctuary of Amon covers an area of approximately 3,600 square yards, to which a further 330 can be added around the sanctuary of Montu (the small enclosure on the right) and the 1,100 around the sanctuary of Mut, below, which is joined to the sanctuary of Amon by the Avenue of Sphinxes.*

152 bottom *The enclosure of Mut included the temples of Amenhotep III and Ramesses III, and the crescent sacred lake. Sacred lakes were used by priests for purification rites and ceremonies linked to the god's bark.*

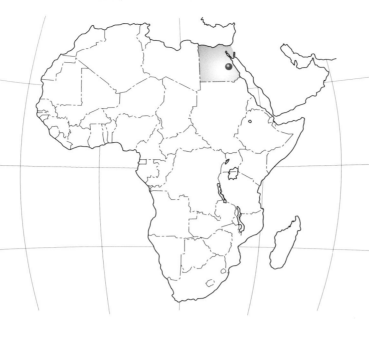

Karnak Temple

LUXOR, EGYPT

by Miriam Taviani

T
he section of the Nile valley where ancient
Thebes was built had no link to the coast of
the Red Sea, but was very green and fertile.
Its consequent growth in prosperity was essential to its rise as
the dominant military power in Upper Egypt, as a result of
which it became the capital of the entire kingdom during the
reign of Mentuhotep III (1997-1991 BC, a pharaoh of the
Eleventh Dynasty.

Homer described treasure-filled Thebes as the 'hundred-
gated city,' relating that two hundred armed men would
periodically ride out in chariots from each gate.

The inscriptions of Amenhotep III (1386-1349 BC) speak
of temples lined with gold and silver, traces of which have
been found. Under Ramesses II (1279-1212 BC), the city was
given a military training camp of 20,000 men. It is also
possible that, given the absence of a city wall, the gigantic
pylons (monumental entrances) of the temples were used as
city gates.

The city of the living stood on the east bank of the Nile
and the city of the dead on the west.

The sanctuary of Karnak was built on the east bank with
three sacred areas ringed by unfired brick walls. The three
areas were dedicated to Montu (an archaic local falcon-
headed warrior god who was soon replaced by Amon), Amon
himself (a ram or man with an headdress crowned by two
feathers), and Mut (Amon's female consort, who wore a crown
and was sometimes represented with a vulture's head). The
temple of Khonsu (Amon and Mut's young son, who wore a
diadem in the form of a crescent moon) was included in the
sacred area of Amon.

The largest of the three sacred areas was dedicated to
Amon. It was a diamond-shaped enclosure surrounded by a
wall 2,625 yards in circumference and 26 feet thick, inside
which stood the Great Temple of the 'lord of the gods,'
Almost nothing remains of its most ancient section (dating to
the Twelfth Dynasty, 1991–1785 BC, Middle Kingdom)
where the pharaohs from the Eighteenth to Twenty-second

*153 top and bottom The colossal
statue of Ramesses II (49 feet tall)
with his daughter Bentanta stands
in front of the Second Pylon. It is
set slightly forward of two others
of the same king at the sides of the
vestibule between the Great Court
and the Hypostyle Hall.*

*153 center The First Pylon is
reached by an avenue lined with
sphinxes. Through a man-made pool,
the sacred bark could reach the Nile
during religious ceremonies.*

154 top The central aisle of the Hypostyle Hall is one third higher than those at the sides. It features enormous abacuses and architraves that support the ceiling at a height of 75 feet, thus allowing space for large rectangular windows.

154 center The sanctuary is reflected in the water of Amon's Sacred Lake. The only two obelisks on the site can be seen on the right; one was erected by Thutmosis I and the other by Queen Hatshepsut.

154 bottom The processional way to the Temple of Luxor leaves from the portal in the Temple of Konsu built by Ptolemy I Euergetes. The entire route was lined with sphinxes with the figure of Amenhotep III between their paws as a sign of divine protection.

155 From the time of the New Kingdom, the Sanctuary of Amon was the most important and economically powerful in Egypt. This aerial view shows the regular plan of the site, with the six pylons, the Hypostyle Hall in the foreground and the temple proper.

Dynasties (including Thutmosis I, Hatshepsut, Thutmosis III, Amenhotep III, Ramesses I, Ramesses II, Seti I, Seti II and Ramesses III) built a complex of sacraria (shrines), obelisks, pylons and vestibules, all of which were characterized by hyperbolic grandeur.

The entrance runs from the west to the east through a series of pylons that gradually decrease in size as the visitor advances. The First Pylon (370 feet wide compared to ca. 164 feet of the Sixth) leads into the Great Court (328 by 262 feet), the largest court in ancient Egypt, which includes the temples of Seti II and Ramesses III.

The Second Pylon leads to the Hypostyle Hall, built by Ramesses II, the greatest builder of the New Kingdom. This hall, which is 335 by 174 feet, is the largest covered area ever built for a temple, and contains a forest of 134 columns carved in the shapes of the papyrus plant; 122 of these are decorated with a capital in the form of a closed calyx and 12 with an open calyx.

Four other pylons follow close together, then the visitor reaches the court of the Middle Kingdom where the earliest sacrarium stood.

The court between the Third and Fourth pylons also gives access to the South Propylaea, which are a development of the complex in a north-south direction. Following this axis through five more pylons, the visitor arrives at the Avenue of the Sphinxes, which connects the sanctuary of Amon with the temple of Mut.

A little to the west, another avenue flanked by ram-headed sphinxes runs the more than two-mile distance to Luxor from the temple of Khonsu. At the start of every new year, a procession walked the length of the avenue carrying the statue of Amon from Karnak to the temple of Luxor (referred to as the Southern Harem of Amon), which was strictly dependent on Karnak and used only on this annual occasion.

The Temples of Abu Simbel

ABU SIMBEL, EGYPT

by Beatrix Herling and Maria Laura Vergelli

In the desert region of the upper Nile valley, known as Nubia during the Roman era, Ramesses II had two underground rock temples built. Today these are considered symbols of the architecture and art of the Ramessid period (1291-1075 BC). Built on the west bank of the river, the façades of both

temples are decorated with colossal statues cut directly out of the rock in which the façades were made.

The larger of the two temples was consecrated to the gods Amon, Ra Horakhty, and Ptah, and to Ramesses II himself. The pharaoh is portrayed in four seated statues approximately 66 feet high, set in two pairs, one on each side of the entrance that extends for 115 feet inside the hillside. The architectural form and decoration were skillfully designed for purposes of royal propaganda: the colossal dimensions of the statues represent the power and strength of the king – who wears the composite crown of Upper and Lower Egypt – and the smiles on the four faces radiate an aura of serene awareness, justice and wise government.

The extravagant and dramatic exterior contrasts with a small, intimate space inside that was dug out of the rock to create a colonnaded 'court,' hypostyle (pillared) room, vestibule and the cella (interior of the temple) that contained the statues of the sovereign and Ramessid triad of gods. The

inclusion of the pharaoh's statues with those of the gods celebrated Ramesses II's apotheosis (while he was still alive) in a design typical of the temples of the New Kingdom but transferred to an underground construction. A parallel can be drawn between the effects created on the façade of the temple by the light, and the carefully contrived lighting effects inside.

156 top *Ramesses II decided to build the two temples of Abu Simbel on sites where previously two caves had been dedicated by the indigenous people to local gods. By building these two temples in honor of Egyptian deities, the pharaoh also wished to emphasize Nubia's subjection to the Egyptian empire religiously. The temples have been part of the World Heritage List since 1979.*

157 center *In this celebratory low relief in the Great Temple, Ramesses II is shown on his war chariot. The walls of the room are decorated with scenes of processions and offerings in honor of the pharaoh and his queen.*

157 bottom *In the pronaos of the Great Temple, eight Osiriac pillars support the ceiling. This type of pillar is characteristic of the Ramessid period (19th and 20th dynasties) and portrays the sovereign on the shaft in the form of a standing mummy. The similarity is to Osiris, who judged the souls of the dead and pronounced on their resurrection.*

156 bottom *Six statues approximately 33 feet high of the pharaoh and Nefertari, his wife, line the facade of the small temple, which Ramesses II dedicated to his favorite consort and consecrated to the goddess Hathor.*

156-157 *Small statues of Ramesses' sons, daughters and wives stand at the feet of the colossal statues of the pharaoh seated and wearing the double crown of Upper and Lower Egypt and the false beard.*

157 top *The cella contains four statues carved in the rock. These are of Ramesses himself and the three gods to whom the temple was dedicated: from left: Ptah, Amon, Ramesses II and Ra-Horakhty.*

The Temples of Abu Simbel

158 This is a close-up of the face of one of the colossal statues of Ramesses at the side of the entrance to the Great Temple. Note the cuts made by restorers to transport the temple when it was saved from the rising waters of Lake Nasser following construction of the Aswan High Dam. Once the temple had been reassembled, finishing details were the responsibility of the restorers from the Egyptian Antiquities Service, who reduced to the minimum every trace of the cutting operation using a mix of sand and synthetic resins.

159 The sectioning and reassembly operations of the temple are in full swing. This rescue project was undertaken in 1960 by UNESCO with the help of many countries and took 5 years to complete.

The pharaoh's regality and divinity were also represented in monumental forms in the smaller temple dedicated to the goddess Hathor (Ramesses' divine consort) and Nefertari (the pharaoh's earthly wife). Composed of a hypostyle atrium and cella, the façade has six statues of the royal couple standing.

The temples were originally built on the slopes of a promontory that faced onto the Nile. They were discovered in 1813 by the great Swiss Orientalist J. L. Burckhardt (1784-1814). However, the area of Nubia made fertile by the Nile underwent dramatic transformation in the 20th century: in

1898 the first Aswan Dam was built and the level of the river rose. In the 1950s, construction of the second dam (the Sadd el-Aali) placed the architectural and artistic heritage of Nubia at risk and the temples of Abu Simbel were due to be lost under the rising waters of Lake Nasser. To save them, UNESCO organized a rescue operation in 1963 that was completed in just four years. The temples were removed from the rock, cut into 30-ton blocks, and then reassembled 215 feet above the water level in exactly the same respective positions and facing the same direction in which they were built in the mid-13th century BC.

The Temples of Abu Simbel

161 Inside the Small Temple Nefertari is shown with a sun disk between the horns of a cow. The queen, who lived in the thirteenth century BC, died many years before her husband, shortly after the temples were completed.

160 Taken from the decorative section in the Small Temple, the scenes show Ramesses II and Nefertari making offerings to the enthroned goddess Hathor (top), while the pharaoh, with his wife behind, kills an enemy (below). Scenes of this kind recur in Egyptian art from the earliest dynasties.

160-161 The Hypostyle Hall in the Small Temple is divided into three aisles by two rows of three Hathoric pillars. It leads into a vestibule followed by the inner sanctuary dug out of the mountain where Hathor, in the form of a cow, is seen protecting Ramesses II. At the center we see the column with the stylized representation of the goddess.

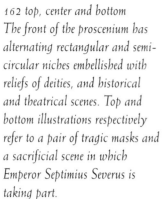

162 top, center and bottom
The front of the proscenium has alternating rectangular and semi-circular niches embellished with reliefs of deities, and historical and theatrical scenes. Top and bottom illustrations respectively refer to a pair of tragic masks and a sacrificial scene in which Emperor Septimius Severus is taking part.

The Theater of Sabratha

SABRATHA, LIBYA

by Miriam Taviani

The theater stands in the east district of the Roman city of Sabratha, which, with the rest of Tripolitania (part of modern Libya), was incorporated in the Roman province of Africa Nova in 46 BC. This event stimulated growth of the city southward and eastward over the earlier Punic settlement. The theater was built in the late 2nd and early 3rd centuries AD, during the community's period of greatest prosperity, and today is the building that best symbolizes the city. It is one of the largest of its kind; its fine state of preservation is partly due to the restoration operations that have been carried out. Standing in a flat zone, the *cavea* (auditorium) of the theater is decorated externally with three orders of arches, framed by Tuscan pillars and Corinthian pilasters. The internal hemi-cycle was divided into three transversal rings, each of which was divided into six longitudinal sections, and was surrounded by a colonnaded portico. The most imposing element in the theater was the *frons scaenae* (proscenium) composed of three large semi-circular niches onto each of which a door opened at the back. It was decorated with three orders of columns built with different types of marble (white and colored) and carved with different shafts (smooth, grooved and spiral). Aligned with the doors, three straight colonnaded corridors interrupted the curve of the niches, creating a compact and *chiaroscuro* effect not dissimilar to that of the Septizodium (a free-standing ornamental façade), which Emperor Septimius Severus had built in Rome. The most original part of the building is the front of the proscenium where the alternate semi-circular and rectangular niches are decorated (rare in this sort of building) with reliefs of gods and mythological episodes, and theatrical scenes. The most outstanding is in the central niche where Septimius Severus is performing a sacrifice in the presence of personifications of the cities of Rome and Sabratha. This may have been an allusion to the concession to the city of the status of a colony.

162-163 The monumental frons
scaenae had three orders.
It dominates the north-facing
cavea and the orchestra,
which are separated by a
semicircular balustrade.
The seats of the proedria
(the seats reserved for VIPs)
stood on three lower steps at
the front of the cavea.

163 bottom left The scenery apparatus
can be seen beyond the outer arches,
which have only been partly rebuilt.

163 bottom right The Judgment of
Paris, center, adorns the right-hand
niche on the front of the proscenium.

164 top *The outer wall of Alexandria Library is called the 'Talking Wall' as it is decorated with letters and ideograms of all ancient and modern alphabets, plus musical and mathematical symbols.*

164 bottom *To the architects, the purpose of the 'segments' of the outside of the Library was to resemble the rising sun (for those who look from the city toward the sea), i.e., the symbol of rebirth and the spreading of the light of knowledge.*

The Library of Alexandria

ALEXANDRIA, EGYPT

by Guglielmo Novelli

The ancient Library of Alexandria was built at the start of the 3rd century BC for Ptolemy I (also known as Ptolemy I Soter, 'the Preserver'). He was a man of letters raised in the culture of Greece and was an enthusiast of the teachings of Aristotle. The set of buildings was created by Demetrius of Phaleron and, with time, turned into a university that prospered until the reign of Cleopatra, the last queen of Egypt. Scholars and students from across the known world gathered to teach or study there.

Some of the more famous were Euclid, the father of geometry, and Aristarchus of Samos and Hipparchus of Nicaea, two of the greatest astronomers of antiquity. Alexandria's was no ordinary library, and was considered one of the wonders of the world, but it was destroyed in several stages by wars and religious fanaticism.

Sixteen centuries later, the new Library was built on the same site as its illustrious forebear in the district of Silsila, and with the same aim: to assemble in one place all of human knowledge.

Designed by the Norwegian firm Snohetta, under the direction of Christoph Kapellar, a Norwegian architect, it was built for UNESCO and twenty or so other countries that signed the Declaration of Aswan in 1990. The building covers an area of 102,000 square yards and is 11 stories high.

In the form of an enormous inclined sun that rises from the sea (a symbol of the renaissance of the ancient Library, and of the diffusion of knowledge and understanding), the building is like a cylinder cut obliquely at 16 degrees. The

164-165 top A plaza in the inner courtyard leads to the main entrance, which is made from concrete, metal and glass. The large sphere of the Planetarium can be seen in the background.

164-165 bottom The drawing of the elevation of the Library shows the large outer wall made from gray granite from Aswan. It is built in the shape of a semicylinder cut obliquely at 16 degrees.

165 bottom The section shows several of the 11 floors in the 100-foot high building. The new Library was designed by the Norwegian architectural firm Snohetta under the patronage of UNESCO.

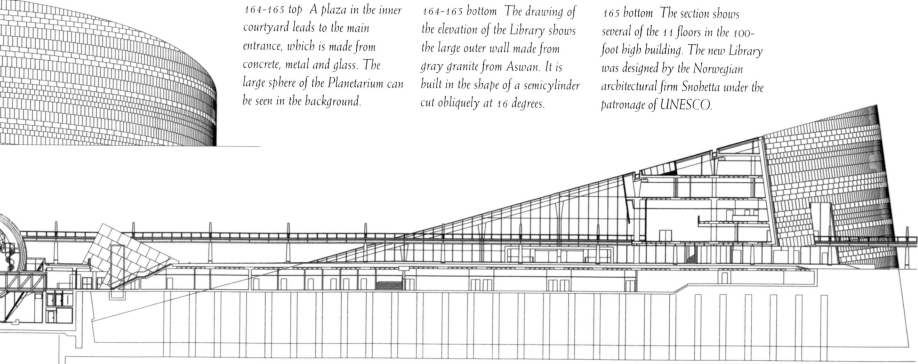

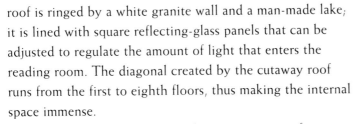

roof is ringed by a white granite wall and a man-made lake;
it is lined with square reflecting-glass panels that can be
adjusted to regulate the amount of light that enters the
reading room. The diagonal created by the cutaway roof
runs from the first to eighth floors, thus making the internal
space immense.

The center of the building is the 215,000 square-foot
reading room made from reinforced concrete and wood. The
2,000 reading places are positioned between 100 or so white
concrete columns up to 52 feet tall, each measuring 27 inches
in diameter and crowned by capitals that resemble the 'lotus
flower' capitals of ancient Egypt.

The Library also includes two museums, an institute for
the restoration of ancient books, a children's library, a
computing school, a conference center, an underground car
park and storerooms.

Ancient manuscripts, rare books and maps are held on the
shelves of the new building, which overall contains over 8
million volumes as well as multimedia and audiovisual
materials.

The exterior of the Library is lined with gray granite from
Aswan, the stone used by the pharaohs. It has no windows
and is decorated with graphical signs from every system of
writing in the world, including rock paintings and
hieroglyphics.

To ensure that the new Library will not be destroyed
by a fire, like the previous one, the engineers have designed
the ceilings in anodized aluminum insulated against the
heat. Architect Christoph Kapellar summarizes the design
of the building as follows: 'The circular structure of the
building symbolizes the knowledge of the world; we chose
the image of a microchip for the roof to indicate that this
institution is not only interested in preserving books, but is
dedicated to exchanging information with the outside world.'

*166 top left The building covers
an area of 800,000 square feet and
contains reading rooms, a restoration
center for ancient books, a children's
library, a computer school, meeting
and conference halls, and an
underground parking lot.*

*166 top right The roof is an
immense inclined semi-circle that
rises to the 7th floor. It is lined
with adjustable glass panels that
modulate and distribute the correct
quantity of light to enter the
reading rooms.*

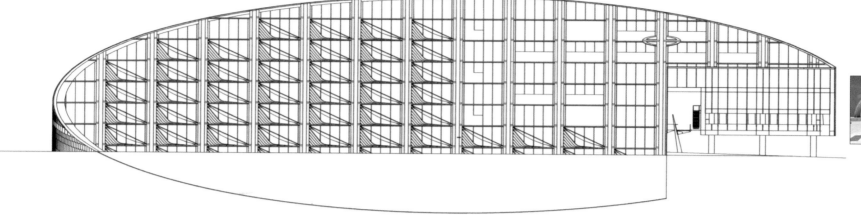

167 center Alexandria Library covers 800,000 square feet. Of the many reading rooms inside, the main one covers 200,000 square feet at the center of the building. It is built from concrete and wood and can seat 2,000.

167 bottom The Library's central reading room has more than 100 white concrete pillars up to 55 feet in height. Their shape vaguely resembles ancient Egyptian columns with lotus flower capitals.

166-167 The sloping roof underscores the Library's modern and efficient appearance. The adjustability of the panels not only ensures good light distribution but also limits problems caused by irradiation of the direct sunlight to which the building is exposed.

167 top The original design was by a team of Norwegian architects led by Christoph Kapellar. It highlights the regular paneling and the 'microchip' form of the roof, which was chosen to symbolize the crucial role that the institution would play in the diffusion of information.

ASIA

It seems almost impossible to cover in a single presentation the huge variety of architectural forms and models of the Asian continent. Though welded to Europe to form a single territorial block, much of the Asian region extending south beyond the Urals is geographically unfavorable to human settlement, and therefore has not been greatly altered by the hand of man. In the west, two narrow straits – the Bosporus and the Dardanelles – separate the continents, and while Asia has been exposed and receptive to Western civilization, the continent has remained somewhat apart from and in conflict with Europe. Similarly, the strip of land that joins Asia to Africa, the area known as Palestine, has for thousands of years been a theater of man-made tension.

In antiquity, the Near and Middle East regions that ring the eastern Mediterranean shared historical and cultural developments with the Western world. Architectural sites that have survived to the present day attest to this important and memorable period.

In Persia, on the road from Isfahan to Shiraz, on the left bank of the Puhar river, the traveler comes across the ruins of Persepolis, the imperial city that Alexander, drunk with wine and victory, gave to the flames. 'This was the end of the capital of the whole of the Orient, [the city] from which many peoples previously demanded laws; it was the homeland of many kings, and the only menace in the past to Greece' (Curtius Rufus, V, 7,8).

"Thus Persepolis watches over the abandoned plain. The space, sky, falcons … and the quality of the Persian light all confer a sort of springing lightness to the great terrace … at the heart of the ruins: the columns hover in the air, without supporting any roof; arched doorways stand open without leading into any room …, in the Hall of a Hundred Columns, a desolate expanse of ruins…. This roofless desolation is dominated by the sun, which creates black square shadows that render the carvings of the reliefs even deeper. Except for dry leaves rustled by a lizard amongst the stones, silence reigns.' Such were the impressions noted by the English writer Vita Sackville-West.

The outcome of the heroic struggle of the Greeks against the Persians in the 5th century BC reverberated a century later in Alexander the Great's expedition. After his conquest of Persia, which had earlier subjected Greece, he continued as far as the Indus river, where the expedition ground to a halt. Alexander's declared intention was to check the security of the border at the mouth of the river, but he naturally had a desire for knowledge. Had Alexander continued eastward toward the Ganges, history would have taken a different course. Although in Central Asia, Alexander's army only conquered Bactria effectively, archaeological studies are turning up the remains of cities from that era along the Oxus; Alexander's biographers had described these, based on tales brought back by Greeks who had taken part in Alexander's expedition.

Alexander's expedition resulted in the diffusion of Greek language, literature, philosophy, art and religion and the reciprocal absorption of Oriental customs, artistry, and religious and philosophical ideas. These two exchanges together formed the basis of what historians call 'Hellenism.' This phenomenon of exchange occurred primarily in the period between Alexander's death (323 BC) and the Roman conquest of Egypt (30 BC). It led to the use of a common spoken language – though at two levels: learned and popular – and a common artistic vocabulary that extended from Gandhara, beyond Bactria, to Iberia.

Syria, Palestine, Egypt and, in the Orient, northwest India were all conquered by Alexander and formed the foundations of the great Hellenistic kingdoms from which Hellenization irradiated. Throughout the era of the Diadochs (Alexander's successors), expeditions and exploration continued, and passed beyond the Indus and Syr Daria rivers as far as the borders of China. Once Greece and Macedonia had been reduced to Roman provinces (147–146 BC), the philo-Hellenism of the Romans, which culminated in the age of Emperor Hadrian (AD 117–138), decided the fortunes of Hellenism beyond the Hellenistic world, namely the lands reached or conquered by the Romans.

In a later cultural shift, the regions in Mediterranean Asia in which Christianity first spread were, in the 7th century

AD, the first areas through which Islam expanded in its advance into the Iranian highlands and Central Asia.

In the 4th century AD Emperor Constantine refounded the Greek city of Byzantium, naming it Constantinopolis. The city became the capital of the Eastern Roman Empire, and gave vigorous life to the Byzantine art that had emerged from the fusion of Classical and Oriental traditions and the need for a new Christian spirituality. Within this polymorphic Graeco-Roman-Middle Eastern region, an intense exchange of technical knowledge mixed with cultural, symbolic and religious elements took place. Here the civilizations of Central Asia and the Far East, developing in parallel, increasingly appear to have been complementary rather than antithetical.

Though suffused with an inherent transcendent magnificence, the works of Asian architecture, no less than those of Western architecture, reflect the history, social structure and economy of the civilizations that produced them. Though architecture was commonly considered a lesser art, with no immediate creativity and burdened by the baggage of technical requirements, the achievements of Asian architecture are so different from those of the West that it may seem fanciful to trace them back to a single approach.

In the regions of tundra, forests, steppes and deserts, architecture was long limited to underground tombs indicated on the surface by rings of stones or mounds, and rare forms of housing. Durable housing was rare because the nomadic peoples and hunters of the north lived in felt tents. Literary sources make reference to 'citadels' fortified with wood and stone, but no trace remains of them. The creation of towns and cities is a phenomenon that occurred only over the last two centuries. Asian architecture was, therefore, produced by the sedentary and agricultural civilizations of the south, in what is now China and in the Japanese archipelago.

It has been noted that cities in Asia have had a diverse and lesser importance for human habitation than villages, which remain the fundamental form of habitat for the sedentary societies of the region. In complex societies – which were predominantly agricultural, without potential, which impeded the creation of private business, and which existed in a difficult balance between the paternalism and despotism of the State (or ruler) – the centralization of power was generally an obstruction to growth. The exception to this situation was in Central Asia. There a mercantile economy was developed by the existence of caravan cities and isolated monasteries, and this led to the creation of refined towns and cities that had strong economic and cultural influence. These centers, however, were radically transformed by the advent of Islam. Another feature peculiar to the region was the theocratic basis of Tibetan society in which architectural forms were determined by mystical and religious beliefs.

It is still the case that the architecture of Asia is mostly religious. As faith and religious practice are universal and metaphysical values of existence are accepted by one and all, religious architecture is charged with symbols and allusions. However, artistic and architectural design are also related to residential buildings, which are traditionally constructed in natural settings. This design in some formal aspects heralded modern architectural style.

In the Far East, buildings are linear and mostly made of wood, while in India and Indianized regions they feature modeling in stone, or are 'built' in different materials or 'carved' out of rock. Thus Asian architecture can also represent the Asian visions of the cosmos. The architectural historian M. Bussagli notes that 'Asian architects are never philosophers or scientists, but their creations almost always reflect a philosophical or religious speculation of which the artist's creative impulse and aesthetic sense are permeated by their essence, fixing it in forms and modules that can, in turn, influence the development of religious thought. Religious thought is also a vision of the world.'

Religious themes are therefore deeply ingrained with the essence of creative thought in Asian architecture, and reflect aspects of 'collective Asian thought.' The various strands of which this consists vary but are also consistent: they have their roots in the relationship between man and nature (feared for its power), and in the predominance of the universal and absolute over the individual.

169 left The Dome of the Rock is the glistening symbol of the old and holy city of Jerusalem.

169 center The Hall of Supreme Harmony in the Forbidden City in Beijing.

169 right The 'sail' of the Burj Al-Arab flies on a man-made island near Dubai in the Persian Gulf.

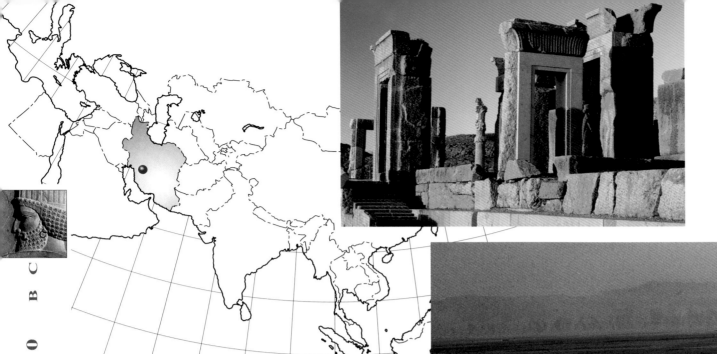

Persepolis

SHIRAZ, IRAN

by Flaminia Bartolini

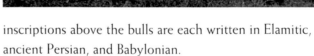

The ruins of the most famous archaeological site in Iran lie on the Isfahan–Shiraz road. The monumental complex was begun by Darius I in 518 BC with the construction of a terrace, an *apadana* (audience hall) and the building known as the 'harem' beneath a rocky spur called Kuh-i Rahmat. Darius' son and successor, Xerxes I (486-465), completed the *apadana* and the *harem*, erected the *hadish* (king's residence) and entrances, and began construction of the Hall of a Hundred Columns, completed by Artaxerxes I (465-424). Artaxerxes III Ochus (358-338) provided the site with a palace, but this remained unfinished in 330 BC, when Persepolis was burned down by Alexander the Great (356-323).

The walls around the city were formed by large square dovetailed limestone blocks. The magnificent entrance portals built by Xerxes I form a square portico with 4 columns and open on three sides. Two gigantic winged bulls over 16 feet tall flank the west gate, and winged bulls with human heads stand on either side of the east gate. Four

inscriptions above the bulls are each written in Elamitic, ancient Persian, and Babylonian.

Passing through the west gate, the visitor reaches the *apadana* begun by Darius I and completed by Xerxes I.

The square central hall originally had 36 columns but only 3 remain. To the sides of this building there are 3 porticoes each of 6 columns, and a few access areas.

The *apadana* was reached by two monumental stairways adorned with large ritual reliefs. These have three registers and represent a procession of Persian, Median and Elamitic dignitaries accompanied by footsoldiers, horsemen and archers marching towards the tributaries of the kingdom.

The tributaries came from 23 vassal satrapies of the empire, and each New Year they presented the Persian king with the best products their respective countries could provide.

The *tripylon* (council hall) is a square room with 4 columns reached by a large flight of steps. The outer walls are decorated with reliefs of sphinxes, lions attacking bulls,

170 top and 170-171 The throne room in the Royal Palace (Apadana), to which Xerxes' Gate (top) leads, covers an area of 50,000 square feet in which the ruins of 100 columns remain. The two flights of steps that lead to it are decorated with three horizontal registers of peoples of the empire bearing tributes to the enthroned king: the Medians, wearing tight clothes, the Persians, wearing loose clothes, warriors bearing spears, and the Melophori, the king's personal guard.

170 bottom and 171 bottom The imposing ruins of Persepolis mark one of the five residences of the Great King of Persia, with Susa, Ecbatana, Babylon and Pasargadae. Persepolis lies on the left bank of the Pulsar river on the desert plateau of Merdacht. The buildings were constructed on a huge rectangular terrace built by Darius I, on which there are several levels connected by a flight of 106 steps. The outer walls are decorated with celebratory and propitiatory reliefs of lions attacking bulls and rows of soldiers armed with spears and shields.

Persepolis

and processions of dignitaries and courtiers holding lotus flowers. The doors are decorated with a low relief of Darius and Xerxes carried in triumph on a throne by 28 tributaries of the empire, and by a winged symbol of the god Ahura Mazdah.

The south gate leads to the stairway of the *hadish* built by Xerxes I. Standing on the highest part of the terrace, it has a central room that was once adorned with 36 columns; they were probably made of wood and lined with stucco, but today all that remains are their bases.

Similar in plan is Darius' *tachara* (audience room), completed by Xerxes. The reliefs on the doors show the king entering or leaving the palace, and fighting a lion, a bull and a winged monster.

The main room has been renamed the Hall of Mirrors on account of the smoothness of the stone with which it is lined. Construction of the Hall of a Hundred Columns in the northeast section of the terrace was begun by Xerxes I and completed by Artaxerxes I.

The square central room had 100 columns, but only the bases were left standing after Alexander's conquest of Persepolis. Here too the doors are decorated with low reliefs of processions and the king fighting wild animals.

173 bottom left The portals and columns of the Apadana are decorated with sculptures of winged bulls, spirits, kings fighting wild beasts, and battle scenes – all typical of the Achaemenid stylistic vocabulary. There are clear links with Egyptian art in the stylization of the forms, and with Babylonian art in the roundness of the solids.

173 bottom right The ruins of Persepolis are only a minimal indication of the grandeur of the Achaemenian empire before the arrival of Alexander the Great (356–323 BC). Plutarch reported that to punish the Persians for the destruction of Athens, the Macedon conqueror ordered Persepolis to be looted, then put to the flames.

175 Scenes of animals fighting – mostly lions attacking bulls – are seen on the portals, steps and walls of Persepolis representing the power of the king. Related to Mesopotamian art in their sinuous lines, arabesques, and filled, harmonious volumes, Achaemenid art was to become a fundamental reference for Indian art in its monumental plasticity, rounded surfaces and sense of dynamism.

174 top left A procession of vassal dignitaries bears tributes to Darius. Achaemenian art was also affected by the plasticity of Greek art, which is something probably assimilated during the repeated wars and dominations between the two regions. The faces, which are more individual than the bodies, appear to reflect the reality of the figures.

174 top right Darius III is followed by servants that protect him in a relief on his tomb. The king was killed in Bactria in 330 BC, then his body was taken to Persepolis.

174 bottom A relief of Darius the Great. King of the Persians from 521 to 485 BC, he was the son of Hystaspes; he extended the boundaries of his empire to the borders of India to the east, and into Thrace, Macedonia and as far as the Danube in the west. His reorganization of his lands into 20 satrapies (districts) is renowned.

176-177 The Great Wall is covered by snow in Jinshanling Pass, one of the less frequented sections. This zone was of great strategic and military importance and was continually strengthened over the centuries with fortifications.

176 bottom Jiayuguan fort at the western end of the Great Wall stands on the old Silk Road in the province of Gansu, which is a broad fertile zone that lies between the Gobi Desert to the north and the mountains of Tibet to the south.

The Great Wall

CHINA

by Beatrix Herling

A symbol of the vast size of China, the Great Wall crosses almost two thirds of the country from east to west, covering a distance of 4,160 miles and bearing witness to the organizational and military power of the Chinese empire and the skill and tenacity of its people.

Construction of the wall is attributed to the emperor Qin Shi Huangdi, the first and last emperor of the Qin dynasty. During his reign in the last quarter of the 3rd century BC, he unified China and established an empire.

Sections of regional fortifications were built from the 8th century BC with the aim of creating lines of defense against the Mongol invasions during the Spring and Autumn Period (722–481 BC) and the Warring States Period (481–221 BC), before Qin Shi Huangdi 's ascent to the throne. However, the new Qin dynasty was aware of the need to defend the unified territory and people, to create employment and to ensure a more stable rhythm of life. Thus in 221 BC, during a military expedition to the north under General Mêng Tian, the work of joining up and strengthening the various regional fortifications was begun.

In a decade, soldiers, prisoners and inhabitants who lived close to the works together built a wall 'of 10,000 li' – in Chinese, *Wan-li-ch'ang*. A li is about 550 yards long so that, according to its name, the wall stretched about 5,500 miles when it was completed.

In its construction local stone was used, or, where this was not available, a double wall was constructed using beaten earth.

Following many restoration and expansion operations, the wall's strategic importance grew in the Ming era (1368–1644). At this time sections were strengthened and raised in height (up to 33 feet), and observation platforms, towers, gates, new defensive means and service structures were added to form an architectural complex that had both military and administrative border functions.

Tradition and pride make the Great Wall a national monument deeply bound to Chinese history and culture. It is said that its winding path through the mountains, valleys and desert, traditionally associated with the body of a dragon, is one of the most clearly visible features on Earth seen from the Moon.

This claim was first published in August 1939, in *The Fortnightly Review* (London), at a time well before either stratospheric flight or Moon landings were possible.

177 top The Great Wall winds along the crests of Badaling. In 1961 the State Council of China declared this section of the Wall a cultural and national asset, and, in 1987, UNESCO declared it a World Heritage site.

177 bottom A magnificent example of military engineering, the Great Wall (seen here in Jinshanling in the province of Hebei) not only allowed troops to be moved quickly but, thanks to a series of forts, permitted rapid communications concerning attacks to be made and reinforcements sent out.

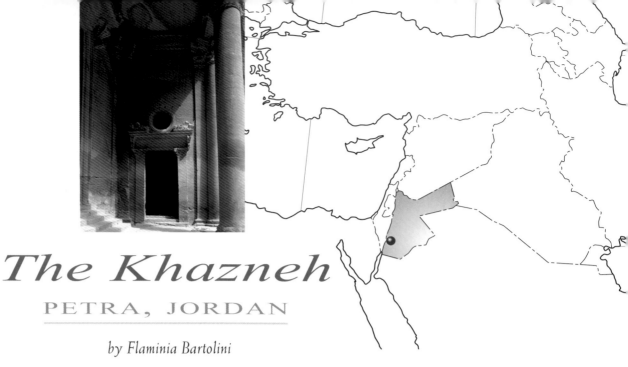

The Khazneh

PETRA, JORDAN

by Flaminia Bartolini

178 top   Three doors in the vestibule of the Khazneh (this is the northwest entrance) lead into the burial chambers. Carved out of the rock, the ruins of Petra are of great interest for the richness and compositional freedom of their architecture.

178 center   Where the Siq opens out, the Khazneh suddenly comes into view, carved out of the sheer rock-face. The ruins of Petra were discovered and excavated in 1812 by J. L. Burckhardt. Further excavation was carried out in 1929 and 1935.

178 bottom   The upper trabeation of the Khazneh has a pediment and a central tholos. The two halves of the pediment, decorated with eagles as acroters, are supported by Corinthian columns.

179   For the freedom with which the architectural elements of the magnificent red façade are articulated, the Khazneh has been compared to the most daring examples of 17th-century Baroque.

Petra ('a rose-red city – half as old as Time'), the capital of both the Nabatean kingdom and the Roman province of Arabia, is situated in the south of what was known as Transjordania. Its location behind the Um el-Biyara made it difficult to reach but allowed it to flourish as a caravan and commercial center. Petra had a route that connected it to the Red Sea and others that connected it to Arabia Felix, Mesopotamia, and the Mediterranean. The ancient city lay among a series of mountains that closed around it like an amphitheater, and on which the Nabataeans built places of worship to gods such as Dushara and Allat. The city included temples, markets, two theaters and many tombs that were dug out of the rock. The only entry point to the city's inhabited area was from the east, along the bed of a dry torrent called the Siq. In the past, the waters of the torrent were diverted into the city aqueduct.

One of the best-preserved buildings that face onto the Siq is the tomb called al- Khazneh ('The Treasury'). The building's façade is 130 feet high and 85 feet wide. It is carved entirely out of the rock and divided into two levels. The lower level is centered on a portico with six columns, four of which stand to the sides of the entrance steps. Only the two central shafts (the left-hand one has been re-erected) are real columns; the remaining four protrude from the rock for only three-quarters of their circumference.

On either side of the portico, two very worn relief sculptures each depicted a cloaked man in front of a horse. The pediment is decorated with volutes (scroll-like ornaments) influenced by Hellenistic art and, at the corners of the architrave, two feline animals function as acroters (ornaments). The upper level of the façade is divided into three distinct parts: a circular architectural feature (*tholos*) in the center is covered by a conical roof that is in turn crowned by an urn; to either side of this is a half-gable supported by two columns, of which the external columns have only three-quarters of their circumference carved, and the others are half-columns, i.e., they have only half their circumferences carved. The central sculpture on the *tholos* is of a woman holding a cornucopia in her left hand. The entrance vestibule leads into two side rooms, which are reached through high portals decorated with low reliefs, and, continuing up a flight of steps, into a central room in which burial niches were cut out of the walls.

180-181 With the unmistakable red of its outer walls, Haghia Sophia looks out over the Bosporus. Despite the building's system of buttresses and load dischargement, the large dome has turned out to be the weakest part of the construction.

180 bottom This three-apse half-dome shows the complexity of Haghia Sophia. Construction lasted six years carried out by craftsmen from throughout the Byzantine empire.

181 top The imposing dome and minarets of Haghia Sophia contrast with the lovely gardens next to the mosque. The minarets were added towards the middle of the fifteenth century when the basilica was converted into a mosque.

181 bottom In this surreal evening picture, the ships transiting the strait seem to tower over the bulk of Haghia Sophia.

Haghia Sophia

ISTANBUL, TURKEY

by Flaminia Bartolini

Ever since its construction centuries before Constantinople became Istanbul, Haghia Sofia has been the city's most famous religious building. Before it was built, the basilica of Constantine II stood on the site. Situated between the imperial palace and the Hippodrome, the basilica was built in AD 360 and known as the Megale Ekklesia ('Great Church'). Burned down in 404 by the followers of John Chrysostomus, it was rebuilt by Theodosius II and completed in 415. The colonnaded portico from the first basilica remained and was incorporated into the new construction. In 430 the name of the church was altered to Hagia Sophia, which means 'Holy Wisdom,' but this new church was also destroyed by fire during the Nika revolts against Justinian in 532.

Justinian then decided to make substantial modifications to the church and chose the architects Anthemius of Tralles and Isidorus of Miletus to design the third basilica. They followed the model of the church of Saints Sergius and Bacchus, also in Constantinople, which the pair probably also designed.

A description of the events of the construction has survived in the writings of Procopius, who narrates how a drawing of the building was shown to Justinian in a dream by an angel.

The structure, based on Greek-cross plan, was crowned by a dome 102 feet in diameter and by two lateral half-domes. Inside, columns and galleries divided the apses of the narthex. Justinian's dome collapsed in 558 (21 years after the church was inaugurated) and was rebuilt by Isidorus the Younger in 562. The new design differed considerably from that of Anthemius of Tralles, in particular with regard to the dome, which was increased in height by 23 feet. Large new glass windows were added in the south and north tympani (masonry drums) to increase the amount of light inside. A golden altar crowned by a ciborium (an ornamental canopy supported by four columns) was positioned inside the apse, the walls of which were lined with silver. The basilica was surrounded by a series of buildings: to the west there was a colonnaded atrium with a fountain at its center; to the north two baptisteries were built; to the northeast there was a circular sacristy; to the south, the church was connected to the palace of the Patriarch and his offices; and an entrance to the southeast connected Haghia Sophia to the imperial palace. The church was used for imperial ceremonies, as two rooms – the *metatoria* – reserved for the personal use of the emperor demonstrate.

The earthquake that struck Constantinople in 869 ruined a

182 bottom left Remains of an earlier fresco, dating to the Christian period, are seen in a smaller dome. Beyond the wall, it is possible to make out Christ on the Cross, various saints and sacred scenes.

182 bottom right The features of Christ blessing, with his long and angular face, and the light and folds of the drapery are clearly Byzantine in style.

183 top The large space beneath the dome is embellished with a row of porphyry and green marble columns, topped by capitals carved with stylized plant motifs.

182-183 The mosque inside is completely lined with mosaics, and stylized plant and geometric patterns on a gold ground. The light enters through a number of windows and reflects on the gold of the tiles to create an effect that seems to dematerialize the walls. The dazzle generated gives the illusion that there is a strong light source inside the mosque.

tympanum, but this was rebuilt as it appears today. In 989, another earthquake caused the collapse of the west arcade with the half-dome annex, and part of the main dome. Reconstruction was undertaken by the Armenian architect Tridat (Tiridates). In 1317, exterior buttresses were added on the north and east sides, but shortly after, in 1346, the east half-dome collapsed with a portion of the main dome. Restorations were carried out in 1353. The decoration in the opus sectile technique of mosaic work from Justinian's time still remains in good condition; it is distinctive for its essentially non-figurative style. In 1453 Haghia Sophia was converted into a mosque and renamed Ayasofia Camii, and four minarets were erected at the corners of the building. Extensive maintenance work was performed in 1573 and again in 1847-49, this time by the Swiss architects Gaspare and Giuseppe Fossati. In 1931 the mosque was deconsecrated on the orders of Atatürk, and the building was turned into a museum.

183 bottom Due to the Islamic prohibition of portraying Allah, the walls of Haghia Sophia are decorated with verses from the Koran on large circular panels made from Iznik clay.

183

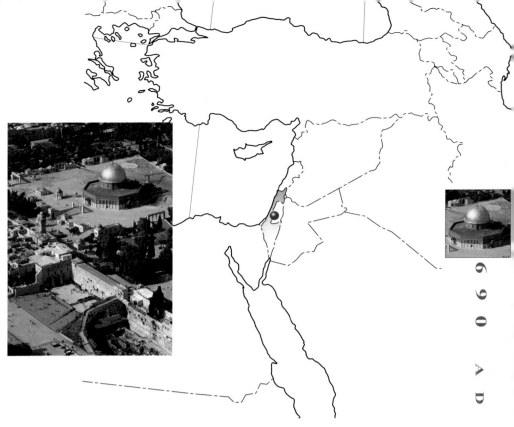

184 *The modern golden anodized aluminum of the dome contrasts deeply with the blue of the arabesque tiles that were used to replace the original ones in the 16th century.*

185 center *The façades have two orders. On four of the eight sides (corresponding to the points of the compass) there are the entrances, with a short corridor on either side. The gold dome rises in the center.*

185 top *The outside of the mosque is covered by a band of marble and majolica tiles ordered by Suleiman the Magnificent in 1552 from Persian manufacturers in Kashan.*

185 bottom *The steps to the mosque lead up to airy porticoes built with three or four fornices in the age of the Mamelukes. These represent the limit of the sacred area.*

The Dome of the Rock

JERUSALEM, ISRAEL

by Maria Eloisa Carrozza

From wherever the visitor looks at the Old City of Jerusalem, from the Mount of Olives to the valley of Hinnom, the Dome of the Rock is immediately apparent, sparkling in the sunlight. Historically and in legend, the hill on which the Qubbet as-Sakhra (Dome of the Rock or, less properly, Omar's Mosque) stands represents the interweaving of three religions. This is believed to have been the site on which Abraham lit the fire when he was about to sacrifice his son Isaac; it was also the place of the 'brazen altar' (Altar of the Holocaust) in Solomon's Temple, the few ruins of which are today known as the Wailing Wall and a place of prayer for the Jews; it was also from here that Mohamed began his journey to Allah on the winged horse that was given to him by the archangel Gabriel. Finally, this was the place where, between 1099 and 1187, the Crusaders swore their faith, transformed Omar's Mosque into a church and raised the symbol of the Cross. The Muslim ruler Saladin removed the Christian emblem when he retook Jerusalem in 1187, and the crescent moon of Islam has never ceased to be visible since.

This hill was also the site of the Temple of Herod, but the Romans razed the structure in AD 70, at the end of the First Jewish War. With this, all trace of the Jewish religion disappeared from the hill and, for several centuries, the zone was popularly considered to be visited by divine ill will, so it was abandoned and neglected.

In the year 638 the territory passed into the hands of the Muslims, but they were respectful of the elements of the Jewish religion that Mohamed welcomed in Islam and also of the site of one of the Prophet's last appearances in Jerusalem. The sacred nature of the hill was re-established definitively in 640, when Caliph Omar ibn al-Khattab built a mosque there, probably of wood; it is only known to today from an account in a pilgrim's diary. This first mosque was replaced in 687

185

186-187 *A rotunda at the center of the mosque, ringed by two ambulacra supported by pillars, contains the sacred rock. The columns were taken from Christian churches.*

187 *The 'golden dome' caps the building. It is formed by two concentric crowns of diameter approximately 67 feet. Inside, the drum is decorated with 11th-*

century floral mosaics and arched windows. The support crown is decorated with stuccoes in gold arabesques and ribbons inscribed with quotations from the Koran.

when the Umayyid Caliph Abd al-Malik built the current mosque, today one of the most important in the Islamic world, on the large esplanade.

The caliph commissioned its design from Byzantine Christian architects. Access is given on all four sides by flights of steps crowned by *mawazin* (arches) on the columns of which are hung, in accordance with Muslim tradition, the scales of judgment.

The octagonal mosque (65 feet long on each side) stands at the center of the esplanade, with its four entrances facing the points of the compass, each 39 feet high. The impression created by the volumes is lightened by the decorative lining of the building: at the bottom are pale polychrome marbles and above are pale blue tiles decorated with arabesques.

The upper section of the octagon is decorated with mosaics in the style fashionable at the time of the original

design, but it was enhanced by Suleiman the Magnificent in 1552 with historiated tiles. These were made in Kashan in Persia. In the 19thth century an inscription in Arabic lettering was added; the dome itself stands at the center of the building on the drum. It is made from wooden coombs and metal sheets, all of which are lined with lead that was gilded in the 1950s.

Inside, the dome is formed by two concentric caps lined with floral mosaics, stuccoes and gold decorated with calligraphic inscriptions.

The plan of the mosque was based on geometric ratios and is split into two concentric ambulatory sections lined by rings of pillars and columns.

The sacred rock itself lies in a round terrace at the center of the mosque. Here, at the heart of the building, is the cave known as the 'well of souls,' where the souls of the dead are supposed to worship Allah, the purpose for the temple.

188-189 The upper platform of Borobudur temple is formed by three circular, sloping terraces on which 72 bell-shaped stupas in concentric circles contain statues of the Buddha in the dharma-cakramudra, the gesture that represents the setting of the dharma (wheel of law) in motion. Outside there are 64 statues of the Buddha in vitarkamudra, the gesture of debate.

188 bottom and 189 bottom The terraces in Borobudur temple are lined with walls that become the balustrades of the upper level; the surfaces are covered by 1,300 reliefs of the life of the Buddha and other legends.

189 top The temple of Borobudur is a colossal stupa built on a small hill in the Kedu valley. Its form and site are symbolic references to Mount Meru, which in Indian mythology represents the center of the Universe.

Borobudur
JAVA, INDONESIA

by Maria Eloisa Carrozza

In the early 19th century, the discovery of the site of Borobudur deep in the Javanese jungle led to the restoration of a large Buddhist temple from the second half of the 8th century, which for almost two hundred years was the center of the Buddhist religion in Java.

The temple, which was probably designed by the architect Gunadharma, covers an entire hill, transforming it into a sort of mountain-sanctuary.

The colossal monument is built in the form of a terraced pyramid that rests on a two-story, square base measuring 124 yards on each side. The pyramid has four terraces on each of which are three-step platforms filled with stupas in decreasing numerical sets (32, 24, 16). Galleries run along the sides of the levels of the monument and are joined by flights of steps. The external walls are decorated with sequences of small niches, each of which holds a statue of the Buddha. And on the top is a central stupa that holds a statue of the Buddha that was deliberately left unfinished.

The decoration of the sanctuary represents the Buddhist universe as it was understood in Java: the hierarchy of gods and demigods consists of the Buddha himself, the images of the Buddha performing symbolic *mudra* (gestures), and *bodhisattva* (enlightened individuals who guide humans on the Buddhist path, and who can in some ways be likened to Western saints).

The cosmogonic inspiration for the site is evident in the rich low-reliefs on the terraces. The lower ones, which were originally open to view, were later covered by a buttress,

190 The high-quality sculptures in Borobudur temple are cut from the surface rock and have a strong visual impact.
The figures shown refer to the real and spiritual worlds of the Buddhist culture.

191 top The objects seen in the low reliefs of Borobudur temple are from Javanese material culture and represent the abandonment of Indian models.

191 center The crowded reliefs on two registers describe the spiritual

nature and everyday life of the temple. The images depict traditional customs and give valuable information on the dress, ornamentation and furnishings of the period.

191 bottom In the rite of the pradakshina (deambulation), the worshiper, starting from the outside, climbed towards the center of the temple following the pattern of the mandala (symbol of the universe). The route was lined on the sides of the stupa galleries with reliefs like the one depicted in this photo.

presumably for reasons of stability. The reliefs on the lowest level reflect Kamadhatu, the earthly plane, and depict man's actions and desires that will be either rewarded or punished in the worlds of paradise or hell to come. However, the strong moral message the artists put across did not rule out aspects of everyday life in Java in the 9th century.

In contrast, images of thought and reason are victorious over the flesh on the twelve higher levels. These monumental low-reliefs narrate the lives of Siddhartha Gautama (the historical Buddha) and the Jataka (the future Buddhas who defeated human evil).

The first gallery is the setting for the life of the Buddha Sakyamuni until the time of his first sermon, but it includes references in popular tradition to his past lives. The second gallery tells the story of the spiritual path of Prince Sudhana, the third the story of Maitreya (the Buddha of the future), while interpretation of the decoration in the fourth gallery is subject to debate.

On the four terraces the many images of the Buddha refer to Rupadhatu (the world of form); the statues in the cardinal points of the compass assume traditional positions that refer to testimony, offering, meditation and reassurance, which are all expressed by the position of the Buddha's hands.

At the top of the steps, a monumental balustrade supports more large stupas that ring the central, closed and impenetrable one that contains the unfinished Buddha. This is the representation of Arupadhatu, the world of pure intellect that cannot be reached by man.

192-193 *The regularity of the layout of the Forbidden City is evident from above. It was Emperor Yong Le who in 1421 transferred the government from Nanking to Beiping ('Peace of the North') and renamed the city Beijing ('Capital of the North').*

192 bottom *After the South Gate, one passes through the first courtyard in a curve from the River of the Golden Waters, which is crossed by five bridges. In the background the Gate of Supreme Harmony leads into the Outer Court (Waichao).*

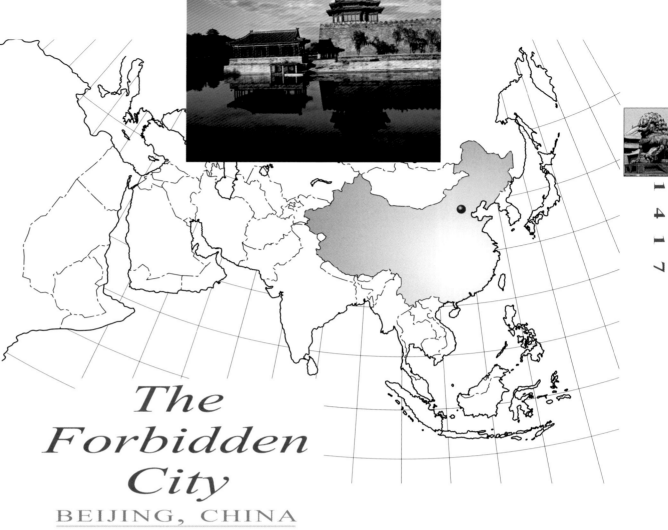

The Forbidden City

BEIJING, CHINA

by Miriam Taviani

Ringed by walls over 33 feet tall and a dike 160 feet in width, the Forbidden City in Beijing is the most outstanding example of the architecture of the imperial bureaucratic system in China. From 1421 to 1911 (the year the Chinese Republic was established) it was the seat of imperial government. It was also the residence of 24 emperors of the Ming (the last native Chinese dynasty) and Qin (Manchu) dynasties: from the Emperor Yong Le to the 'Last Emperor,' Pu Yi.

Covering 178 acres, this city within a city was reserved for the emperor's family and court, and therefore prohibited to common mortals, hence its name. Yet it is difficult to consider the site as being completely isolated as its 9,000 rooms were probably inhabited by between 8,000 and 10,000 people.

The myriad buildings inside the walls (made from wood on stone platforms and covered by sloping roofs with golden-yellow tiles) were located in two areas: in those in the south zone, political functions were carried out; those in the north zone were reserved for private life. Four gates provided entry from the outside world: three led into the south zone and one, the Gate of Divine Military Genius on the north side, entered directly into the residential area. The most important buildings lay on a north-south axis and were referred to by highly poetic names. Entering from the South Gate (once reserved for the emperor's exclusive use), a visitor crossed the first court, through which the River of the Golden Waters flowed. Passing through the Gate of Supreme Harmony, the visitor entered a second enormous court capable of holding at least 90,000 people, onto which the stepped terrace of the Three Great

193 top At the corners of the ring of walls around the Forbidden City there are four elegant, three-story towers that, though strategic, seem no different to the pavilions inside.

193 bottom The Gate of Divine Military Genius lies near the Inner Palace (Neiting) on the same axis as the South Gate on the other side of the walls. The Imperial Garden (Yuhuayuan) lies between the gate and private palaces with its many pavilions and sculptures.

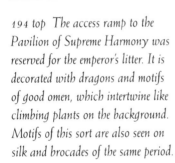

194 top The access ramp to the Pavilion of Supreme Harmony was reserved for the emperor's litter. It is decorated with dragons and motifs of good omen, which intertwine like climbing plants on the background. Motifs of this sort are also seen on silk and brocades of the same period.

Pavilions faced. The first of the three, the Pavilion of Supreme Harmony, was the largest in the entire Forbidden City. Seated on the Dragon Throne at the center of this building, the emperor governed his empire and oversaw official ceremonies.

The other two great pavilions were the Pavilion of Central Harmony and the Pavilion of the Preservation of Harmony, while the Gate of Celestial Purity behind led into the maze of pavilions, palaces and gardens reserved for use by the imperial family. The nucleus of imperial private apartments was designed to be a mirror image of the Three Great Pavilions, and centered on the three palaces of Celestial Purity, Union, and Earthly Tranquility. Lying behind these was the traditionally Chinese imperial garden that covered two acres and had the Pavilion of Imperial Peace at its center. The residential quarters of the eunuchs and concubines, lodgings of the servants, and temples, libraries, theaters and more gardens lay to the east and west.

The attractive appearance of the complex was created by the combination of bright colors: the white marble of terraces, stairways and balustrades contrasted with the red of the wooden parts, the golden-yellow of the tiles, and the various colors of the brackets and decorative features. The brackets were often decorative rather than structural, but the ridges of the roofs were often so heavily laden with wooden sculptures that it was necessary to build a colonnade to support their weight. The buildings that visitors see today mostly date to the 19th century. In addition to looting and destruction carried out in 1664 by the Manchu invaders, the wooden buildings were often destroyed by fires, whether accidental – easily assisted by the wind from the Gobi Desert – or organized by unscrupulous dignitaries who wished to gain personally from restoration work. Fires also destroyed books, paintings, and furniture of inestimable historic and artistic value but, despite the losses, the Forbidden City has retained its beauty and fascination and continues to impart an aura of stately authority.

194 bottom Like all birds, this crane, on the other side of the entrance to the Pavilion of Supreme Harmony, represented light and the spirit. To the Chinese even bats were a good omen.

194-195 One side of the entrance to the Pavilion of Supreme Harmony is guarded by a turtle, a symbol of long-life, with the head and paws of a dragon, a creature that represented the male principle (Yang). The shell of this bronze turtle could be removed to reveal an incense burner in the creature's back.

195 bottom left Sculpted lions are frequent in the Forbidden City. This animal, like the tiger and other wild beasts with a hairy coat, symbolized the Earth and Yin (the female principle).

195 bottom right A tangle of dragons adorns the ramp of the Pavilion of Supreme Harmony. From the 13th century, Chinese art had a strong influence on Western culture.

The Forbidden City

196 top The Six Eastern Palaces and Six Western Palaces stand symmetrically at the sides of the Palace of Celestial Purity. It's where political decisions were taken and court intrigues hatched. The rooms communicate with one another and the central axis (in this case of the Western Palaces) has a series of painted portals.

196 center The structural wooden elements on the inside and outside are finely carved and painted with bright colors. The smooth columns painted with red lacquer are made from highly-prized camphor wood imported from Yunnan and Sichuan.

196 bottom The defensive walls and external building walls in the Forbidden City are painted bright red to symbolize royalty; the yellow on the surfaces of this portal has the same significance, but was a color that could only be used by the emperor.

196-197 In some cases the sentinels at the entrances to the Forbidden City seem to be hybrids. Two gilded bronze lions in front of the Gate of Supreme Harmony have open jaws, pointed manes, and the tails and paws of a dragon. The globe beneath the front paw alludes to the power of the emperor and his control over his territory.

197 right Belonging to the 'lady of the interior' (nei), the throne of the empress in the Pavilion of Union (Jiaotai Dian) behind the Palace of Celestial Purity could only be placed in the 'inner' part of the city.

197 bottom A procession of imaginary creatures on the roof ridge of one of the largest pavilions is preceded by a figure riding a phoenix. They look down on the gutter, with its rounded antefixes and drips, both decorated with dragons and, at the corner, a large drip in the form of a dragon's head.

198-199 The magnificent vault of the Hall of Prayer for Good Harvest is an unequaled masterpiece of carpentry charged with symbolic images. It covers the point where, in 1420, the geomancers of Emperor Yong Le established the point of contact between Heaven and Earth.

199 top This was the room in which Ci Xi, the emperor's widow, governed for 52 years until the death of herself and her grandson Guang Xu. Among the stories about her, it is said that she dealt with a concubine hostile to her by having the woman wrapped up in a carpet and thrown into a well.

The Forbidden City

199 center Ceremonies and public audiences were held in the Pavilion of Supreme Harmony where the Throne of the Dragon stood. Here in the Palace of Celestial Purity, the emperor, seated on another elegant throne, received his private counselors and sometimes gave receptions.

199 bottom The inner (private) rooms were large and richly decorated but sparsely filled with furniture. Objects that were essential, however, were incense-burners and enormous bronze vases filled with water for use in the event of fire.

The Registan

SAMARKAND,

UZBEKISTAN

by Maria Eloisa Carrozza

The ferocious Mongol leader Timur-i-Leng (1336-1405), better known as Tamerlane, who conquered much of Central Asia and northern India to his rule, chose the site of Samarkand as his capital. He built a city that symbolizes the power of an overlord and still exists as a masterpiece of the Timurid Renaissance.

Timurid architecture was characterized by domes and minarets built using bricks formed of straw, clay, desert sand and camel urine were lined with magnificent faïence tiles tinted every hue between pale blue and turquoise, Tamerlane's favorite colors. It was these dazzling tiles that earned Samarkand the name the 'blue city.'

The Registan – literally the 'square of sand' – is a large open area lined with buildings. Such squares were typical of Timurid architecture; they were the site of the market and provided a setting for the political and judicial events in the city's life. Even today the Registan is very beautiful, and the fact that it is now a giant museum does not diminish the evocative power of its buildings. The façades of *madrasa*s (scientific and religious schools) stand on three of the square's sides, with their enormous portals and dazzling domes. The design draws upon several inspirations: the layout of the buildings comes from Uzbeki and Safavid architecture, the typology of the buildings is Seljuk in origin, and the traditional plan of the *madrasa* with their four *iwan* (vaulted rooms) around a courtyard lined with arcades follows the classical design of aristocratic houses. The cells and rooms where the teachers and pupils lived and studied was derived from the monasteries of Zoroaster, and the monumental portals were inspired by Sassanid architecture.

Ulugh Begh, Tamerlane's grandson and an astronomer and mathematician, was responsible for the oldest of the three *madrasa*, which was built between 1417 and 1420 on the west side of the square. Flanked by two columns, the tall entrance on the façade is framed by two spiral pillars. The decoration of the building surfaces has typically Islamic geometric, calligraphic, floral and arabesque motifs. Originally the building had 2 stories, 50 cells and 4 corner domes but time has taken its toll.

200 top A rather coarsely featured tiger, is seen at the corners of the entrance to Tilakari madrasa.

200 center Lining the Registan are three monumental religious institutions. From the left, the three madrasa of Ulugh Begh, Tilakari and Chirdar.

200 bottom In the madrasa named after him, Ulugh Begh taught mathematics and astronomy.

201 The decoration of the dome and minaret of Chirdar madrasa is Uzbeki in style. The mosaics and painted tiles are refined but not at the level of Timurid ceramics.

203 center Tilakari madrasa, the most imposing of the Registan institutions, was built by the Uzbek ruler Yalantuch Bahadur. To the left of the portal, above the 400-foot long facade there appears the magnificent dazzling turquoise dome that crowns the mosque.

203 bottom and 204-205 The entrance to Tilakari madrasa is over 100 feet high but its huge projection achieves its aim of reducing the visibility of its interior. Inside, the curvilinear space is crowned by a half-dome lined with mosaics and brick, and decorated with geometric and floral motifs. Porches by the walls frame passages and windows.

The Registan

The other two *madrasas*, the Chirdar (or Cher dor and the Tilakari (or Tilla Kari), were commissioned by the Uzbek ruler Bahadur, and date to the 17th century. The first was built between 1619 and 1636; it stands on the east side of the square and is also known as the 'madrasa of the lions' owing to the presence of the traditional Persian emblem on the corner stones of the portico. The Tilakari stands on the north side and was constructed between 1647 and 1660. Its name means 'gold *madrasa*', which it earned from the abundance of the precious metal that decorates it. There is also the dazzling turquoise dome of the great mosque, with its two minarets crowned by small blue cupolas. The mosque was built inside the school to symbolize the growing cultural interest in religious studies. The two orders of arcades mirrored the students' cells.

The fourth side of the square, to the south, is empty and has only a single column at the corner.

As the visitor admires the Registan, it is easy to understand why in the West the name Samarkand has always been associated with the exotic treasures of the East.

202 The prayer niche in the mosque of Tilakari madrasa (restored in 1979) is enhanced by the luminous blue and gold decoration. The papier-maché ornamentation is very rare, with only two other examples in the world, both in Samarkand.

203 top The dome on the mosque of Tilakari madrasa has concentric decorations of sinuous plant motifs. In the drum there is a succession of arches joined by decorated spandrels that alternate with windows and strongly illusionistic architectonic elements.

206-207 Similar to a fort, the Potala is anchored to the Marpo Ri (Red Mountain) by massive scarp walls that seem to make the stairways on the south side of the slope into a further buttress. The different colors of the plaster (white lower down and red in the central section) correspond to two construction phases and different use of the building: The residential section is white and the religious section red.

206 bottom left Once inside the east gate, a huge court has for centuries been a place to catch one's breath before tackling the ascent inside the Potala. It was here that monks used to perform sacred dances in costumes and masks.

206 bottom right In the upper section of the lower part of the White Palace, rows of windows and small balconies look out over the bare landscape of the Tibetan plateau. Below we see the top of a flight of steps.

207 The external decoration of the Potala is limited to small variations in color, a few spires on the roofs or terrifying animals from the Buddhist pantheon at the corners, whose task it is to protect the building.

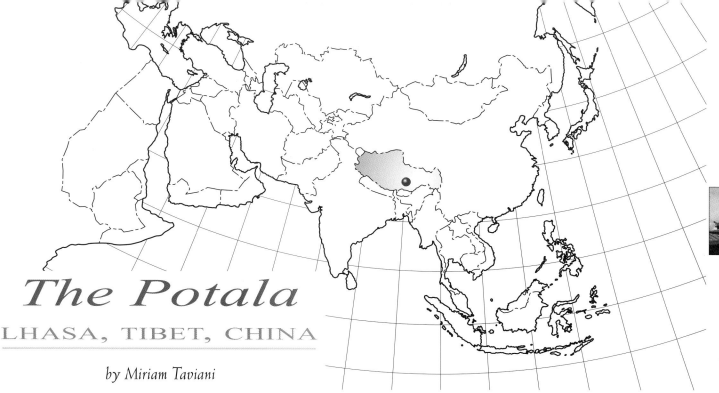

The Potala

LHASA, TIBET, CHINA

by Miriam Taviani

An imposing white and ocher fort with golden roofs, for four centuries the Potala was the abode of the Dalai Lamas. The highest building in one of the highest cities in the world (12,140 feet above sea level), it is the visual announcement to pilgrims and travelers that they are approaching the sacred city of Lhasa.

Potala is a name of Indian origin and recalls the place where the *bodhisattva* Avalokiteshvara lived, of whom the Dalai Lama is believed to be the living incarnation. The palace's remote origins date back to King Songtsen Gampo who, having married a Nepalese princess and a Chinese princess, both of whom were Buddhist, completed unification of Tibet in the 7th century, introduced Buddhism to the country, and moved his capital to Lhasa. When the fifth Dalai Lama decided to move his government from Drepung monastery in the mid-17th century, the choice fell on the red mountain – Marpo Ri – where Songtsen Gampo's palace had been built. Even though the Potala was used only as a winter residence

following the construction of the Norbulingka summer palace at the end of the 18th century, from that time the Potala was the seat of the government of Tibet and the Dalai Lama (the spiritual and temporal leader of Tibet) until 1959, when the army of the People's Republic of China occupied Tibet.

Work began in 1645 on the Potrang Karpo, the nine-story White Palace, and took only three years to complete. The palace was immediately used by the Dalai Lama as his new administrative seat and later he retained it as his residence. Construction of the Potrang Marpi – the Red Palace – was longer and more complex and did not end until 1694. This building was to be used for religious purposes so when the fifth Dalai Lama died in 1682, the news was only announced publicly when construction was complete (12 years later) for fear that the work would be halted.

Overall the palace has 13 stories, is 384 feet high, has more than 1,000 rooms, roughly 10,000 temples, 200,000 statues and the burial stupas (*chorten*) of 8 Dalai Lamas (from the fifth

The Potala

208-209 The top of the Red Palace is covered with golden domes and spires. The prevalently yellow curtains and canopies have two functions: decorative and to shield the interior from the sun, which at this altitude is very powerful.

208 bottom left A row of mythological dogs designed, like many of the divinities in the Buddhist cosmogony, to terrify. Placed on the architrave of the portal of the Red Palace, their function is to protect the building within.

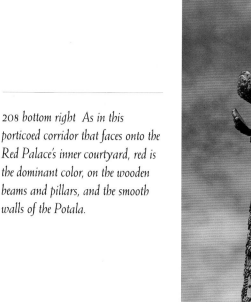

209 top *The gilded bronze cylinders – called* kenchira *or* ganjira *– that crown the access facade of the White Palace contain strips of paper on which sacred mantras are written.*

209 bottom *The portal of the Red Palace is made from carved wood and decorated with various colors. It is flanked by polystyle columns and crowned by polylobate capitals with double brackets.*

1645-1694

to the thirteenth, excluding the sixth). The Potala is reached up two steep flights of steps 427 feet high that lead from the village of Stöl up the south slope of the hill. Entering the east entrance and crossing the outer courtyard (*Deyang Shar*), the visitor arrives at a stairway that leads into the White Palace and the rooms where the Dalai Lamas used to live. From there visitors pass into the Red Palace, which stands in the middle of its White counterpart, like an enormous raft, and is the most visually dramatic part of the complex.

The interiors of the Red Palace are impressive for their rich decoration and spirituality. The Hall of the Western Audiences is a ceremonial room with a floor area of 7,800 square feet; it still contains the throne that belonged to the sixth Dalai Lama. The majestic Chapel of the Tombs of the Dalai Lamas (the fifth, tenth and twelfth) is dominated by the funerary *stupa* – 45 feet high and covered with 8,157 pounds

of gold – of the founder of the Potala. Then there are the *chorten* of the seventh, eighth, ninth and thirteenth Dalai Lamas, and the Chapel of the Holy Born that contains the tomb of the eleventh Dalai Lama; the Chapel of the Three Dimensional Mandalas that contains the mandalas studded with precious stones of the three principal Tantric deities; and the Chapel of Victory over the Three Worlds, where precious Manchu texts are kept in the library. The Chapel of Arya Lokeshvara (the most venerated chapel in the Potala) is particularly beautiful and said to have belonged previously to the palace of Songtsen Gampo like the Chamber of Meditation on the floor below. An immense nave carved out of the mountain, the Potala represents the most original type of Tibetan art: its massive but simple architecture is in perfect harmony with its environment, and seems to have emanated from the hill on which it stands.

The Castle of Hime-ji

HIME-JI, JAPAN

by Miriam Taviani

210 top The geometric pattern created by undulating sloping roofs and dormer windows in the Daitenshukaku gives the impression from the outside of five floors, whereas in fact there are seven inside. The alternation of concave and convex lines provides an elegant decorative effect, which is embellished by zoomorphic acroters on the ridge of the tympana and practical bronze drips at the ends.

210 bottom The interior of the castle is entirely made from wood. The lower floors are supported by massive wooden beams reinforced by huge brackets.

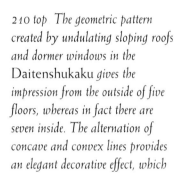

Known as the 'Castle of the White Heron' for its elegant form and the dazzling white of the plaster that lines the walls, the castle of Hime-ji is a product of Japanese military architecture, and one of only six that have survived entire. Situated in the town of Hime-ji about 30 miles west of Osaka, the castle is an excellent example of how tactical requirements can be combined with artistry, for example, the white plaster was used to protect the wooden buildings from fire. The castle was built in 1346 and rebuilt in 1580; it owes its current appearance to the designs of General Ikeda Terumasa, who between 1601 and 1609 transformed it into a better protected fort on the model of the residence of Emperor Azuchi.

The castle comprises more than 80 buildings and is built within three concentric walls, each of which has its own dike and is strengthened by towers and fortified gates. The walls are 50 feet high and so hide the buildings inside; the internal labyrinth of alleys and passages, some of which are blind, was designed to disorient an enemy force that had succeeded in passing the many previous obstacles unharmed.

At the center of the innermost wall, in the highest section of the castle, stands the Daitenshukaku, the main tower. This five-story building was the residence of the *daimyo*, the feudal lord. Built on solid rock and covered by sloping roofs with undulating gables, it stands next to three smaller towers called Shotenshukaku.

The middle wall circled the residential quarters of high-ranking officers, and the outermost wall circled the lodgings of the middle and low-ranking soldiers and servants, temples, and stores for munitions and food.

The beauty and solidity of Hime-ji castle has survived all kinds of natural disasters over the 400 years of its history, including typhoons and earthquakes, which are frequent in the area.

210-211 *This view from the southwest highlights the defensive system of dikes, walls and gates that surrounds the castle. The main tower (Daitenshukaku) is 150 feet tall and stands over the surrounding towers (Shotenshukaku). The dazzling white construction as a whole suggests a white heron (Shirasagi).*

211 bottom *The upper floors and windows are united with extreme gracefulness: the elegance of the interiors makes it hard to imagine their use for military purposes.*

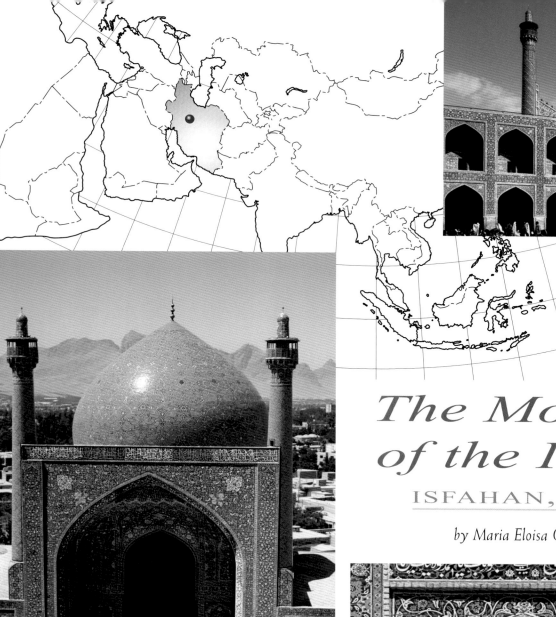

The Mosque of the Imam

ISFAHAN, IRAN

by Maria Eloisa Carrozza

The blue Masjid-i-Imam (the Mosque of the Imam, constructed 1612–38) is a superb example of the power of religious values proclaimed through architecture. The enormous principal and slightly flattened dome was built with a double concentric shell, and its lining of tiles decorated with floral patterns produces changing and surprising effects with the change of the light. The extraordinary arc of the outer portal is flanked on either side by a minaret and, curiously, follows the layout of the square before it. The body of the mosque is oriented so that the building faces west toward Mecca.

The opulence of the design is clearly revealed inside the mosque. The breadth of the interior does not diminish in any way the simplicity of Islamic conceptions or the call to prayer. A tour of the building begins at the main entrance where the portico is adorned with a magnificent half-dome featuring the characteristic *muqarna*, or 'stalactite' elements lined with enameled mosaics. The door lined with incised gilded-silver plaques leads into a short passage and a circular vestibule that functions almost as the hub around which the building revolves. From the vestibule, the visitor passes into the central court surrounded by four *iwan* (huge colonnaded atria) that lead to vaulted prayer rooms.

At the center of the court the water in the washing

212-213 *From above, the Masjid-i-Imam faces onto the Maidan-i-Imam, the 'Square of the Imam.'*

213 *top right Walls with two orders of arcades ring the large central court of the mosque.*

213 *center left Two minarets stand at the sides of the south iwan in the court of the Masjid-i-Imam.*

213 *bottom right Sparkling abstract and plant motifs adorn the external surfaces of the building.*

fountain reflects the multi-colored façades of the *iwan*. The northeast *iwan*, which seems to be almost a continuation of the vestibule due to the non-alignment of the building compared to the portal, is particularly magnificently decorated.

The west *iwan* is characterized by a *goldatesh*, the pulpit from which the imam makes the call to prayer; the east *iwan* has a large portico lined at the bottom by marble and, at the sides, by blue enamel tiles. Next comes an interior with majolica-tile surfaces and a half-dome vault embellished with enameled *muqarna*, and a last room crowned by a dome.

The south *iwan* is the most impressive: it is flanked on either side by a minaret with brackets supported by arrangements of stalactites, and actually imposes itself on the main prayer hall. The main *mihrab* (the niche that indicates the direction of Mecca) in the prayer hall dates to 1666. The square plan of the hall is transformed into the dome above by means of four octagonal spandrels, which transmute into the drum.

Two wide passages accentuate the sense of lightness of the entire building and lead to other rooms with small domes where there are two secondary *mihrab*. The mosque is completed at the corners by *madrasas* (Koranic schools).

The Mosque of the Imam

214 top The principal space in the mosque is lined by two rectangular prayer rooms joined to the shrine through large archways.

214 bottom The archways between the rooms are ornamented with enameled floral motifs, patterns and bands of calligraphic decoration.

214-215 A lustral pool in the courtyard reflects the colors and shades of the ceramic tiles in all tones of blue. A majestic pointed arch leads into the iwan.

215 bottom The Entrance to the east and west iwan in the Mosque of the Imam is a vaulted space with a half-dome and magnificent enameled stalactites in blue and gold.

216-217 The ceilings of the Mosque of the Imam are lined with dazzling blue and gold tiles painted with geometric and floral patterns. The surfaces are embellished by arabesques and curved moldings, and the succession of concave spaces is joined by spandrels and pendentives.

217 top The prayer niches inside the mosque have concave surfaces decorated with enameled ribbing, and white quotations from the Koran on a blue ground.

217 bottom The cloudy blue of the tiles reinforces the sense of lightness conveyed by the mosque; it is a fluid structure designed to dissolve the building's solidity and mass.

218-219 *The Taj Mahal is the mausoleum built by Shah Jahan in memory of his wife Arjumand Banu Bagam, known as Mumtaz Mahal. It stands inside a large four-sided garden, which was a favorite geometric figure in Islamic art as it symbolizes perfection. The facade of the mausoleum is reflected in a pool at the center of the garden. The Taj Mahal stands on a platform 23 feet high. Its corner minarets, the dome at the center and its dazzling white marble together produce its unmistakable appearance.*

218 bottom *The north, three-floor portal has a large, inward curving arch on each of its four sides; this motif is found in all the buildings in the complex. Around this arch there is a rich decoration on a white ground that contrasts with the red sandstone lining. Fine inlays in black marble and colored stones (at least 43 types) create patterns of plants and verses from the Koran. As these increase in size as they rise, they appear to the observer below to be all the same size.*

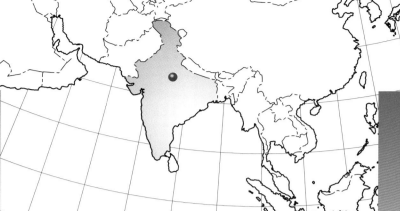

The Taj Mahal
AGRA, INDIA

by Beatrix Herling

A superb memorial to eternal love, the white marble and red sandstone architecture of the Taj Mahal stands on the right bank of the Yamuna river in Agra, northern India. To commemorate his favorite wife, Mumtaz Mahal, the 'Chosen One of the Palace,' Shah Jahan, the Mogul emperor, dedicated seventeen years (1631-48) and enormous resources to the construction of this magnificent mausoleum.

It stands in the northern part of a vast rectangular enclosure that has an octagonal pavilion at each corner. The greater part of the enclosed area is occupied by a four-part garden (the Char Bagh). This is a representation of the Garden of Paradise of Persian tradition, based upon a symmetrical design in which squares of different sizes are laid

219 top This view of the Taj Mahal is taken from a ruin on the other side of the Yamuna river. The masterpiece of Mogul Islamic art was abandoned after the death of the last descendants of Shah Jahan and fell into ruin. Thefts and looting continued for about two hundred years, when the building was restored and consecrated definitively to eternity.

219 bottom Twin mosques stand at the sides of the mausoleum. Both are built from marble and red sandstone and have three bulb-shaped domes. The west mosque was the only one to be used for worship; the east one, known as Ja-Wab ('The Reply') as it was symmetrical and identical to the other, was only built for aesthetic reasons and therefore has never been used.

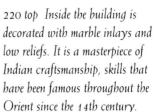

220 top Inside the building is decorated with marble inlays and low reliefs. It is a masterpiece of Indian craftsmanship, skills that have been famous throughout the Orient since the 14th century.

220 bottom Though solid, the structure of the Taj Mahal is softened by its forms and delicate inlays; thanks to the whiteness of the marble, it dominates the surrounding countryside.

out and framed by canals that run at right angles to the central square pool.

Two buildings stand symmetrically halfway along the long sides of the gardens, and the geometrical correspondences are completed by the mosque and the identical building that stand on either side of the mausoleum. The magnificent entrance to the complex on the south side of the enclosure provides a view of the entire complex toward the mausoleum. Dark sandstone inlaid with white marble, and white marble inlaid with colored stones, produce outstanding color effects that culminate in the pale glow of the mausoleum. Raised on a base with a minaret at each of the four corners, the building is crowned by a bulbous dome that is the characteristic element of the whole edifice. It towers over a spacious open area at the center of which, in an enclosure ringed by lacework marble walls, lies the cenotaph of Mumtaz. Beside it, and off-center, is the cenotaph of the emperor, which was added after his death against his wishes. Reflecting the same asymmetry, the actual royal tombs lie immediately below in

the royal crypt. In addition to the careful arrangement of volumes and division of surfaces, the building's visual harmony and unified design are highlighted by the repetition of elements in the architectural design, such as spires, cornices and tiny details, and by the sequences of geometric, calligraphic, and plant motifs in the decoration.

Even though the Taj Mahal has been looted of its most precious objects, it remains an insuperable example of the sumptuous architecture of the Moguls, in terms of its organization of space around the intersection of squares and crosses, and for its innovative fusion of the Persian-Islamic tradition – seen in the courts, internal spaces and bulbous domes – with Hindu architecture, evident in the massive use of stone.

The enchanting melancholy of the site remains unspoiled even though the changing environmental conditions place the condition of this famous monument at risk. One example is that the course of the Yamuna was changed so that the surface of the river could reflect the beauty of the building in the clear light of morning.

The Taj Mahal

220-221 Amanat Khan was a famous Iranian master of calligraphy who executed the marble inscriptions on the facade of the Taj Mahal. He was the only artist to sign his work in the building.

221 bottom The precious materials used in the decorations were imported from afar: jade and crystal from China, turquoise from Tibet, lapis lazuli from Afghanistan and chrysolite from Egypt.

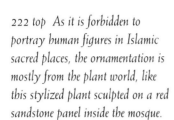

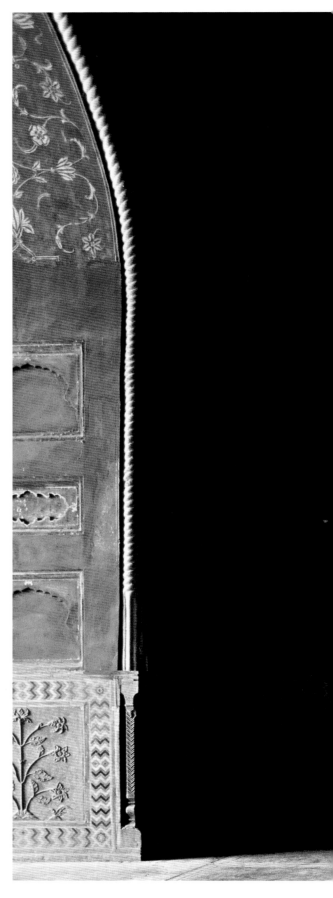

222 top As it is forbidden to portray human figures in Islamic sacred places, the ornamentation is mostly from the plant world, like this stylized plant sculpted on a red sandstone panel inside the mosque.

222 center Construction of this rich and magnificent complex lasted seventeen years and required roughly 20,000 workmen. To accommodate them, a town, Mumtazabad, was built nearby that was also dedicated to the memory of the dead consort.

222 bottom Rectangular twin mosques each with three bulb-shaped domes, flank the mausoleum. The red tufa used to line them was quarried in caves nearby and provides an excellent contrast with the white marble of the domes and inlays on the facades.

222-223 The internal decoration of the mosque follows the Islamic tradition of geometric figures and plant motifs distributed harmoniously along the walls, and sacred inscriptions taken from holy texts.

223 bottom The mihrab is a typical Islamic feature of a mosque. It is a niche in the Qibla (the wall that faces Mecca) from where the imam directs the prayers of the faithful. The mihrab represents the center of worship and traditionally is a derivation of the place where Mohammed used to recite his prayers in his own home.

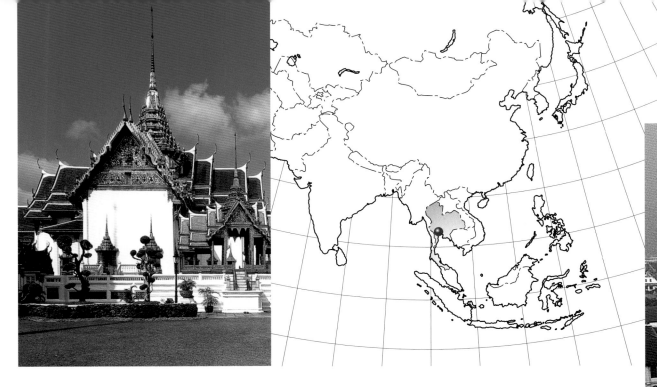

The Royal Palace
BANGKOK, THAILAND

by Maria Eloisa Carrozza

Construction of the Phra Borom Maha Rajawang (Great Palace) on the banks of the Chao Phraya river in Bangkok began in 1782 under Rama I, the founder of the Chakri dynasty. Today the dynasty is still in power and the palace is still the royal residence. However, over the centuries each sovereign has wanted to make his own contribution to the palace by adding his own pavilion.

The result today is that the complex is made up of buildings from different eras and in different styles that offer an overall view of Thai architecture.

Pale bare walls with plain portals topped by slender spires run through the monumental area; they were not built exclusively to bound an enclosure but are themselves a form of architecture. Another recurring theme in the palace is the roofs, which are embellished with curved and decorated elements in dazzling orange, the customary color in Thailand.

An external court leads to the Wat Phra Keo (the temple) in an enclosure that contains many buildings not dedicated to the cult of a god but, in accordance with Thai tradition, are associated with meditation and the preservation of sacred objects and relics. The designs of the buildings pay tribute to ancient Thai culture while also highlighting their distant Indian origin.

Everything calls out for attention: the bright colors of the polychrome ceramics, the mosaics, the painted lime walls, the statues of gigantic demons and the decoration of figurative motifs like the *garuda* (mythical birds ridden by the god Vishnu), *yasha* (guardian spirits), *kinnara* (creatures with human faces and birds' legs) and celestial nymphs.

Wall paintings illustrate the *Ramakien*, the epic poem of Indian literary tradition, which is interpreted here eclectically with elements taken from Indian, Singhalese, Burmese, Chinese, Khmer and European cultures.

224 top The Dusit Maha Prasad (Throne Room) in the Royal Palace has the traditional roof formed by decorated, overlaid sections, beneath a part decorated with volutes, and crowned by a gilded chedi.

224 bottom A wall encloses the Wat Phra Keo. This is topped by spires *of* chedi, mondop *and* prang, *and colored roofs.*

224-225 The Wat Phra Keo stands close to various types of building: prang *in the foreground, which are derived from Indian* shikhara, *and the* chedi, *which are the equivalents of* stupa.

225 bottom left Inspired by the Italian Renaissance during the late-19th-century revival, the Chakri Residence was given Thai roofs on the orders of King Rama V.

225 bottom right The Chakri Residence neighbors the Dusit Maha Prasad (back) and the Maha Montien (once the Court of Justice and then residence of many kings).

226 *The buildings in the Royal Palace are decorated with pediments and gilded wood carvings on colored tiles.*

227 *left This golden chedi is supported by Yaksa (demons converted by the doctrine of the Buddha) and towered over by the* prang *in the Royal Palace.*

227 *right Sculptures in the courtyards of Bangkok's Royal Palace represent mythological beings of supernatural, human and animal appearance. The* kinnara *and* kinnari *are respectively figures with the face and trunk of a man or woman, and the legs of a lion. The statues are painted dazzling gold.*

1782 - 1882

The most famous building on the site is the Royal Chapel (1785). It has a rectangular *bot* (the room where new monks take their vows) reached by steps guarded by bronze lions, and it contains a magnificent green jasper statuette known as the Emerald Buddha that may date to the 15th century.

On a terrace north of the *bot* there are equally interesting buildings: the Prasad Phra Thepbidorn is a pantheon and sacrarium (or shrine) of the Chakri gods; with a plan in the form of a Greek cross, it has a multi-level roof lined with orange tiles bordered with green. The Golden Chedi built by King Mongkut was named after its roof of small gold leaves. The Library is a square building with four massive stone statues of the Buddha at the corners sculpted in the 14th century. On the Library's multi-level roof there is a *yot* (a typical spire).

Passing out of Wat Phra Keo through a double door the visitor comes to the largest area in the Great Palace, an internal courtyard where the official ceremony room and residences of the monarchy stand. The Dusit Maha Prasad is a magnificent example of local architecture with the traditional plan of a Greek cross and a five-story roof topped by a crown-shaped spire. It was built by Rama I for his own coronation and various ceremonies.

The Maha Montien was built by King Rama III in the first half of the 19th century to contain the Amarinda (ancient throne room), while the Chakri Maha Prasad was commissioned from an English builder in 1882 by King Chulalongkorn; this unusual building is in Neo-Renaissance style but has a typical Thai roof. Finally, the Sivalaya garden is the site of the royal apartments and the Crystal Buddha Chapel built by King Mongkut.

The Royal Palace

228 top The orange covering of the Wat Phra Keo walls is watched over by the guardians of the temple. These are warlike statues with the faces of demons whose task it is to protect the sacredness of the site.

228 center The decoration on the buildings, spires and shrines in the Royal Palace is rich and varied, and includes polychrome mosaics of geometric and floral motifs, shiny tiles and relief ceramics.

228 bottom In the Wat Phra Keo the huge statues of the Yaksa demons are decorated with motifs sculpted in relief and painted. The color of their skin may be white, red or, as in this case, green.

229 Northwest of the enclosure stands the large Phra Sri Rattana chedi. This sacred reliquary conserves a fragment of the Buddha's breastbone.

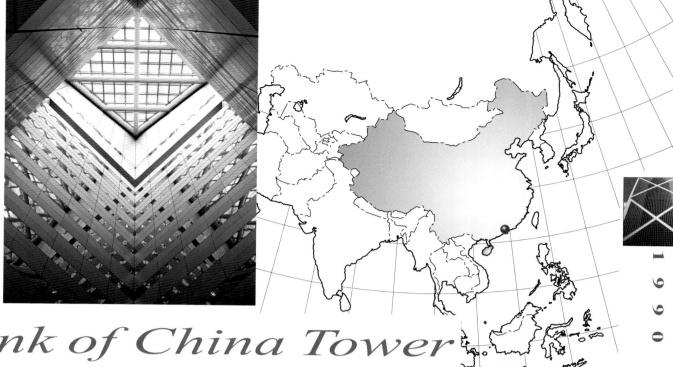

230 *A triumph of cleanly defined geometrical lines, the Bank of China skyscraper is unusually 'light' to be one of the tallest buildings in the world.*

231 top *A large rhomboidal light-well crowns the open area inside the skyscraper.*

231 bottom *Outlined by the night sky, the purity of the Bank of China's form dominates Hong Kong's skyline.*

The Bank of China Tower

HONG KONG, CHINA

by Guglielmo Novelli

Rising 70 stories to a height of 1,211 feet, the Bank of China skyscraper in Hong Kong is one of the tallest buildings in the world. Such a height was required because of the limited space available on the site, and because of the desire to make it the tallest building in the city (the skyscraper was built close to its rival tower of the Hong Kong Shanghai Bank).

The tower was designed by Ieoh Ming Pei as an elegant monolith on a square base, composed of four triangular prisms. Construction was completed in 1990. Its attractive profile blends with the sky, and its sculptural composition, inspired by the natural shapes of bamboo, is rigorously geometric. The novelty of this architectural masterpiece is the frame of the building, seen on the skyscraper's exterior.

The building's skeleton distributes the weight onto the four large corner pillars, thereby eliminating the need for internal vertical supports. This design meant that huge savings were made in the quantity of steel required for a building of this height. The function of the huge cross supports is to ensure that the structure resists the force of the frequent local typhoons; it is calculated that the skyscraper can withstand winds of 143 mph. The dialog between the skyscraper and the rest of the city is provided by an enormous atrium on two levels that can be entered from opposite sides. Its function is one of a large covered plaza.

Pei's sculptural building belongs to the generation of skyscrapers that reacted against the 'long reign of the glass prism in the style of Mies van der Rohe,' designs of which were based on the formal (at times rigid) relationship with the streets around them. The Bank of China Tower's sculptural minimalism is one of the most brilliant examples of architectural composition adopted in the attempt to solve the difficult problem of the relationship between a skyscraper and its urban context.

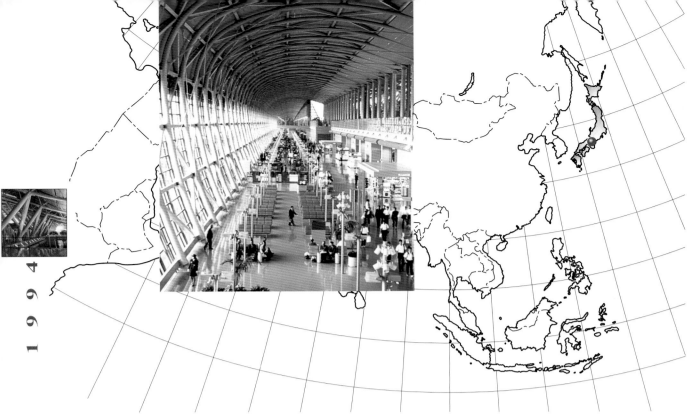

The Air Terminal Kansai

OSAKA, JAPAN

by Guglielmo Novelli

232 top The curves of light-filled Kansai Air Terminal suggest the skeleton of a sea creature. The building's relationship with the sea is the most direct one as it stands on a man-made island.

The futuristic Kansai Air Terminal in Osaka is the first airport in the world to be situated in the sea. It stands on a man-made island 2.7 miles long and less than 1 mile wide.

The requirement existed for an airport close to the city that was second in size to Tokyo's airport and able to handle both passengers and goods, but the terrain made it impossible to find the necessary space between the mountains and the coast. In consequence, it was decided to undertake the colossal task of building at sea.

Two and a half miles from the shore a project was undertaken to consolidate the seabed (at a depth of 60 feet) and then cover it with 215 million cubic yards of earth. A highway was built between the shore and this island, and then the architectural project began in earnest. In addition to the airport, the island hosts a seaport where ferries and hydrofoils can dock.

The enormous building site lies in the earthquake-prone waters of an unfriendly sea, which is feared and worshipped by the Japanese.

The design competition was won in 1991 by Renzo Piano, who, in order to tackle the task in as straightforward a manner as possible, first defined methodological guidelines to work from.

To summarize, the entire design was to be based on a layout that could be widened serially along at least one of the axes as space requirements demanded. This approach also made it simpler to deal with construction and the airport was completed in just three years.

The design was based around a building 1,860 yards long that runs north-south. The central section is the Main

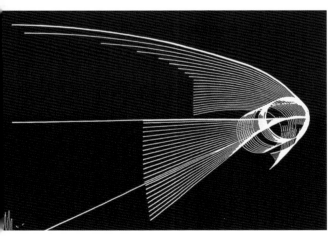

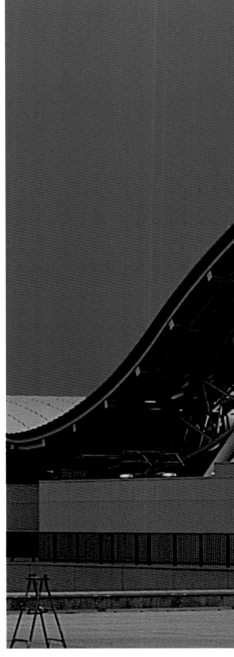

232 center Wind tests show the aerodynamic qualities of Renzo Piano's structure. Wind is a steady feature of the site, which is also subject to frequent seismic activity.

232 bottom The undulating roof covering offers another link with the sea, and alters depending on the currents of air inside the building.

232-233 *Twilight accentuates the beauty of the Air Terminal, increasing visibility of the interior 'wrapped' in its magnificent shell of metal girders.*

233 *center and bottom right The arrangement of tensoactive structures reveals the modularity of the design, based on the integration of the elements of the construction.*

233 *bottom left At the center of the picture, Kansai Air Terminal breaks the linearity of the buildings around it.*

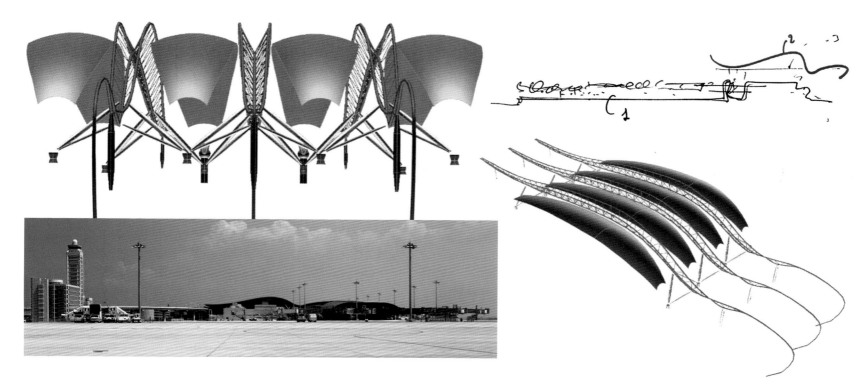

234 bottom right The interior of the Terminal covers 29 acres; the main space measures 1,043 x 502 feet and each wing 138 x 2,220 feet.

235 top This view inside an atrium shows the simplicity permitted by the technology used in the building. A total of 4,100 tons of steel was used.

234-235 Trusses support the Terminal roof on the top level of the structure. The Teflon velars that distribute the natural light are partially visible on the left.

234 bottom left Besides performing a structural function, the large inclined supports in the departure hall form a 'portal' that welcomes travelers.

235 bottom *The overall height of the various levels inside the Terminal comes to 120 feet. The structure is designed to handle 25 million passengers a year, thereby substantially lightening the load on Tokyo Airport.*

The Air Terminal Kansai

Terminal Building, and on either side are wings containing the Passenger Boarding Bridges. The three parts are perfectly integrated by a sinuous, stainless steel covering designed to optimize the air-flows inside the building. The huge atrium contains the entire height of the building, from the ground to the broad metal ceiling.

Taking his inspiration from the sea, Piano designed the covering in the shape of a wave, creating a fluid structure that reflects the co-existence of nature and technology, and the balance between the interior and exterior.

Natural light penetrates the high-tech building through the structures that support the large steel-and-glass façade and provide a view over the sea. The result is that as travelers walk through the building, they have the sensation that they are inside the skeleton of an enormous sea creature.

The roof, in the shape of a glider, seems to hover in the air. It is lined with 82,000 steel panels and supported by reticular girders. Positioned between the girders are Teflon curtains that have the dual function of optimizing the air conditioning and, during the night, of reflecting artificial light uniformly into the space below.

Renzo Piano has succeeded in fulfilling the requirements of such a huge and demanding project with the human quality typical of an architect's design studio. It reflects the Italian architect's claim that 'imagination must be combined with technical ability.'

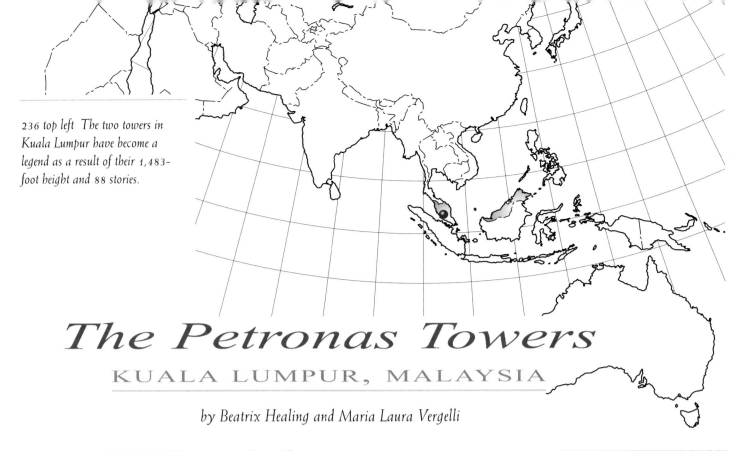

1998

The Petronas Towers

KUALA LUMPUR, MALAYSIA

by Beatrix Healing and Maria Laura Vergelli

The profile of the Petronas Towers in Kuala Lumpur, the Malaysian capital, is unique and distinctive, almost distended by their huge height. Completed in 1998 to be the tallest building in the world, the towers are still a legend for their enormous upward projection (1,483 feet). Their 88 stories are mostly filled with offices (Tower One is occupied by Petronas, the national oil company) and served by an innovative system of elevators able to move people at high speed. Figurative and symmetrical, with a 9:4 ratio between their height and breadth, the two buildings were designed with the formal characteristics of Islamic culture. They soon became national and cultural icons, representative of the country's political and economic power, and of the public image of Malaysia.

The towers' architectural design draws on the legacy of Muslim forms and decorative motifs, with repeated intertwined and geometrical arabesques, and curved and angular lines that intersect the structure to define its volumes and surfaces. The eight-pointed star on which the plan is based originated from the overlaying of two squares; and the curved and pointed vertical bays combine to create the towers' characteristic and ornamental scalloped façade. Giant twins, the two towers are connected by a sky bridge between the 41st and 42nd stories underpinned by steel struts in the shape of an upturned V.

In the mind of the Towers' American designer, Cesar Pelli, the axis of the composition lies at the center of the empty space over which the sky bridge is suspended. The sky bridge itself is supposed to represent 'an entrance to the sky, a door on infinity.' Steel and concrete provide the necessary stability for the structure of the extraordinary building, and steel and glass clad the sides, filtering and diffusing the intense equatorial light with great versatility. Surrounded by acres of gardens and concrete, the Petronas Towers dominate a large platform that houses a concert hall and shopping mall. They are the distinctive emblem of Kuala Lumpur City Center (KLCC) and the symbol of the country's newly achieved modernity.

236 bottom left The exterior of the Petronas Towers is completely clad with stainless steel sheets and darkened glass to protect it from the intense equatorial sun.

236 right Cesar Pelli's drawing shows the axis running between the two towers, through the center of the skybridge.

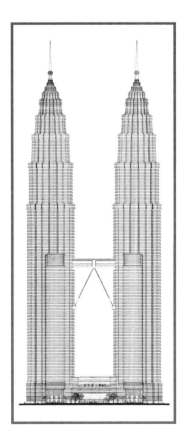

237 To meet the requirements of the client, Pelli's design for the Petronas Towers had to make reference to Islamic culture and include forms typical of Southeast Asian architecture.

238 Inside the tips of the towers there are large areas used for offices and commercial activities. They are conical and have no apparent means of internal support.

239 top The sophisticated structure of the Petronas Towers allows high-ceilinged rooms at the top of the building within which there are other structures.

239 center On April 15, 1996, the Council of Tall Buildings declared the Petronas Towers to be the tallest building in the world, shifting the title from the Sears Tower in Chicago to a new continent. In agreement with the consortium of financiers that backed the project, led by the Malaysian oil company Petronas, Cesar Pelli's aim was not to beat

the height record but to create a proportionate relationship between height and breadth (9:4) that would capture the public imagination.

239 bottom In 2020 the interior of the Petronas Towers (not yet completed) will be fitted with a mosque, a shopping center and a concert hall.

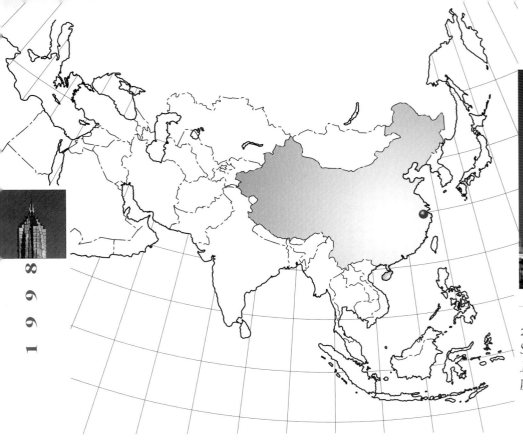

240 top left Designed by Skidmore, Owings & Merrill, the Jin Mao Tower is the gravitational hub of modern Shanghai.

240 top right and 242-243 An observation terrace at the top of the Jin Mao Tower looks directly down to the atrium of the Grand Hyatt Hotel.

The Jin Mao Tower

SHANGAI, CHINA

by Beatrix Herling and Maria Laura Vergelli

240 bottom The organic design of the internal framework of the Jin Mao was studied to absorb violent seismic tremors and strain placed on the building by gusts of wind.

241 The glass and metal cladding of the building reflects the changes of the weather on the exterior of the Jin Mao Tower, creating an effect of total integration with the natural environment.

Standing on the east bank of the Blue River, in front of the historic center of Shanghai, the gigantic Jin Mao Tower dominates the skyline of city's financial and commercial area in the new district of Pudong.

At a height of 1,312 feet and with 88 stories, the tower is still the tallest in China and the fourth highest in the world. Of the 88 stories, 52 are dedicated to office space (served by 60 elevators and 19 moving staircases) and the remaining 35 are occupied by the new Grand Hyatt Hotel. Anyone visiting the observation deck on the top of the building is tempted to admire the sheer drop of 21 stories to the atrium of the hotel. The speed with which the two elevators carry visitors from the first floor to the extraordinary view from the observatory is astounding, taking less than a minute. The top of the steel tower is covered by a glass dome that reflects daylight into the hotel.

The architecture of the Jin Mao Tower makes reference to Asian tradition: its four-sided, tapered shape is intended to be a contemporary form of the pagoda and, as such, an explicit tribute to Chinese history and culture. Construction took only four years and the tower was opened in 1998. Its position among the highest towers in the world is about to be lost, however, as the 'Tower of Babel saga' never lets up and another tower in Shanghai has been announced. It will take the record of the world's tallest building away from the current holder in Taipei, and bring it back to mainland China.

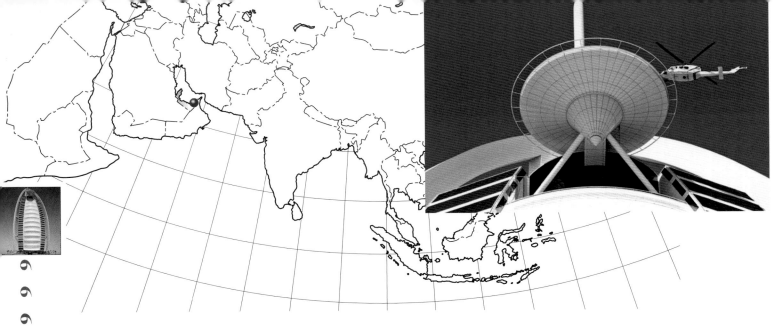

The Burj Al Arab Hotel
DUBAI, UNITED ARAB EMIRATES

by Guglielmo Novelli

The Burj Al Arab (literally 'Tower of the Arabs') is the only seven-star hotel in the world. The area in which it stands underwent rapid and far-reaching transformation to allow development of the 'Dubai of the future.' The hotel was the idea of Sheikh Mohammed Rashid Al Maktoum, and the result of the imagination of 3,500 designers. Following four years of work, the Burj Al Arab was inaugurated at the end of 1999, and quickly became the symbol of the city.

Built on a nautical theme, the building is worthy of inclusion in *A Thousand and One Nights*. Its structure resembles a ship's mast 1,053 feet tall attached to which a 'sail' of fiberglass and Teflon swelled by the wind dazzles the eye, white by day and all the colors of the rainbow at night.

This, the tallest hotel in the world, stands on a man-made island in the Arabian Gulf, 350 yards from the shoreline. Frequently guests arrive by helicopter, landing on the pad at the top of the hotel. Those that arrive by plane are transferred to and from the airport by Rolls Royce and reach the hotel along a very closely guarded roadway over the water.

The view on entering is very impressive: the enormous hall is almost 600 feet high and a fountain shoots geysers 100 feet high every half-hour. Inside, unbridled luxury is the order of the day. The hotel does not have rooms but 202 suites that range from a minimum of 1,830 to a maximum of 8,400 square feet, installed with dozens of telephones, plasma-screen televisions, computers, etc.

The style is updated Empire and Arab Eclecticism interpreted in Brazilian and Italian marbles, silks and walls lined with 22-carat gold leaf. Every architectural feature in the building was designed to 'surprise' and create an explicit display of opulence and lavishness for the pleasure of a very few!

244 top A helicopter lands on the futuristic helipad at the Burj Al Arab at the top of the guest section.

244 center This view shows the curve of the two pylons that face the coast 330 yards away, and the road at bottom right.

244 bottom and 244-245
A surprising combination of reflections and geometrical patterns, the tower stands 1,053 feet high. The three vertical pillars are connected by horizontal girders further strengthened by diagonal trusses. The structure is made from steel and glass, and is clad with white Teflon.

245 bottom Luxurious and dizzying, the immense atrium in the Burj Al Arab provides a spectacular view from the top. Arriving guests are welcomed on the yellow first floor dominated by huge gold structures. Everything is designed to conjure up the impression of princely splendor, for the privilege of which guests have to pay tens of thousands of dollars a night.

The Burj Al Arab Hotel

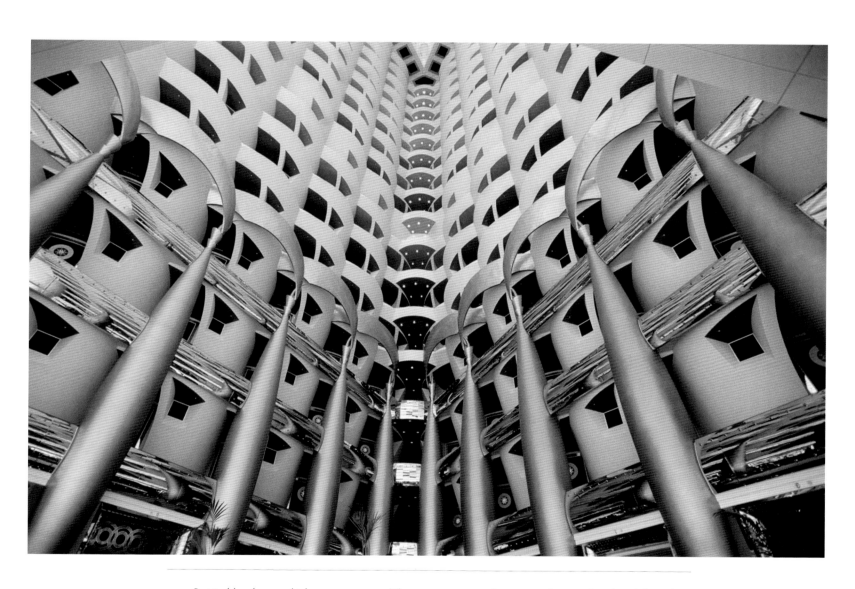

246 Inspired by the sea which surrounds and seems to support it, the Burj Al Arab imitates the form of a sail. Note the join between the 'mast' (the vertical pylon) and one of the two curved pillars that represents the 'edge' of the sail.

247 top The various sections of each floor are connected by straight walkways along the outer edge of the 'sail.' The space in the center of the building acts as a light-well 54 floors deep, which therefore makes the hall beneath a full 591 feet high.

247 bottom Seen from below, the interior of the Burj Al Arab is like a honeycomb of suites. The gigantic, brilliant gold, tapered pillars are topped by arches inspired by traditional Islamic architecture.

NORTH AMERICA

The seemingly boundless expanse of the United States of America is protean in nature, with vast landscapes, huge but diverse metropolises of breathtaking skyscrapers, and areas with extremes of population density. It is also a metaphor of power and, now, also of tragic destruction.

Almost two centuries passed following Columbus' first voyage in 1492 before European settlers ventured to create their own residential environment rather than exist in rudimentary structures, if not those offered by nature itself. Towns expanded organically from the first settlement or adopted the grid pattern of streets, like the celebrated plan of Philadelphia (1682) that was replicated across the entire country from coast to coast. Though developed from and related to European traditions, colonial architecture produced original prototypes that followed a progression of styles and revivals from the last decade of the 18th century to the period after World War II. The alternative to anti-academic eclecticism, and reflecting the taste of elites, architectural orders and canons seen through the lens of Neoclassicism and Neogothic, American styles contrast with a free and empirical formulation of 'architecture without architects' (Bruno Zevi). In domestic construction, wooden mobile houses evolved into the standardized technique of 'balloon framing' (G. W. Snow, 1833) based on a vertical wooden frame; this was to have a long-lasting influence, provide high standards of comfort and used to experiment with spaces and volumes until the advent of the organic architecture of Frank Lloyd Wright.

The expansion of towns and the industrial economy were important and interdependent factors that stimulated the growth and development of city planning at the start of the 19th century, for example, the establishment of private towns that were exclusively dependent on a particular company or business concern. Midway through the century, industry and the railroad infrastructure were both linked to the progressive pushing back of the frontier, and were a further catalyst in the new phenomenon of urbanization on a wide scale.

Contemporaneously, a trend towards an organic integration of nature and artifact was occurring, for instance, the laying out of The Mall in Washington in 1851 was a precursor of the theme of the public park which, with the completion of Central Park in New York (1862) was to become increasingly important in the planning of American cities and towns after the end of the Civil War.

During the same period urban centralization was countered by residential decentralization, or the flight to the suburbs of the city's inhabitants. Chicago was the leading exponent of this phenomenon though it was common to other American cities. This led to the development of a new type of urban building that was made possible by technological innovations in construction: the skyscraper. Products of the 'functional specialization of urban centers,' skyscrapers increased the space available on building plots of limited size. They appeared in the U.S. in the 1880s having been preceded by construction experiments in New York that defined their typology and use, and encouraged the development of the techniques required to build them. This is Wright's description: '... carefully designed, a steel building of great height transcribed in architectural terms: tall coherently and synthetically ... an event more important than the papal dome because in it utility is turned into beauty through the sheer triumph of creative imagination. ... As a work of art, the skyscraper had been born.' He was referring to the Wainwright Building in St. Louis of 1890, designed by the 'lieber Meister' Louis Henry Sullivan. In modern and contemporary America, architecture 'indulges in an experimentalism that is as fascinating in individual examples as it is corrosive and decaying overall.' It affected the whole of the modern movement, which, 'oscillating for decades between mannerism and utopia ... and open in its congenital mutability' is capable of fulfilling 'Wright's prophecy of a human, anti-authoritarian and joyful habitat' (Bruno Zevi).

If, less than three centuries ago, we had climbed into a huge and very light balloon and flown from the center of the Old Continent westward, first touching ground in Iberia, then in the Azores, we would next have landed in the United States before continuing to Japan. Today many obstacles and buildings would make such a trip impossible, first and foremost the Sears Tower in Chicago; the enormous height of this futuristic lookout and defense tower might even send the balloon back again toward the Atlantic. The proliferation of skyscrapers in the United States might be considered a metaphor of the country's existence: unlike icebergs, seven-eighths of which are hidden, skyscrapers emerge nine-tenths above ground and are in this sense a symbol of the history, world presence and openness of the United States since the country's very inception. We see almost everything there is to see, and what remains hidden is insignificant. A careful captain would maneuver the balloon so as to suspend it at a height of approximately 1,520 feet, in other words, just above the tallest building in Chicago. At that height there would be no other obstacles to negotiate and we could take advantage of the winds to visit the next two tallest buildings in the country, the Empire State and Chrysler buildings. Like the Sears Tower, both are dedicated to the world of work and are monuments to the entrepreneurship and industriousness of America. Verticality and the competition to build the tallest skyscraper partly originated on the small island of Manhattan, but the height of skyscrapers, not only in New York, is a spin-off of wealth; it is a tangible sign and symbol of the power of money. Yet the indifferent majesty of these buildings endows them with two negative qualities: through the transparency of their glass facades they are exposed to the public gaze, and their very height means they are so very distant from city life. At their feet the great pulsing metropolis is no more than an expanse of tiny objects.

We descend, in our balloon, to fly over Central Park, and are made curious by the round building that appears anomalous in the grid pattern of New York. This is the Guggenheim Museum, a dreamlike helix and unforgettable architectural form that winds its exhibition space in a spiral continuum. As we continue on our imaginary journey over New York toward the Atlantic, we make out the solemn Statue of Liberty, the city's portal, a metaphor and promise of freedom for the land of America and the whole world. Then we slip down the East Coast and head inland when we come to the Potomac. Here we have to release a little of the gas in the balloon to descend so as to appreciate the Neoclassical grace of Washington's Capitol Hill, designed as an updated version of the styles and forms of ancient architecture.

Continuing inland, the balloon skims over the trees of Pennsylvania where we catch sight of the building integrated with the wilderness of Bear Run. This is the longitudinal house Fallingwater, designed by Frank Lloyd Wright. The architect wrote, '... I was born an American, a son of the earth and space' (*The Natural House*), and it is the qualities of freedom and protection by which the house is characterized, representing the point of departure for an imaginary 'architecture of democracy' that implements the original ideals of the nation. One of these ideals is the constitutional right of every citizen to aspire to happiness, perhaps the interior and intellectualized one of an art museum, or perhaps the participatory and transitory one produced by a staged event. And, as we pass over in our balloon, we may be attracted by the gigantism of a sports stadium or the spectacular transparency of a museum of the new millennium.

To the west, far off, we make out the titanic orange structure of the Golden Gate Bridge. This product of determined American civil engineering will be the point for our departure across the Pacific, following the route to the Orient that Columbus searched for. It has been an imaginary trip between great architectural works of America, the history and meaning of which seems to echo in the words of Scott Fitzgerald: '*America [...] a design for the whole human race, the last and the greatest of all human dreams — or nothing.*'

Alessandra Capodiferro

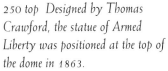

250 top *Designed by Thomas Crawford, the statue of Armed Liberty was positioned at the top of the dome in 1863.*

250 bottom *The allegorical figures on the tympanum of Capitol Hill, designed by Luigi Persico, were replaced by copies in 1959–60.*

Capitol Hill

WASHINGTON D.C., USA

by Maria Laura Vergelli

Amagnificent expression of American Neoclassicism, the Capitol in Washington, D.C., is a work of unquestioned power. However, as a result of events during construction, it is marked by a certain architectural conformity. The seat of the Senate, the Chamber of Representatives and the Supreme Court of Justice, the immense and visually powerful white marble building stands on the hill at the east end of The Mall. Dominating the entire building, the hemispherical dome rests on a drum of equidistant columns and has been described by the Italian architectural critic Bruno Zevi as 'a symbol of the sovereign law that stipulates the equality of all citizens.' In 1792, two years after the choice of the site had been made and Pierre Charles L'Enfant had been assigned the task to plan a new federal capital, the Frenchman had abandoned the job.

Thomas Jefferson, the Secretary of State and an enthusiastic supporter of the prevailing Greek Revival style, suggested that a competition should be held for the design of a Capitol. The competition closed without a winner: none of the seventeen plans that were submitted received approval. In October of the same year, with the competition well and truly over, William Thornton, a Scottish doctor and amateur architect, received approval to submit his own design. Palladian in concept, the design was of a building with a circular central body crowned by a low dome, and of two symmetrical rectangular buildings for the Senate and Chamber of Representatives. Approved by the Commissioners of the Federal Buildings and by President Washington, work began in 1793.

The first long period of construction concluded in 1828. Completed in stages and with delays in the execution, the building seems to be the result of a fairly unsuccessful collaboration between the inexpert Thornton and a series of architects (Stephen H. Hallet, George Hadfield, James Hoban, Benjamin Henry Latrobe and Charles Bulfinch) who assisted him, either trying variously to modify the plans, or limiting themselves to carrying out the project. Major expansion plans and monumental modifications of the original form, such as the addition of wings and an iron dome, were incorporated between 1850 and 1868, resulting from five different proposals coordinated by Thomas U. Walter and, at the end, by Edward Clark.

The statue of Armed Liberty by sculptor Thomas Crawford was placed on the top of the dome in 1863; it seems to symbolize the strong civic and patriotic passion that had characterized the long period of construction.

250-251 Capitol Hill stands at the east end of The Mall on what was known in the 18th century as Jenkins Hill, though today it is referred to simply as 'the Hill.' The solid, white marble body and majestic dome, also seen in the Capitol Reflecting Pool in front of the building, are the outcome of many contributions made during the 19th century (especially between 1851 and 1868) and, more recently, in 1962.

251 bottom Rural America is tinged with Neoclassicism in the sculptural groups on this pediment of the Capitol. It shows farmers, herders and laborers.

252 Statuary Hall (top), formerly the Chamber of Representatives, today holds a collection of statues of famous citizens. The Apotheosis of Washington, in the lantern, was designed by Costantino Brumidi.

253 The portico of the main entrance to the Capitol was the setting, until the 1980s, of the swearing-in ceremony of the President of the United States. This has since been moved to the more attractive west front, on The Mall.

The Statue of Liberty

NEW YORK, USA

by Flaminia Bartolini

254 The symbol of the United States, the Statue of Liberty was a gift to the American people from France and the defiant French Republic. Edouard de Laboulaye, whose idea it was, conceived the statue as an allegory of the 'Liberty that lights the world.'

255 top Frédéric-Auguste Bartholdi was born in Colmar in 1834 and died in Paris in 1904. A famous sculptor, he erected

many statues in his home town and created a statue of the Marquis Lafayette for New York, which now stands in Union Square.

255 bottom Completed by Richard Morris Hunt in 1875, the statue's pedestal is made from a concrete block decorated with friezes and ashlar plinths, and a Neoclassical loggia made from granite and concrete.

The symbol of the New World, the Statue of Liberty stands on Liberty Island in the New York Bay. The sculpture was donated to the United States by France in 1885 to commemorate 100 years of independence.

The statue is of a young woman clad in flowing robes, wearing a seven-pointed crown and holding a torch in her right hand. At her feet are the broken chains that symbolize the end of her slavery, and her left hand clasps a book with the date of her independence incised upon it: 4 July 1776.

The sculpture is by Frédéric-Auguste Bartholdi, who began work on the terracotta model in 1875. Later he built a wooden model 150 feet tall and made the sheet-metal cladding.

When the work was completed, the gigantic figure was taken to pieces and shipped to New York in 214 chests.

Strong winds made the assembly of the colossus problematical. Bartholdi then sought the assistance of Gustave Eiffel who designed an internal frame for the statue. The four vertical supports that form the load-bearing axis intersect with horizontal and diagonal struts to create a mesh.

The 150 feet high star-shaped pedestal was designed by the architect Richard Morris Hunt and made from concrete reinforced with granite.

In 1983 restoration work began on the statue to remedy deterioration caused by its exposure to the wind and rain. The electrolytic reaction created by rainwater and the metal had caused the most damage; in addition, water had succeeded in infiltrating the torch in many places.

A number of internal pins were replaced with new stainless-steel supports, while restoration of the lady's clothing required more extensive repairs.

256-257 and 256 bottom Liberty wears a seven-pointed crown representing the seven seas of the world and bears the flame of freedom. In her left hand she holds a tablet on which the inscription 'July IV MDCCLXXVI' represents the date July 4th 1776, when the U.S. obtained its independence from the United Kingdom.

257 top In 1885 the Statue of Liberty was dismantled into 350 pieces, packed into 214 chests and shipped to New York. It was unloaded in Upper New York Bay, onto a small island that has become known as Liberty Island.

257 center To erect the statue (151 feet tall) the sculptor Frédéric-Auguste Bartholde asked the engineer Gustave Eiffel to produce a support frame made from iron and steel and then lined with embossed copper.

257 bottom During the Exposition Universelle in Paris in 1878, the Statue of Liberty was visible for a certain period in Paris, where it was assembled in four months and inaugurated on 28 October 1886.

The Chrysler Building

NEW YORK, USA

by Beatrix Healing and Maria Laura Vergelli

258 top In 1925 Walter Percy Chrysler (1875–1940) founded an automobile company, the Chrysler Corporation, and at the height of his success he built a skyscraper to celebrate its triumph.

258 bottom The Chrysler Building was one of the second generation of skyscrapers and, at 1,047 feet high, it was the tallest building in the world until the Empire State Building was completed shortly after.

Walter Percy Chrysler was a perfect example of the self-made man American-style: from a simple master machinist he raised himself to become one of the barons of the U.S. automobile industry, enabling him to finance the construction of the Chrysler Building in New York. In keeping with the progressive spirit of the times, during the Depression Chrysler bought the land lease and architectural plans for a speculative venture initiated by the developer William H. Reynolds. Chrysler wanted the building to be an iconic skyscraper in the heart of Manhattan that would magnify the grandeur of the modern age and which would rival other buildings for height. Chrysler realized his ambition when the building was completed in 1930. Its glorious but short-lived record as the world's tallest building (1,046 feet) was dependent on its unmistakable and innovative slender spire, and was taken from it by the Bank of Manhattan in late 1930.

Designed by William Van Alen, the Chrysler Building is one of the most successful interpretations of Art Deco in the United States as a result of the stylization of its architectural structure and its decorative design. Nor has the passing of time erased the building's sensational modernity, which achieves its greatest expression in the spire that almost seems to perforate the sky, in its architectural form, its exquisite decorative details, and the innovative use of steel in the cladding. The thrust of the central tower is highlighted at the 31st floor by four metallic corner elements like giant radiator caps, similar to the winged helmet worn by Mercury, and by a frieze round the outside of the building decorated with the wheels and fenders of a car. Eight steel gargoyles in the form of stylized eagles' heads project threateningly on the 61st floor. The spire, decorated with triangular windows and with radiating metal panels, resembles the grill of a car radiator. In its early decades the Chrysler Building dominated midtown New York; its distinctive components and automobile marques symbolized the supremacy of the Chrysler company and also celebrated the rhetoric of the triumph of the individual and financial power. Indeed, as Bruno Zevi stated, the Chrysler Building 'threw the surrounding buildings into shadow.'

The Chrysler Building

260 Designed to resemble a gigantic automobile grill, the Art Deco Vertex is like a nascent star with its radiating panels. The star, in this case, was the Chrysler Corporation.

261 top The interiors of the Chrysler Building have outstanding Art Deco decoration; for example, the doors of the elevators are embellished with eight types of wood from around the world.

261 bottom A frieze on the 30th floor simulates wheels and fenders and, at the corners, enormous radiator caps. On the 61st floor, eight steel drips in the form of eagles' heads project menacingly into the void.

The Empire State Building

NEW YORK, USA

by Guglielmo Novelli

The Empire State Building is one of the symbols of New York and of American culture. Who does not remember it in the 1933 film when King Kong climbed the tower fighting off airplanes?

John Jackob Raskob, vice-president at General Motors and the building's main client, launched a challenge to his rival Walter Chrysler (owner of the Chrysler Building) by building a higher skyscraper.

Set in the heart of Manhattan, the massive building soars on the site of the original Waldorf-Astoria Hotel. Excavations of the foundations began a few weeks before the Wall Street Crash in October 1929 and the building was completed in just 18 months with the help of 19,000 workers. The plainness of the architectural style and the serious economic crisis meant lower costs than the designers had expected, but when the skyscraper was inaugurated in 1931, only half of the space had been leased, which brought it the nickname Empty State Building. On the other hand, the Empire State had exceeded the height of the Chrysler Building by approximately 200 feet, making it the tallest building in the world.

The 102-floor colossus is characterized by a massive base that engulfs the first six floors. As it rises the building tapers progressively at the 25th, 72nd and 81st floors. It is crowned by an antenna about 200 feet high, completely lined in metal, which was originally designed to be a berth for dirigibles but which has only ever been used as a tower to receive radio and television signals.

Until the 1970s, the Empire State was the tallest building in the world at 1,453 feet. To give an idea of the bulk that this icon of the American myth represents, consider that it has a useable floor area of 51.6 acres and that it contains 37 million cubic feet of total volume. A unique sight by both day and night is given by the steel fixtures; the thirty highest floors are also illuminated from 9pm to midnight by powerful spotlights with colored filters that vary depending on the circumstances.

Another important fact is that the Empire State Building was the first skyscraper to include an observation deck open to the public.

262 top With the 'defeated' Chrysler Building to the left, a worker continues to make the Empire State Building even higher.

262 bottom The last few feet: seen from below, what was to have been the berthing place for dirigibles is about to be completed.

263 Standing atop the 10 million bricks used to construct the Empire State, the radio and television antenna spears the sky at a height of 1,453 feet. The elegant Empire State Building is composed of elements that gradually taper towards the top.

264-265 *From above it is easy to appreciate the 'telescopic' form of the building. The vertical bands of windows increase its apparent verticality.*

265 top left *The Empire State Building is an evocation of the optimism of the age in which it was designed, but the confidence was short-lived: in 1931, the year it was completed, the Great Depression was at the door.*

265 top right *Visitors to the skyscraper's entrance hall are regaled with a magnificent gilded model of the building in which the top is shown as a lighthouse illuminating the world.*

265 bottom *Gigantic and spectacular, the 6,500 windows (which cover more than 494 acres) reflect spectacularly when the sunset illuminates the symbol of New York.*

The Empire State Building

Fallingwater

OHIOPYLE,
PENNSYLVANIA,
USA

by Guglielmo Novelli

Called 'one of the greatest masterpieces of all time' by Bruno Zevi, this sophisticated house was commissioned from Frank Lloyd Wright by Edgar Kaufmann, a wealthy businessman from Pittsburgh.

Construction took place between 1934 and 1937 at Bear Run in Pennsylvania on a site of great beauty in the middle of a wood. Crossing the site is a torrent that forms a small waterfall at a certain point.

The house has a central nucleus of visible stone load-bearing walls anchored to the rock from which concrete planes project into space toward the waterfall. Horizontals prevail in the composition; Wright defines these terracings as 'the branches of a tree that come away from the trunk.'

To arrive at the house, the visitor crosses a small bridge and passes through a narrow passage between the back of the house and the rock wall to reach a small entrance. This leads into the spacious, luminous living room in which rocks emerge from the floor to evoke the natural environment outside. The focus of the living room is the stone hearth

266-267 and 266 bottom Set against the backdrop of Pennsylvania's woods, Fallingwater emphasizes the horizontal, a 'natural' dimension inspired directly by Japanese architecture.

267 top Frank Lloyd Wright in a photograph from 1938.

267 center and bottom Like the exterior, the interiors of Fallingwater harmonize with nature: large open areas and natural materials.

typical of American frontier life, around which the rest of the house revolves. The various rooms and activities were arranged by the great American architect in a particular fashion: the living room faces south toward the waterfall, the eastward-facing entrance and westward-facing kitchen lie on either side of it; the area of the stairs and dining room face north. A small room that houses the boiler and the stores lies beneath the main level. The upper floor accommodates the bedrooms and bathrooms and serves to counterbalance the projection of the living room northwards by means of a progression of volumes that decrease from east to west.

This surprising building was constructed using the most modern materials available at the time (concrete, iron, and glass). They blend successfully and harmoniously into the beautiful natural setting. Fallingwater is certainly one of the best examples of the integration of nature and architecture. The plasticity of the projections toward the surrounding environment creates a certain interpenetration between the building and its natural context. The stone ashlars of the vertical walls that enter the house are a reference to nature, and the large windows help to reduce the definition of the building.

The ambitiousness of the construction was not an end in itself but the instrument through which the architect arranged man's work in symbiosis with nature. The house 'lives' in its environment as though it had grown spontaneously. Even the colors are 'suggested' by the rocks, earth and trees, and the window and doorframes are the same color as the autumn leaves.

Technically the building was very advanced for its time; for example, the reinforced-concrete platforms built over drops of up to 16 feet. However, structurally these platforms have created problems from the start and have had to be heavily rebuilt. At the time, of course, construction using reinforced concrete was a technique not very well known.

Fallingwater recently underwent structural restoration, thus saving it from probable ruin, and now that the danger of yielding has been permanently warded off, the house-cum-museum can be visited once again.

This brilliant creation has fascinated and influenced generations of architects and art enthusiasts for the tangibility of its organic architecture. Undoubtedly it is one of the greatest examples of architecture's integration with nature, and perhaps even its 'continuation.'

269 The distance between the two shores, the instability of the seabed, the frequent and turbulent tides and the strong currents created substantial difficulties during construction of San Francisco's Golden Gate Bridge.

268 These three photographs from the 1930s evoke the 'pioneering' atmosphere of the construction of the Golden Gate Bridge; they show the examination of the model and the works in progress, with cables and wheelbarrows.

The Golden Gate Bridge

SAN FRANCISCO, USA

by Maria Laura Vergelli

'At last the mighty task is done'; this is the start of the celebratory poem written in May 1937 by Joseph Baermann Strauss, the engineer who designed and built the Golden Gate Bridge. Baermann wrote the lines when the job was completed. The events of the construction had seemed to mark the changing of an era and, on the two inauguration days, swarms of people and cars had crossed the bridge. The difficult but intriguing task of building a bridge across the Golden Gate – the wide and stormy stretch of sea that marks the entrance to San Francisco Bay from the Pacific Ocean – was first proposed in 1872. The

idea was relaunched through a press campaign led by the editor of the *San Francisco Call Bulletin* in 1916: 'It is possible to build a bridge across San Francisco Bay at various points. But in only one place could such an undertaking represent a universal benefit: at the Golden Gate.'

Strauss was won over by the challenge to find the technical and financial means required to build a structure considered to be at the limits of the engineering capabilities of the time and a to be high economic risk. His experience and skills as a designer enabled him to present a preliminary plan within a couple of years, along with arguments to

270-271 Two workers paint the stay bars the bridge's characteristic vermilion-red. The view that takes in San Francisco, Alcatraz and the Marin Headlands, one of the most spectacular in the world, is no longer just available to motorists but cyclists and pedestrians too.

270 bottom The two tapered towers of the Golden Gate on the San Francisco side stand 743 feet above the water. The two gigantic steel cables at their summit are the biggest ever produced (diameter 3 feet); the thousands of stays suspended from them support the deck of the bridge.

271 These two details of the iron frame that supports the bridge and metal cables connected to the deck give an idea of the bridge's gigantic proportions. The towers and

massive structure and characteristic color make the Golden Gate Bridge one of the world's most famous suspension bridges.

support the feasibility of the project and a limited cost estimate. Having been made responsible for raising the finance for the project, Strauss succeeded in persuading the city administration to form a Golden Gate Bridge and Highway District in 1928. This administrative and territorial body played a decisive role by providing organizational and financial support in the critical years of the American Depression. In January 1933 the work began, financed by the issue of bonds for $35 million between 1930 and 1932, despite the clear difficulties represented by the geography of the site, and, in just 4 years, 'the bridge that couldn't be built' was completed. Having overcome the substantial differences of interest involved and the dogmatic assessments of the skeptics, the bridge that Strauss had dreamed of became reality. Once the suspension concept had been perfected, the original

design was masterfully revised and transformed into the elegant and refined Art Deco structure that it is by architects Irving and Gertrude Morrison.

In total the bridge is 8,980 feet long, 4,200 of which are represented by the main span and 1,125 feet by spans at either end. Two tapering towers rise 745 feet above the water to support the two gigantic cables from which the deck is suspended. These cables are then anchored at either end to massive blocks. Each cable is composed of 92 strands, and each strand is composed of 27,572 metal wires.

The harmony of the design transcends the bridge's individual parts and is perfectly inserted in the landscape of San Francisco Bay. The image of the Golden Gate Bridge – with its sinuous orange-vermilion arcs suspended over the Pacific – is the icon of the city, but also belongs to the world.

272-273 *Despite the economic difficulties and skepticism of his contemporaries, Strauss managed to complete construction of the Golden Gate Bridge faithful to the original* *plan. Due to the fog, for which San Francisco Bay is famous, the U.S. Navy proposed painting the bridge black and yellow so that it was more clearly visible to passing ships.*

 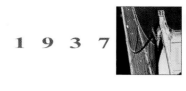

274 top left Spacious and luminous, the entrance hall of the Sears Tower leads into an internal space several floors high designed to meet the client's exact needs.

274 center left The different heights of various elements of the Sears Tower stand out against the Chicago skyline.

The Sears Tower
CHICAGO, USA

by Maria Laura Vergelli

The Sears Tower is the result of the collaboration between the architect Bruce Graham and the engineer Fazlur Khan. With 110 floors and a height of 1,453 feet it is one of the world's tallest skyscrapers. Between 1974 and 1997 it held the record, having exceeded the height of the Twin Towers, but it lost its supremacy to the Petronas Towers in Kuala Lumpur. The actual top of the Sears Tower is still debated as the height calculated to date (1,453 feet) does not include the television antennas, which are an integral part of the structure. Therefore the title of tallest building remains in doubt. One thing is certain, the Sears Tower is the tallest skyscraper in Chicago as regards the heights of both the topmost inhabited floor and the roof.

The building's framework based on a 'bundle' of individual towers of different height is a revolutionary structural technique used by Graham on other skyscrapers. The body of the tower is formed by the assembly of 9 large tubular elements, with walls composed of a thick and rigid mesh of girders and columns. The first two elements halt at the 49th floor while the others continue. More stop at the 64th and 90th floors leaving only two to continue to the very top of the building. The result is surprising: even a rigorously Modernist skyscraper can be elegant if its conformation varies when viewed from different points.

Furthermore, a structure formed by the 'bundling' of several elements has a particular functional purpose: that of strengthening the building to withstand the violent buffeting it receives in the Windy City. As each element is exposed on one or two sides to wind pressure, they are better able to resist its force. Nonetheless, the oscillations produced on especially windy days are one of the skyscraper's characteristics. The Skydeck Pavilion opened in 1985 at the top of the tower offers marvelous views over Lake Michigan and the green flat land of Illinois, Indiana, and Wisconsin. Designed primarily to accommodate offices, the Sears Tower is entered each day by about 25,000 people, roughly double the number forecast.

274 bottom left The Sears Tower has the largest number of private offices in the world, distributed across 100 floors. The scalar framework made of tubular elements has a square section measuring 75 feet on each side; it is lined with bronzed glass on the outside.

274 right Only two of the nine towers in the tubular load-bearing structure of the Sears Tower reach right to the top. The height is then increased by the antennas on top of the building.

275 Designed to be the 'people's tower,' the Sears Tower has a floor area of 450,000 square yards and is served by a series of very fast elevators.

The Louisiana Superdome

NEW ORLEANS, USA

by Maria Laura Vergelli

Dean Gerald McLindon of the University School of Environmental Design has called the New Orleans stadium – the Superdome – the most functional public building ever designed. Construction began in 1971 and its gates opened officially exactly four years later in August 1975.

The Superdome stands 273 feet high, has a total of 27 stories and covers 13 acres. The stadium's covering is the largest steel dome ever built.

The building's most interesting characteristic is its versatility: built as a stadium for the Superbowl, the final of the American football championship, it also has the following facilities: 53 meeting rooms, 3 banqueting halls and a television studio. It is also used to hold concerts, shows, trade fairs, conventions, theatrical performances and every kind of event that attracts large numbers of people. Many famous artists have performed there.

The technology used in the plants and grandstands is very innovative and sophisticated. Depending on whether musical performances, meetings, exhibitions or the Superbowl is being held, the grandstands have a mechanism that allows them to turn towards the relevant part of the arena.

Every section of the stadium is perfectly visible thanks to two giant screens (95 x 121 feet), and there is an innovative telescopic camera system that can pick up the tiniest detail.

The Superdome is connected via a ramp to the commercial district where the Center Mall, Hyatt Regency and Poydras Plaza Office Complex are located, and also linked via two other ramps to the New Orleans Arena (a 18,500-seater opened in October 1999). As a result, the Superdome has helped to create a sporting and cultural center that has boosted the image of New Orleans.

This futuristic stadium has been a powerful tourist attraction: since it opened hotels within a mile of it have reported a 180 percent increase in their bookings.

276-277 The Superdome in New Orleans (Louisiana) is one of the most famous stadiums in the world. The gigantic but compact form, similar to a flying saucer, was inaugurated in August 1975 and has become a part of the skyline. It has contributed to turning the city into a center for sports, culture and all kinds of entertainment.

276 bottom The dome is a metal frame 688 feet in diameter that rises approximately 272 feet above the ground. It is the largest steel vault ever built. Around the building is a large parking lot.

277 One of the most futuristic buildings of the last century, the Superdome was built in the record time of four years. Construction began on 11 August 1971 and ended on 3 August 1975.

278 top and 278-279
A powerful electric plant with about 400 miles of cable, including optic fiber, provides the stadium with all its energy. The lights (inside and out), the 2 audiovisual panels (95 x 121 feet each), an innovative telescopic system, 42 moving staircases, 14 elevators and all other public services are powered by this system.

279 top Built to hold the Superbowl, from its opening to 2002 the Superdome in Louisiana has hosted 6 (a record) and also been used for many other events. The versatility of its facilities is famous, allowing it to host concerts, trade fairs and spectacles of every kind. The building also contains conference halls and recording studios.

The Guggenheim Museum

NEW YORK, USA

by Guglielmo Novelli

280-281 A work of art designed to contain art, the Guggenheim Museum building represents Frank Lloyd Wright's attempt to overcome the 'passivity' of traditional architecture using functional forms that actively involve the observer.

One of the most important museums of modern and contemporary art in the world, the Guggenheim in New York is part of the Solomon R. Guggenheim Foundation, which heads other institutions around the world (Bilbao, Berlin, Venice, etc.). The collection, held in the famous building completed in 1959, by Frank Lloyd Wright includes works belonging to all the most important international genres from French Impressionism to the modern day. A sculpture in itself, the museum is one of the works that most intimately represents the poetics of Wright's architecture. It is a conception that distanced itself from the dictates of the Modern Movement and imbued the building with an 'organic' quality. He intended to establish a dialectical relationship between the functionality of the building and its form (as happens in the natural world).

On that score the Italian critic Bruno Zevi wrote, 'it is important to note how Wright's space comes down to its simple functions and establishes itself, not in geometric terms, but in immediately plastic ones.' Situated at 1071 Fifth Avenue at 88th Street, seen from outside the building contradicts the standard orthogonal, checkerboard plan of New York. This fact stimulated the imagination of the inhabitants of the Big Apple, who dreamed up many names for the museum: snake, tornado, wedding cake, skateboard ramp, multistory parking lot, etc. However, these initial attitudes soon turned positive. The great projecting curve of the first floor creates a plastic movement that invites the passerby to enter.

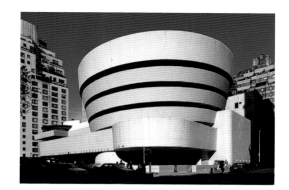

282 and 283 center The attractive 'shell' inside the Guggenheim Museum is illuminated by a dome with a window like a spider's web. The shell is formed by a spiral walkway that forms the museum's gallery.

283 top From the outside, the building seems to taper downward. Originally criticized, the appearance of the building, with its window that runs the length of the spiral, is now universally appreciated.

283 bottom This view shows the intersection of the entrance and the spiral. The overall layout is changing and almost unpredictable.

Exterior and interior have a direct relationship by means of the loggia beneath the bridge that joins the two sections of the museum building. The dynamic appearance of the exterior is reflected internally in the upward movement created by the continuous spiral that projects from the gallery walls. Starting from a basin in the central bay of the first floor, the spiral walkway offers the visitor an uninterrupted experience of spatial vitality. The continuity of the spiral halts at each level near the elevator tower where the concave lines of the ramp are reversed to become convex.

The diameter of the spiral increases as it rises so that the light entering from the large transparent dome is able to illuminate the large central space and each level of the gallery. The various exhibition areas are also lighted by the ribbon window that follows the length of the spiral.

Wright developed the building organically, rejecting the traditional approach of the passive layering of floors and its consequent neat distinction of spaces.

He concentrated on the relationship of the observer with the work of art: the route to be followed in the museum, designed to start at the top and work downward, guides visitors but also allows them to stop in front of the works displayed.

Visitors are also given different perceptions of the internal space, which expands or contracts according to the level on which the observer is standing, and from the outside it is impossible not to notice how this shell-like building breaks up the monotony and straight lines of the surrounding skyscrapers.

This was the intention when Hilla Rebay (Solomon Guggenheim's art advisor) wrote to Wright saying 'I need a fighter, a lover of space, an agitator, a tester and a wise man. . . . I want a temple of spirit, a monument!'

Milwaukee Art Museum

MILWAUKEE, USA

by Maria Laura Vergelli

284 top and bottom The tail of an enormous whale, the hull of a futuristic ship ... as one's perspective changes, the surprising Quadracci Pavilion appears differently to the visitor. Seen from the west, the entrance to the pavilion is dominated by the cable-stayed bridge that joins it to Wisconsin Avenue.

Milwaukee Art Museum is one of the most surprising examples of modern architecture, and its dynamic yet grandiose structure has become the symbol of the city's renewal.

The variety of the materials with which it is built (glass, Carrara marble, maplewood and concrete), the superb view over the lake and the extraordinary panorama of the city make the museum itself a work of art.

The current structure is the outcome of distinct phases. The original building dates to the postwar period when, to honor the dead, public opinion demanded the construction of a War Memorial Center. Some years later it was decided to build a memorial along the shores of Lake Michigan with space for works of art to be exhibited.

The design was commissioned from the Finnish architect Eero Saarinen, and construction began in 1955. Two years later the museum was opened when the Milwaukee Art Institute and Layton Art Gallery merged their collections to create the Milwaukee Art Center.

In the 1960s, Peg Bradley offered the center her entire collection of 600 modern American and European works of art and donated $1 million to expand the building.

The new project was the work of three architects – David Kahler, Mac Slater and Fitzhugh Scott – who in 1975 gave the complex a theater, educational center and the exhibition area known as the Bradley Galleries.

From the 1980s, when the museum changed its name to the Milwaukee Art Museum (MAM), the fame and prestige of the institution began to grow and the number of visitors rose to 200,000 a year.

This popularity made necessary a further extension, this time commissioned from the Spanish architect Santiago Calatrava. His contribution, which is the real attraction of the complex, is the Quadracci Pavilion, a spectacular, pale,

284-285 Similar to large white wings, the Brise Soleil ('sunbreak') is a dramatic mobile piece of architecture, seen here in its open position. The South Terrace extends toward the observer like the bow of a ship, and is dominated on the left by the huge inclined 'mast' that supports the bridge.

285 bottom *Calatrava's model shows the Quadracci Pavilion in its entirety. The bridge runs left from the central structure and is supported by stays to the mast in the center of the picture. Seen in a complex configuration, the Brise Soleil stands over the museum's reception area on the east side. Calatrava's works often make use of mobile elements and curves inspired by natural shapes.*

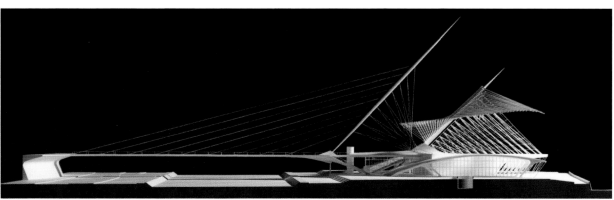

transparent structure opened in May 2001. This light, dynamic construction is made in glass and topped by an architectural form called 'brise soleil' that resembles wings. Fitted with an internal mechanism, this construction can move up and down to cover the entire hall of the museum below with its shadow.

A bridge suspended by metal stays from an inclined pylon 200 feet high connects the Quadracci Pavilion to one of the city's principal streets, Wisconsin Avenue. Like an arm extended towards the city center, this bridge represents the opening up of the museum to the

world and its link with Milwaukee.

Inside, the museum is a typical modern art center with meeting rooms, auditoria, restaurants and terraces that look out over Lake Michigan, and outside there are beautiful gardens designed by Dan Kiley.

The Quadracci Pavilion has succeeded in satisfying all the demands made of it: the conventional one of expanding the museum space, the functional one of regulating the natural light that enters, the symbolic one of welcoming visitors, and the iconic one that has made the museum the unmistakable symbol of the city.

286 top Night-lighting accentuates the originality of the Quadracci Pavilion, and its whiteness is brought out even more strongly than during the day.

286 bottom and 287 bottom The attractive and ordered symmetry of the interior of the museum offers views of great purity.

286-287 Large windows light the interior of the museum's reception area, seen here from the south. The Brise Soleil, partially seen above, can throw its shadow over the entire construction. The appeal of this structure lies in the absolute silence of its movement.

Milwuakee Art Museum

CENTRAL AND SOUTH AMERICA

It is difficult not to be attracted by the massive and unadorned stone buildings scattered throughout Mesoamerica where, before the Spanish conquest and European exploration, a number of indigenous civilizations had developed.

The remarkable heritage that forms the basis of the term 'Mesoamerican culture,' as defined by Paul Kirchoff, a specialist on the region, is characterized by recurring architectural and artistic elements, farming techniques, numeric and calendarial calculations, writing, the folding (like an accordion) of manuscripts, social structure, the political order, and a deep sense of religion.

At the time Mesoamerica was ruthlessly occupied under the leadership of the Spanish conquistador Hernán Cortés, and concluded in 1521 with the conquest of Mexico, the region was defined by natural boundaries: rivers to the north and south, and the oceans to the east and west. This large region now covers much of Mexico, Guatemala, El Salvador, Nicaragua, Costa Rica and part of Honduras. The east coast, which is sheltered from the Atlantic Ocean by islands and archipelagoes, faces toward the Caribbean Sea and the Gulf of Mexico, and the Pacific Coast is lined by the gulfs of Tehuantepec, Nicoya, and Fonseca.

The geography of Mesoamerica features mountains, deserts and tropical forests, and was the decisive factor that led to the foundation of separate and independent city-states. Their position and relations formed the basis of the territorial organization and trading network of the Mesoamerican cultures, and their exposure to unexpected, powerful natural phenomena is recognized as being a determining aspect of the formation of their intellectual knowledge and art.

The geographic determinism of Mesoamerican art is summed up admirably by Paul Gendrop and Doris Heyden: 'In the coastal region, where life is easier and weather conditions encourage agriculture, we find the smiling figurines of Veracruz, which are images of an extrovert people. In the harsh highlands, however, not even Xochipilli, the Aztec god of song, dance and flowers, is shown smiling. The smile of the Aztecs is almost a grimace' (in *Mesoamerican Architecture*).

The period during which the formation and first development of Mesoamerican culture occurred (called the Archaic Period, 7000–2000 BC) was marked by the beginning of the cultivation of maize (5000 BC), the cereal that lay at the basis of Mesoamerican diet, and by the manufacture of pottery (2500 BC). The following epoch is divided into three periods: the Pre-Classic (2000–200 BC), the Classic (200 BC–AD 900) divisions are further split into various phases.

In the state of Veracruz in the Pre-Classic Period, the Olmec civilization developed from about 1500 BC. This is referred to as the 'mother culture' as it affected the intellectual, religious, social, political, technical, and artistic development of other cultures. Over the arc of a thousand years (1200–200 BC) the basic models of Mesoamerican stone architecture developed in the Central American highlands. The Olmecs built platforms of pressed earth in their ceremonial centers which they transformed into modest masonry bases with the quarrying and dressing of stone and the use of adobe bricks and mortar. These constructions were the forerunners of the pyramidal structures.

The appearance of stairways, and inclined surfaces or protection ramps (*alfardas*) completed this development and culminated in the magnificent site of Teotihuacán,'the place of the gods,' where, according to myth, the gods gathered at sundown to create a new god. The origin of the monumental architecture of the Proto-Classic Period, at the start of the Christian era, began here with the construction of the Pyramid of the Sun.

This led to the advance from the early forms to the mature stepped pyramid, in which the series of levels formed a monumental base for the temple placed on the top and reached by one or more stairways. The many temples built in the Classic Period in the various Mesoamerican sites reflect the existence and importance of a priestly class, the increase in the pantheon of gods, and

the relationship between artistic expression and religious thought.

Dominating the highland plateau, rearing above the vast tropical forest, or snuggling between the low hills and dense vegetation, the tall stepped pyramids were an expression of a specific and original architectural language. Though similar structurally to the ziggurats of Mesopotamia and the stepped pyramid of Saqqarah in Egypt, they differed functionally, particularly from the latter as this was a funerary monument dedicated to the memory of a pharaoh.

In Palenque in Mesoamerica, there is a rare exception to the general model of the temple pyramid: the Temple of the Inscriptions was built with a tomb in its base. Structural analysis suggests that, rather than a pyramid proper, the construction was a superimposition of geometric shapes that together symbolized the celestial stratification considered by religious beliefs to be the succession of levels (almost always thirteen) where the gods dwelt. The driving impulse seems to have been the requirement to raise the temple that contained the statue of the god up to the sky. Small in size and not accessible to common mortals, the temple at the top of the pyramid could only be entered by the priests in charge of the cult. The priests celebrated the religious rites, sometimes cruel, from the top of the pyramid to emphasize their superiority over the community of worshipers. The verticality of the temple building and the hierarchy of the cult officials seem to reflect one another; this element was accentuated by the further steepening of the building, the progressive reduction in the pyramids' architectural mass, the centrality of the stairways, and the modeled decorations on the ridge of the temple, like at Tikal, where it seems such elements originated.

In the flourishing cities in the Maya region – now covered by Tabasco, Honduras and El Salvador – the buildings were embellished with sculptural and mosaic decorations. New artistic techniques were introduced, such as stuccowork, which is admirably represented at Palenque.

In the Puuc region, the sites of Uxmal and Chichén Itzá in the Yucatán peninsula reveal the organic fusion of decoration and architecture in the Late Classic Period.

The Mayan-Toltec culture developed in Chichén Itzá following the conquest of the city by a group of people of Toltec origin that arrived from the Mexican highlands. Migrations of peoples from the north resulted in the establishment of new indigenous cultures during the Post-Classic Period, but their supremacy was wiped out by the destruction caused by the subjection and colonization imposed by the Spanish.

It has been shown how at the time of the invasion the Spanish did not act on their intention of integrating the urban dimension with nature, with the result that the invaders applied the European standard in which the countryside and the city were separate entities.

More than 400 years later, in another region equally marked by the dramatic experience of colonization, the European notion of the compact city returned to inspire the foundation of the new political and cultural capital of Brazil. In the center of the South American forest, Brasília is laid out on the basis of a cross in which the allegorical forms of a bird, airplane or bow and arrow have been recognized. Along the straight, central axis, the administrative and governmental quarters are built, whilst the longer, curved arm that crosses it is where the large, square, residential 'superblocks' are sited.

The creative dimension of the city is remarkable, which lies at the limits of sustainability: it is an 'ideal city' tinged with sophistication. Lucio Costa designed the city plan, and Oscar Niemeyer produced the inventive and original building designs of which a characteristic is that they share various repetitive elements. The result has been much debated: 'Brasília is a Kafkian, surreal metropolis that reflects a diktat, an authoritarianism which the city plan and architecture transcribe without attempting to alter the meanings,' stated the Italian architectural critic Bruno Zevi.

Alessandra Capodiferro

289 left *The pyramid of El Castillo (the temple of Kukulcán) in Chichen Itzá, Mexico.*

289 center *The Pyramid of the Inscriptions in the archaeological site of Palenque, Mexico.*

289 right *The towers of the Palace of Congress and the Plaza of the Three Powers in Brasília, Brazil.*

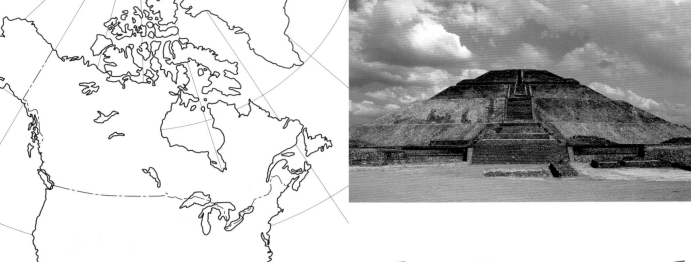

The Pyramid of the Sun

TEOTIHUACÁN, MEXICO

by Maria Eloisa Carrozza

Teotihuacán is one of Mesoamerica's most important archaeological sites. It lies at a height between 7,380 and 9,350 feet in a valley to the northwest of Mexico City, in a volcanic zone enclosed by mountain chains.

The climate (temperate in parts and sub-humid in others), the abundance of water and its fertile soil were the conditions that encouraged the establishment around 100 BC of a large settlement. Unquestionably the first city in Mesoamerica, Teotihuacán reached its peak between AD 150 and 300.

The layout of the city is on a geometric plan that was probably based on astronomic reasoning. The city's main axis – the Avenue of the Dead – runs north-south and intersects with a large east-west axis to divide the city into four quadrants. At the center of the city plan is the Pyramid of the Sun, the largest and most important building on the site, and a stop on the ceremonial route followed by pilgrims from the center of the city along the Avenue of the Dead to the Pyramid of the Moon.

The Sun Pyramid is 207 feet tall and has a volume of 35 million cubic feet. It is a four-stage truncated platform that originally supported a small temple on the top. The main façade faced west in the direction of the setting sun.

The sacredness of the pyramid is strong, and its symbolism has been furthered by the discovery of a natural cave, beneath the pyramid, which the ancient inhabitants excavated into the form of a cloverleaf. A

290 top *Pilgrims from faraway places toil up the steep stairway, originally to the temple at the top, that links the five levels of the Pyramid of the Sun in Teotihuacán.*

290 bottom *The square base of the Pyramid of the Sun measures 736 feet per side. Including the temple on the top, the pyramid's overall height was 235 feet, which made it the tallest building in pre-Hispanic America.*

290-291 *The massive Pyramid of the Sun stands at the focal point of ancient Teotihuacán. Its design was calculated on astronomical principles and the wish to harmonize it with the landscape of the plateau.*

symbol of creation and the birth of life, the cave was certainly at the origin of the great religious importance of the pyramid-temple. For the inhabitants of the city, the cave was a sort of belly from which the ancestors of tribal society originated, and it was around this cave that the entire city grew up.

Other important buildings stand on the Avenue of the Dead: the Citadel, which was probably a royal palace; the five-level Pyramid of the Moon, with its large staircase; the Palace of Quetzalpapalotl, the Temple of the Feathered Shells and the Palace of the Jaguars.

The civil buildings of the aristocracy were also to be found in the ceremonial center. These were of different size but collected in groups of buildings decorated with pictures,

corridors, porticoes, open areas and small internal temples. All the buildings were constructed using the local materials of mud, stone and wood. The stone was worked, decorated with stucco and painted. The decorations provide valuable iconographic information on the game of *pelota*, the cult of the dead, the feathered snake (the symbol of the god Quetzalcoatl), and jaguars decorated with feathers and shells that were associated with the god Tlaloc.

Weakened by a large fire, the cause of the end of the city in the late-8th century AD is subject to debate but may have been caused by concurrent events: the invasion of nomadic peoples from the north, a terrible famine, the ruinous struggle between dominant groups, and a people's rebellion against the rulers.

292 *A steep flight of steps without balustrades* (alfardas) *leads to Temple I, crowned by a high carved 'crest.'*

293 top *An early example of local architecture, Temple I (or Temple of the Great Jaguar) lines the east side of the Great Plaza.*

Temple I
TIKAL, GUATEMALA

by Maria Eloisa Carrozza

uring the period of their greatest splendor, the Maya were distributed among at least fifty politically independent, populous kingdoms formed by a capital city and a collection of smaller, subordinate inhabited centers. In the heart of the rainforest of El Petén, the city of Tikal was one of the largest, numbering hundreds of architectural complexes. Most of the sets of buildings that comprised the North Acropolis stand around the Gran Plaza. This was the square in which the kings had their burial temples built, and constructed the group of buildings known as the Mundo Perdido, which was the earliest Mayan astronomic center. The civil buildings of the city are concentrated in the Central Acropolis, where they had residential and ceremonial functions. Those that stand out are the Palace of Windows, also known as the Palace of the Bats, Group G or the Palace of the Grooves, and other buildings that ring the plaza of the Seven Temples. The monumental architectonic style – the acme of Tikal's architecture – occurred in the Classic Period between AD 700 and 800. The great pyramidal temples have a major visual impact and political significance and are conventionally named with numbers from I to VI. The heart of the site is thought to have been Temple I, or the Temple of the Great Jaguar, where the tomb lies of Ha Saha Chaan Kauil, the king of the city from AD 682 to 734. The monument was built after his death by his son Yax Kin Chaan Kauil in accordance with his father's instructions. The nine-story pyramid 150 feet tall stands on a wide base, with its various platforms inclined to emphasize the heightened elevation of the building. The temple is on the top of the pyramid, crowned by a cornice of stuccoes. It is irregular in plan and has three entrances with solid wooden architraves. This is where the king was buried, together with his grave goods.

References to the divine are strong in Tikal architecture, as well as the symbolic tension linked to the landscape created by the gods, and images of the journey to the supernatural world. The places dedicated to rites of communication and reinforcement of magical powers were determined by the movements of the stars. The gods, though, did not save the city from its dramatic political and cultural decline which consigned its splendors to wild nature.

293 center *There are nine – the magic number of the Mayan culture – levels that make up the base of the pyramid. The steep inclined sides have strongly angular corners decorated with moldings and grooves.*

293 bottom *The top of the Temple of the Great Jaguar stands out above the thick forest opposite Temple II. The Maya were builders of wonderful cities and constructed at Tikal temples taller than the surrounding jungle.*

294-295 *The Palace, at the center of this view of Palenque, stands on a large platform. It is thought that the four-story tower that overlooks the royal residence had functions of defense and astronomical observation.*

294 bottom *Set in the green forest, the Pyramid of the Inscriptions stands over the tomb of Pacal the Great. At the top, the temple is crowned by characteristic decorative crests.*

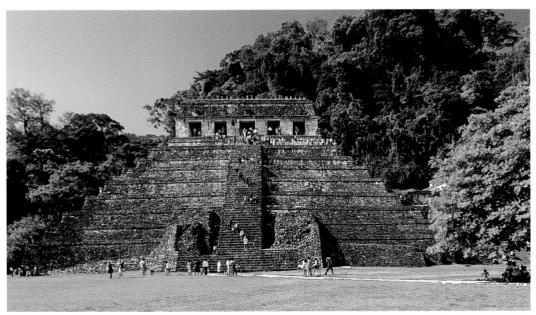

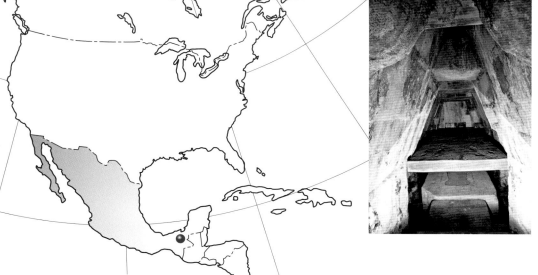

295 top and bottom The crypt containing the sarcophagus of Hanab Pacal II (bottom) is covered by a slab decorated with reliefs. It is reached down a stairway 78 feet long inside the pyramid.

The Pyramid of the Inscriptions

PALENQUE, MEXICO

by Flaminia Bartolini

Situated at the center of the Mexican state of Chiapas, Palenque is one of the largest and most important Mayan sites. According to hieroglyphs, the city's peak was reached in the Late Classic Period (AD 600–900) when the city of Lacam Ha ('Great Water'; Palenque is a modern name) was the flourishing capital of the kingdom of Bak. Excavation of the city since the end of the eighteenth century has shown that the monumentalization of the city we see today was the work of the sovereigns Hanab Pacal II the Great (AD 615–683) and his son Can Balam II (AD 684–702). The buildings stand in a natural setting of lush vegetation and were designed with the clear political and ideological intent of glorifying the rulers through the immanence of stone constructions decorated on the facades or internally with stucco reliefs or stone carvings.

The hieroglyphs in the main buildings list the rulers of the city, indicating their desire to legitimate their dynasty and to strengthen its validity through having it set down in writing. The harmony of the forms, stylistic elegance and rich sculptural decoration – which would have been accentuated by bright red, blue, ocher and green colors – are unique examples of this dynastic and self-celebratory architecture. The pillars and walls of the Temple of the Inscriptions are covered with hieroglyphs, including the famous dynastic lists. The building is the funerary temple of Hanab Pacal II, construction of which he himself began whilst still alive, though it was completed by his son Can Balam II.

The temple proper stands at a height of 79 feet on a base at the top of a stepped pyramid. The pyramid is formed by eight tapering levels that has a stairway on the south side. Five entrances lined by pillars decorated with stucco lead into the first large chamber; the second is divided into three parts. A stairway that leads down through the temple floor is split into two flights of steps. It leads to the crypt, the walls of which are decorated with stucco reliefs of nine figures (ancestors or perhaps the Lords of the Night in Mayan mythology). Pacal the Great's sarcophagus is adorned with low reliefs on the sides and covered by a huge finely carved slab. The slab has one of the most famous and deeply studied Mayan reliefs: a series of figures symbolizing the eternal cycle of death and resurrection surround the king on the point of death, represented with divine attributes on the point of falling into the darkness that leads to the Infraworld. The cosmic cross-shaped tree grows from his belly.

Discovery of the sarcophagus beneath the crypt floor – built at the center and below the base of the pyramid – is clear evidence that the building was constructed to contain the king's sarcophagus, though also to represent him as an individual.

296-297 Uxmal lies on the
Yucatán plateau in the Puuc sierra
and is a fine example of Maya-
Puuc architecture.

296 bottom left The pyramid is the
result of the overlaying – over
hundreds of years – of five temples.

The Pyramid of the Magician

UXMAL, MEXICO

by Flaminia Bartolini

Uxmal, in the north of the Yucatán peninsula, is perhaps the most important Mayan settlement in the Puuc sierra in the modern Mexican states of the Yucatán and Campeche. In this area, hills often not more than a few scores of feet in height and length are often the most suitable sites for urban settlements due to their favorable climatic conditions. The cities in Puuc territory stand out for their artistic and architectural qualities; the buildings were made using advanced techniques and are distinctive for their perfect geometric composition elegantly associated with an elaborate decoration carved on the facade. In the high friezes, motifs and figures (often with symbolic and religious value) are either repeated continuously or in groups. The remains of the imposing and refined stone architecture are from the era of Uxmal's greatest size and splendor (Classic Period, 3rd to 10th centuries AD).

The city seems to have a fair scattering of man-made platforms and four-sided buildings like the Nunnery Quadrangle, residential buildings made from massive stone blocks like the Governor's Palace, well-proportioned buildings like the House of the Turtles, and elevated temple bases like the Pyramid of the Magician. As Uxmal had a certain superior economic and political status, and its connections with nearby smaller cities were provided by the road that left from east of the Governor's Palace, passed through Chetulix and Nohpat, and reached Kabah where the grandmother lived of the dwarf to whom legend attributes construction of the Pyramid of the Magician. The elliptical plan (279 x 164 feet) stands over the remains of previous constructions built in five different stages. The structure of the Pyramid is formed by unequal sections on top of one another with an overall height of about 115 feet. Two steep stairways lead to two temples at different levels. The east stairway leads to Temple IV on the first level that has a facade rather like a 'dragon's mouth.' The stairs are lined by a sequence of large masks of the god Chac on a level set back from the steps. The east stairway leads to the upper temple known as Temple V or the Temple of the Magician. The façade is decorated with a series of small columns and a frieze in which stylized Mayan huts are carved in the stone in typical Puuc style.

296 bottom right The Nunnery lies in front of the Pyramid of the Magician and is an example of Puuc architecture. It is formed by four buildings that stand at the four compass points around a court that has entrances at the corners.

297 top The portal designed as a mask of a monster was a modified element of the Chenes architecture that developed in the north of Campeche. This motif is an example of the cultural exchange between Uxmal and other Mesoamerican regions.

El Castillo

CHICHÉN ITZÁ, MEXICO

by Maria Eloisa Carrozza

298 top left The upper temple of the pyramid in the Castillo has a double corridor and vestibule that opens to the north, with three entrances separated by columns.

298 top right The corridor at the rear, in the cella of the temple at the top of the Castillo, is supported by pillars decorated with low reliefs.

298 bottom left The Chac Mool (foreground) and the Red Jaguar (background) in the temple of the Castillo are stone sculptures in Toltec style.

298 bottom right Four steep stairways at right angles to the base lead up to the Castillo.

298-299 and 299 right The majestic proportions of the pyramid of the Castillo are accentuated by its position at the center of a large open area. Various elements of the building's design seem Toltec in derivation, such as the sculpted decoration at the top that replaced the Mayan crest, and on the inclined surface (talud) that strengthens the walls.

As the conquistadors emerged from the jungle of the Mexican lowlands, they saw the remains of Chichén Itzá, the most spectacular Mayan city in north Yucatán. The first part of the name means 'on the edge of the well', in which the well refers to the local *cenote*, or natural well that made water in the deep water-table accessible and which the Maya considered an entrance to the world underground. The *cenote* became sacred and a place of

pilgrimage, and propitiatory rites were performed there, for example, sacrifices of human beings, who were thrown in along with precious and simple objects as offerings. The second part of the name – Itzá – refers to an ethnic group of mysterious origin and complex structure that had been present in the area, probably since AD 435. Contact with the sub-culture of the Puuc (the inhabitants of the 'red hills' to the south) gave rise between AD 750 and 900 to a prodigious and flourishing culture, but in the thirteenth century the city unexpectedly fell at the hands of its rival Mayapán. The site has a central area and a network of minor

centers joined by paved pathways (*calzadas*). The elegant Las Monjas complex, with an abundance of decoration, the Caracol round tower (or Observatory), the pyramid known as the Ossuary and the residential annexes were all built by the Maya-Puuc culture, whereas other complexes have a completely different style. These were the works of the Toltecs, a new people that arrived in the tenth century, who took the culture of the Maya and developed it with stylistic innovations. This led to Maya-Toltec architecture which centered on vast open spaces rather than plazas. A group of Maya-Toltec buildings adorned with reliefs stand on bases often in the form of stepped pyramids on a large esplanade enclosed by a wall. Il Castillo (the Temple of Kukulcán) at the center of the Toltec area is perhaps the most interesting monument in the new style. This is a temple pyramid of nine levels (which decrease in area as they rise) that stands on a square base 180 feet long on each side. The temple stands on the topmost level 79 feet up. Each façade has its own flight of steps

that joins the various levels of the building. The structure clearly has a cosmological significance: the inclination is to east of magnetic north in accordance with tradition in the region, the nine levels represent the nine levels of the infraworld, and there are 365 steps, like the days in a year. The stone balustrades on the north stairway are carved in the form of rattlesnakes with heads that seem to slither onto the plaza. At the top the temple has two corridors, a cella lined with Mayan-style low reliefs, a vestibule with three access bays separated by columns carved to represent snakes, false vaults, and large masks of the god Chac in Maya-Puuc style. A gallery behind the temple has three doors that open towards the east, west and south. The decoration on the beams and columns throughout the complex emphasizes the Serpent which is a characteristic element of Toltec iconography. To the northeast of El Castillo there is the Group of the Thousand Columns, and the Temple of the Warriors, which is adorned, like the Temple of Kukulkán, with the traditional Toltec decoration. At the top is the Chac Mool, a half-reclining sculpture of a mysterious creature.

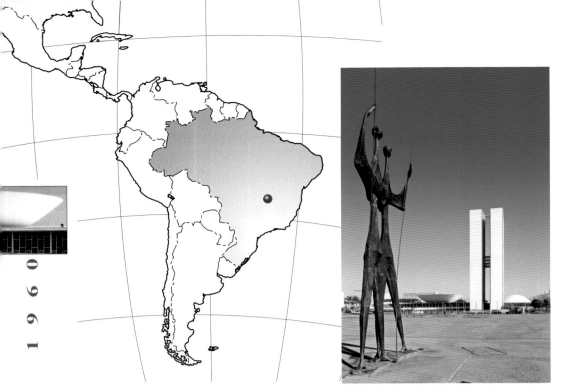

The Palace of Congress

BRASÍLIA, BRAZIL

by Guglielmo Novelli and Maria Laura Vergelli

In Brazil in 1957 the need to move a proportion of the population and economic activities from the coast to the interior was recognized. A site was located on a desert plateau in the state of Goias and thousands of workers arrived from the northeast of the country to build the new capital. A condition of the city was that it had to reflect the country's political and economic programs but also encapsulate the innovations in contemporary architecture.

As a representative of Novacap (an organization that studied the construction plans for Brazil's new capital), the architect Oscar Niemeyer was part of the judging panel in the competition for the urban development plan and was assigned to construct the first two buildings: the governor's residence and the hotel used to put up official guests.

The city layout was designed by Lucio Costa. He made use of two principal techniques: that of the modern highway and that of inserting many gardens and parks.

Brasília is built on two axes, one slightly curved, which intersect to form a cross in vaguely animal-like form (the location plan is in the form of a bird). This new and gigantic urban landscape acts as a dignified setting for the sculptural buildings (for example, marble elements smoothed like animal bones) charged with semantic significance.

The Monumental Axis – along which all the government buildings stand – intersects the residential axis of the city. At the end of the former lies the Plaza of Ministries, which is reached down a wide avenue lined with 16 parallelepiped buildings.

Two of Niemeyer's masterpieces stand at the sides of the square: the Ministry of Foreign Affairs, which is reflected in a large pool of water, and the Ministry of Justice, where small artificial waterfalls represent the many natural waterfalls in the territory of Brasília. From the end

300 top left The towers of the Palace of Congress (in the background) dominate the Plaza of the Three Powers and the monument to the workers who built Brasília.

300 top right At the foot of the towers, one of the two domes of the Palace of Congress, the Senate one, stands on the base of the building's covering.

300 bottom A concave hemisphere forms the corresponding 'dome,' which Niemeyer wanted to have on the Chamber of Deputies.

300-301 The stylistic motif used by Niemeyer is the contrast created by a combination of curved, undulating and oblique planes with strong, square surfaces.

of the Monumental Axis you enter the Plaza of the Three Powers, which is filled with symbolic and political significance. Its name refers to the three divisions of constitutional power: the Executive, which is exercised in the 'Planalto Palace' on the left, the Judiciary, represented by the Supreme Court on the right, and the Legislative, seen in the National Congress Building with its famous twin towers. At the base of the towers there is a low building crowned by two hemispherical domes, one is upturned to represent the Chamber of Deputies, and the other is upright and represents the Senate.

As a city, Brasília has a concentration of good quality architecture and design, seen in its prestigious buildings and monuments of modern art. Two examples are the

splendid concrete and glass cathedral designed by Niemeyer in the form of a crown, and the cube-shaped sanctuary of Don Bosco, with walls lined with blue and indigo glass.

In tribute to the thousands of workers who built the city, Bruno Giorni was commissioned to produce the monument *The Warriors*, and another brilliant work (also by Niemeyer) is the *Plombal*, a dovecot in the curious form of a large clothes-pin.

The residential zones are huge urban estates that have allowed the city fabric to be loosely woven. This 'rarefaction' is also seen in the structure of the facades. Simplicity is the keyword in every aspect of Brasília, so that this huge city is easy to navigate and easy to understand.

AUSTRALIA AND OCEANIA

'The waters of the seas rose until they closed over the tips of the tallest eucalyptus trees. The earth turned into a vast blue plain. Only the peaks of the mountains stood above the water. In the end, even the summits disappeared. The world was turned into a vast flat expanse of water and the Nurrumbunguttia (the spirits of men and women) no longer had a fit place to live. Many of them drowned, but others encountered a vortex of air that lifted them up to the sky, where they turned into stars, while those that were gods on Earth became gods in heaven' (from 'The Great Flood' in *Tales of Time and Dreams*, edited by M. R. Buri and A. Magagnino).

The development of the autochthonous cultures of Australia and Oceania in prehistory and history has been long and complex. The processes of population, differentiation of cultures and languages, and the creation of settlements and the social system have taken place over a time-span of at least 40,000 years. Until 10,000 years ago, when the Pleistocene hunter-gatherers occupied the western territories of Melanesia, Australia was joined terrestrially to Tasmania and New Guinea by a structural platform known as the Sahul Shelf. This has since sunk beneath sea level. Over the generations, Australian aboriginals have transmitted their memory of primordial events orally from generation to generation, creating and drawing on a rich and multiform heritage of fables and legends. Their stories refer to a mythical period that was a 'time before time,' when the mythical beings of the Dreamtime appeared during various epochs. They came from the sky, the earth, and the unknown, and were the creators of the 'first human men and women.' The early humans were placed in certain areas reserved for them and their descendants under the protection of specific gods, as Magagnino relates. An indissoluble link joined man to the land on which he was born. There, he was able to recognize the various elements of the landscape which represented transformations ('mythical traces') of ancestral beings and conserved their spirits.

The aboriginals still follow the Songlines, renewing their creation cycle, when 'the Men from Ancient Time wandered through the whole world singing: they sang the rivers and the mountains, the salt-flats and the sand dunes. They went hunting, fed and made love, danced, killed: in every point on their paths they left a trail of music' (B. Chatwin, *The Songlines*).

Hundreds of aboriginal groups inhabited the Australian continent. They had developed an extraordinary capacity to adapt to the environment, an intimate coexistence with the wildlife of unique original phenomena when, at the start of the 16th century, Dutch expeditions first reached the continent but soon left.

Sailing east via the Indies, having crossed the boiling waters of the strait that divides the Atlantic from the new South Seas (which Balboa had glimpsed from the Central American isthmus a decade earlier), Magellan sailed across the calm ocean that he called the Pacific and touched on the 'Islands of Thieves' – the Mariannas. As one of his chroniclers noted, 'the vastness of the Pacific is such that the human mind has difficulty in grasping it,' and other expeditions that recounted the beauty and natural wealth of the South Seas endlessly plowed the infinite horizon of this new-found ocean.

The difficulty of orienting oneself in all that solitude and expanse of water strongly encourages reveries and mirages. There are only strips of land; multitudes of islands appear unexpectedly, or, on the contrary, rise only just above the surface though they appear definitively on maps, or are only imaginary in the watery immensity of the ocean. These are the 'Wandering Isles' of the 18th-century geography of the South Seas.

The dangerous and extenuating search for a huge unknown land mass – the Terra Australis – whose very existence was also in doubt, was undertaken on several occasions by courageous and visionary navigators, emissaries of the great European powers whose interests were strongly underpinned by imperialist, commercial, spiritual and civilizing aspirations. Captain Cook's systematic exploration and his drawing of excellent maps during his three expeditions (1768-71; 1772-75;1776-79) transformed the legendary and idyllic image of the lands and peoples of the South Seas into

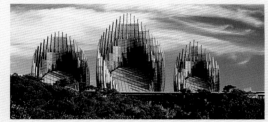

geographic knowledge, and the 'extremely strange and romantic sights' offered by the landscapes and people who inhabited them were depicted by the expeditions' artists.

Once they had moved out of the realm of imagination, the islands of the Pacific, particularly those of Polynesia, became objects of scientific study and entered the historical epoch of a slow colonization blended with the sometimes cruel process of evangelization. Once the Enlightenment myth of the 'noble savage' had been abandoned, during the 19th-century Western occupation was carried out in repressive ways and the customs of the indigenous communities were overturned by the interests of the new white inhabitants.

The apparent desolation of Australia had placed it outside of the image of terrestrial paradise witnessed elsewhere throughout the Pacific. No-one had ventured into the inhospitable land. Cook explored the east coast, and claimed possession of it as it was *terra nullius*, noting at the same time that the local peoples wanted him to stay rather than leave, and by the mid-19th century, thousands of British convicts had been dropped on the Australian continent so it might be colonized.

Artists and literary men described the South Seas' enchantment as being of dazzling beauty but 'the slightest thing and the dream dissolves and is transformed into its opposite, a nightmare. Paradise becomes hell, and calm solitude a fearful abyss'. Melville speaks as though it might happen unexpectedly, 'as occurs in the magical gardens in the stories of fairies' (M. Dini, *The Islands of Eden*).

If the path of history could be retrodden, if our ancestors could return to bask in the sun, if the venerated Captain Cook could return to sail the waters of the Great Barrier Reef along the coast of New Holland, in sight of the white concrete sails of the Opera House in Sydney Harbor, would the former sing the praise of that strip of land where the new building stands looking like a freshly cut fruit? And would the great explorer respect the *genius loci* and keep his promise not to occupy lands without the consent of its inhabitants?

Today, domination of the harbor – ascribed by some to the magical powers of the verses of the song, by others to the violent right of the conqueror – seems naturally to belong to the attractive volumes of the Royal Opera House, which has aspects of the primitive in the bare, 'inert cavities' of its shell.

Before the modern era or even the colonial one, there were no buildings that lasted, as construction by the Australian tribesmen was essentially a re-creation of the landscape and a representation of the territory. The relevance of the myth once more: natural forms are the creation of animal ancestors, the sinuous slither of the mythical serpent is the reflection of a winding water course, and knowledge of the geomorphology of the land and its symbolism rooted the group in the area in which it was able to 'periodically find the paths, wells and places rich with game,' thereby avoiding boundary violations and disputes with other groups (E. Guidoni, *Primitive Architecture*).

With its high conical roof crowned by a decoration, and a round plan with a central pillar, the 'large hut' typical of New Caledonia dominates the village and is the immutable symbol of the power of the chief and the unity of the clans who built it. It is the 'men's house,' which is understood today in the sense of 'public building.' The door opens on the village clearing where group life is lived and dances and festivals are celebrated. The family houses stand on either side. 'Curved structures similar to huts, made from wooden trusses and listels: archaic-looking shells…' (R. Piano), similar to the Kanaka villages, are harmonized with the thick vegetation on the promontory east of Noumea. What is universal in the design is its recourse to traditional materials and techniques, whereas the risk lies in its similarity to and diversity from traditional architecture, and between its refined solidity and use of natural, perishable materials.

And here we are back in the present. After centuries in which man has dreamed of the knowledge and wealth represented by the legendary, idyllic and wild New World, it now tells us its own story: 'At the end of this sentence, rain will begin./ At the rain's edge, a sail…/ A man with clouded eyes picks up the rain/ and plucks the first line of the Odyssey' (D. Walcott, *The Map of the New World*).

Alessandra Capodiferro

303 *left The bristly structures of the J. M. Tjibaou Cultural Center stand in a natural park in New Caledonia.*

303 *right The series of shells of the Opera House stand on Bennelong Point just south of Sydney Harbour.*

304-305 *A source of inspiration for decades, the Opera House has represented the city of Sydney for more than forty years. Before construction of the building, there was a huge green area, as seen in the photograph, with the Governor's Palace at the center.*

304 bottom *Seen from above, the similarity of the unusual architecture of the Opera House to the sea in front of the building is evident.*

305 top left *The overlapping shells of the Opera House culminate in the upper ogive at a height of 179 feet.*

305 top right *The tiles on the external surfaces 'play' with the light, creating ever-changing subtleties.*

305 bottom *The stalls in the small auditorium lie on the building's main level, ringed by boxes and with the stage in front.*

The Opera House

SYDNEY, AUSTRALIA

by Guglielmo Novelli

In 1957 the Danish architect Jorn Utzon won the international competition to design the new Opera House in Sydney. The superb site and the lack of all restraints in the specifications allowed the imagination of every entrant to soar. The design produced by the young and promising architect, and presented with a dozen or so simple but poetic drawings, appealed to everyone from the first moment for its very beautiful external profile that resembled a squadron of sailing boats.

Construction began in 1959 but Utzon was obliged to retire from the commission in 1966 due to the many administrative problems he encountered, and in 1973 the project was completed by other architects. The spectacular building was based on a simple and logical concept far removed from the rigors of Modernism.

The overlapping shell-like coverings are derived from the decomposition of a single geometric figure: a virtual sphere of diameter 246 feet. Utzon's inspiration for the building and its architecture was mostly drawn from natural forms and structures (waves about to break, the beak of a seagull, the dorsal fin of a shark, etc.).

The roof that covers the two main rooms and the restaurant is formed by three primary elements: principal shells, lateral shells, and ventilation shells, which differ depending on their function. Each is composed of two symmetrical parts around the central axis of the room they cover, structured by a series of special concrete ribs that fan out from the base.

The transversal section of the roof consists of ogival arches of different height, the largest of which measures 179 feet. The result is an elegant series of overlapping volumes that both oppose and balance one another.

An entire generation of designers experimenting with new possibilities in reinforced concrete was struck by the design, which became the symbol of a renewal in contemporary architecture.

The covering is freed from what it protects, so allowing the interior and exterior to be modeled separately; the building thus becomes a sculpture from any direction in which it is viewed.

Utzon's masterpiece was the outcome of a need for imagination, dreams and a propensity for expressive forms.

The decoration is inherent in the nature of the building and the ornamentation seen directly in the design of essential elements. The result is a transparent building, a framework without filling or visible mechanical constructs. Utzon commented, 'Think of a Gothic cathedral: that is what I was trying to achieve. The sun, the light and the clouds will make it a living thing. You will never tire of it.'

Unfortunately, only a part of this extraordinary, controversial project remains faithful to the original design as it was finished by others: those parts are the tiled 'sails' and a plinth, of which not even the cladding was carried out as originally planned.

The windows, auditoria and the internal finishing were not part of Utzon's conception and it is difficult to reconstruct them from his plans as it is his custom to modify his designs continuously. In spite of all this, the Opera House has become the symbol of Sydney and brought the city international renown.

The Opera House

306 top Cranes and scaffolding surround the ribbing of the roof, which was being completed at the time of this photograph. The administrative problems caused by the building's construction obliged the architect, Jorn Utzon, to resign from his appointment.

306 center A lateral section of the building demonstrates Utzon's basic idea modified by other architects between 1966 and 1971. As can be seen, the basics of the design were generally respected but the original design was only partly conserved.

306 bottom At the end of the 1950s, Jorn Utzon illustrates a model of the Opera House at Sydney City Council. Innovative for its era, the modernity of the magnificent set of buildings was still in keeping with the times.

306-307 The long curve of Harbour Bridge seems to pay tribute to the elegant shells of the Opera House, which extend eastwards towards the Pacific Ocean. The design of the tile lining, visible here, radiates from the base of each shell.

The Tjibaou Cultural Center

NOUMEA,

NEW CALEDONIA

by Guglielmo Novelli

Owing to its isolation, the French overseas territory of New Caledonia has retained much of its traditional atmosphere and beauty, as well as its extraordinary biological diversity. The French government provided funding for the construction of a cultural center designed to commemorate the past of the first inhabitants, the Kanakas, the island inhabitants before the arrival of the missionaries. The center was named after Jean-Marie Tjibaou (the local leader of the independent protest movement killed in 1989.)

The elegant design produced by Renzo Piano stands among long, white and pink beaches, blue and turquoise lagoons and tall pines, and was inspired by the traditional architecture of New Caledonia.

Situated on a promontory in a nature park about eight miles from Noumea, the capital, the center consists of a walkway that connects ten 'huts' that vary between 63 and 92 feet in height, each of which is dedicated to a particular activity or art typical of the local population. The set of buildings covers an area of 2 acres and houses the local cultural heritage of legends, stories, contemporary indigenous literature, pottery and decoration. Part of the complex is used to display temporary and permanent exhibitions, and the rest is reserved for offices, a library and an auditorium. In this last building, traditional music and dance is performed, though music plays in all the huts as well along the walkway.

The lightness and precariousness of local architecture are reflected in the wood, steel and glass 'shells' arranged in the same traditional social structure as Caledonian huts. The buildings are oriented so as to filter sunlight and to provide protection from the prevailing trade winds.

The huts are formed by a double layer of wood 'ribs' connected together by a series of steel ties, all of which is 'padded' by a skin of iroko wood that functions as a sun-break.

309 top In the evening, electric lights turn the Cultural Center into a magical place, effecting a transformation in which both the light and the buildings play a part. The higher sections of the pavilions faces the sea in order to rebuff the trade winds.

309 bottom right A sketch by Renzo Piano shows the foundation of his concept; he drew in the 'huts' and the intersection of the horizontal and vertical lines that characterize their surfaces.

308-309 Surprising human artifacts integrated into the natural surroundings, the pavilions of the J.M. Tjibaou Cultural Center are made mainly of wood. The pavilions contain displays of the traditional crafts and arts in New Caledonia.

308 bottom When the pavilions designed by Renzo Piano are seen from the sea, surrounded by the lush vegetation of New Caledonia, it is easy to see how they are based on the traditional huts of the island.

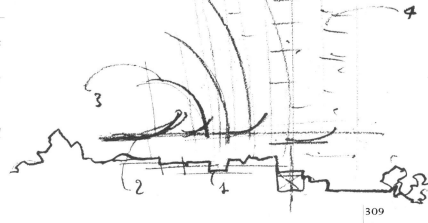

310-311 The fragility of the huts in the J. M. Tjibaou Cultural Center is only apparent. Wood is a resistant and flexible material and has always been perfectly suited, even in traditional architecture, to withstanding changeable and adverse weather conditions.

310 bottom Sculptures that are sacred to the local people – the Kanakas – are displayed in one of the Center's pavilions. Each hut deals with a specific aspect of local culture.

311 top This simple detail of the structural 'weave' reflects the close relationship between the design of the pavilions, their materials and the natural environment.

311 bottom In contrast, the metal parts that give the buildings solidity, which are placed between the wooden shells and ribs that form the outer and inner walls, are invisible to the observer.

The Tjibaou Cultural Center

The huts are a modern technological version of the traditional conical huts; standing above the lush vegetation, they alter the skyline of the site but not the natural balance. Piano's respectful design has produced a cultural center that has the noble task of safeguarding and diffusing the history and beauty of the place. The principal inspiration behind each building is given by the uniqueness of its context.

Piano's respectful design has produced a cultural center that achieves the noble task of both safeguarding and diffusing the beauty of the place.

INDEX

PHOTOGRAPHIC CREDITS

Page 76 bottom AISA
Pages 76-77 Alamy Images
Page 77 left Diego Lezama Orezzoli/Corbis/Contrasto
Page 77 right AISA
Page 78 top left Angelo Colombo/Archivio White Star
Page 78 top right Sandro Vannini/Corbis/Contrasto
Page 78 center Robert Polidori/RMN
Pages 78-79 Alamy Images
Page 79 Sandro Vannini/Corbis/Contrasto
Page 80 Bill Ross/Corbis/Contrasto
Page 81 top Sandro Vannini/Corbis/Contrasto
Page 81 center Dave G. Houser/Corbis/Contrasto
Page 81 bottom Yann Arthus-Bertrand/Corbis/Contrasto
Page 82 top AISA
Page 82 center top Archivio Scala
Page 82 center bottom The Bridgeman Art Library/Archivio Alinari
Page 82 bottom Sandro Vannini/Corbis/Contrasto
Pages 82-83 AISA
Page 84 left Erich Lessing/Contrasto
Page 84 bottom Philippe Renault/Hemisphere
Pages 84-85 AISA
Page 85 top Erich Lessing/Contrasto
Page 85 bottom AISA
Page 86 Francesco Zanchi
Pages 86-87 Dave G. Houser/Corbis/Contrasto
Page 87 top Angelo Colombo/Archivio White Star
Page 87 center Diego Lezama Orezzoli/Corbis/Contrasto
Page 87 bottom Giulio Veggi/Archivio White Star
Page 88 top Steve Raymer/Corbis/Contrasto
Page 88 center Dave Bartruff/Corbis/Contrasto
Page 88 bottom Giulio Veggi/Archivio White Star
Page 89 Alamy Images
Pages 90-91 Francesco Venturi/Corbis/Contrasto
Page 91 top Giulio Veggi/Archivio White Star
Page 91 center top Francesco Zanchi
Page 91 center bottom Dave G. Houser/Corbis/Contrasto
Page 91 bottom Giulio Veggi/Archivio White Star
Page 92 top left Vittoriano Rastelli/Corbis/Contrasto
Page 92 top right Angelo Colombo/Archivio White Star
Page 92 center Alamy Images
Page 92 bottom Vittoriano Rastelli/Corbis/Contrasto
Pages 92-93 Sandro Vannini/Corbis/Contrasto
Page 93 Vittoriano Rastelli/Corbis/Contrasto
Page 94 top Vittoriano Rastelli/Corbis/Contrasto
Page 94 bottom Sandro Vannini/Corbis/Contrasto
Pages 94-95 Vittoriano Rastelli/Corbis/Contrasto
Page 95 Sandro Vannini/Corbis/Contrasto
Page 96 top left Angelo Colombo/Archivio White Star
Page 96 top right Gregor Schmid/Corbis/Contrasto
Page 96 bottom Yann Arthus-Bertrand/Corbis/Contrasto
Page 97 Archivio Iconografico, S.A./Corbis/Contrasto
Pages 98-99 Ray Juno/Corbis/Contrasto
Page 99 James Sparshatt/Corbis/Contrasto
Pages 100-101 James Sparshatt/Corbis/Contrasto
Page 101 top Patrick Ward/Corbis/Contrasto
Page 101 center James Sparshatt/Corbis/Contrasto
Page 101 bottom Patrick Ward/Corbis/Contrasto
Page 102 Marcello Bertinetti/Archivio White Star
Pages 102-103 Yann Arthus-Bertrand/Corbis/Contrasto
Page 103 top Angelo Colombo/Archivio White Star
PAGE 103 bottom Owen Franken/Corbis/Contrasto
Page 104 Bettmann/Corbis/Contrasto
Pages 104-105 Todd A. Gipstein/Corbis/Contrasto
Page 105 Sebastien Ortola/Rea/Contrasto
Page 106 top left Angelo Colombo/Archivio White Star
Page 106 top right Marcello Bertinetti/Archivio White Star
Page 106 bottom Patrick Ward/Corbis/Contrasto
Pages 106-107 Alamy Images
Page 107 Mary Evans Picture Library
Page 108 top Marcello Bertinetti/Archivio White Star

Page 108 center Charlotte Hindle/Lonely Planet Images
Page 108 bottom Marcello Bertinetti/Archivio White Star
Pages 108-109 Alamy Images
Page 109 Marcello Bertinetti/Archivio White Star
Page 110 top left Angelo Colombo/Archivio White Star
Page 110 top right Bauhaus Archive Dessau
Page 110 center Bauhaus Archive Dessau
Page 110 bottom Bauhaus Archive Dessau
Pages 110-111 Bauhaus Archive Dessau
Page 111 top Bauhaus Archive Dessau
Page 111 bottom Bauhaus Archive Dessau
Page 112 top Angelo Colombo/Archivio White Star
Page 112 bottom Gianni Berengo Gardin by kind permission of the Renzo Piano Building Workshop
Pages 112-113 Gianni Berengo Gardin by kind permission of the Renzo Piano Building Workshop
Page 114 by kind permission of the Renzo Piano Building Workshop
Pages 114-115 Yann Arthus-Bertrand/Corbis/Contrasto
Page 115 top Gianni Berengo Gardin by kind permission of the Renzo Piano Building Workshop
Page 115 bottom Michel Denancé by kind permission of the Renzo Piano Building Workshop
Page 116 top Livio Bourbon/Archivio White Star
Page 116 center Marcello Bertinetti/Archivio White Star
Page 116 bottom Marcello Bertinetti/Archivio White Star
Pages 116-117 Livio Bourbon/Archivio White Star
Page 118 Livio Bourbon/Archivio White Star
Pages 118-119 Scott Gilchrist/Arcivision
Page 119 top left Owen Franken/Corbis/Contrasto
Page 119 top right Angelo Colombo/Archivio White Star
Page 119 center Cuchi White/Corbis/Contrasto
Page 119 bottom Scott Gilchrist/Arcivision
Pages 120-121 Robert Holmes/Corbis/Contrasto
Page 122 top left Angelo Colombo/Archivio White Star
Page 122 top right Stuart Franklin/Magnum Photos/Contrasto
Page 122 center Dennis Stock/Magnum Photos/Contrasto
Page 112 bottom Wolfgang Kaehler/Corbis/Contrasto
Pages 112-123 Yann Arthus-Bertrand/Corbis/Contrasto
Page 123 left Pavlovsky Jacques/Corbis Sygma/Contrasto
Page 123 right Pavlovsky Jacques/Corbis Sygma/Contrasto
Page 124 Pavlovsky Jacques/Corbis Sygma/Contrasto
Pages 124-125 Tibor Bognar/Corbis/Contrasto
Page 125 top left Rene Burri/Magnum Photos/Contrasto
Page 125 top right Rene Burri/Magnum Photos/Contrasto
Page 125 bottom Dennis Stock/Magnum Photos/Contrasto
Pages 126-127 Yann Arthus-Bertrand/Corbis/Contrasto
Page 128 top left Angelo Colombo/Archivio White Star
Page 128 top right Adenis/GAFF/laif/Contrasto
Page 128 bottom Adenis/GAFF/laif/Contrasto
Pages 128-129 Adenis/GAFF/laif/Contrasto
Page 129 left Hoehn/laif/Contrasto
Page 129 right Reimer Wulf/AKG Images
Page 130 top David P eevers/Lonely Planet Images
Page 130 bottom Boening/Zenit/laif/Contrasto
Pages 130-131 Hahn/laif/Contrasto
Page 131 left Brecelj Bojan/Corbis Sygma/Contrasto
Page 131 right Bojan Brecelj /Corbis/Contrasto
Page 132 left by kind permission of the Santiago Calatrava S.A.
Page 132 right by kind permission of the Santiago Calatrava S.A.
Pages 132-133 by kind permission of the Santiago Calatrava S.A.
Page 133 top by kind permission of the Santiago Calatrava S.A.

Page 133 center left Angelo Colombo/Archivio White Star
Page 133 center right Juergen Stumpe
Page 133 bottom by kind permission of the Santiago Calatrava S.A.
Page 134 left by kind permission of the Santiago Calatrava S.A.
Page 134 right by kind permission of the Santiago Calatrava S.A.
Pages 134-135 Juergen Stumpe
Page 135 top left by kind permission of the Santiago Calatrava S.A.
Page 135 top right by kind permission of the Santiago Calatrava S.A.
Page 135 bottom by kind permission of the Santiago Calatrava S.A.
Page 136 by kind permission of the Santiago Calatrava S.A.
Pages 136-137 by kind permission of the Santiago Calatrava S.A.
Page 137 top by kind permission of the Santiago Calatrava S.A.
Page 137 center by kind permission of the Santiago Calatrava S.A.
Page 137 bottom by kind permission of the Santiago Calatrava S.A.
Page 138 left Boening/Zenit/laif/Contrasto
Page 138 right Adenis/GAFF/laif/Contrasto
Pages 138-139 Reimer Wulf/AKG Images
Page 139 top left Dieter E. Hoppe/AKG Images
Page 139 top right Angelo Colombo/Archivio White Star
Page 139 center Langrock/Zenit/laif/Contrasto
Page 139 bottom Langrock/Zenit/laif/Contrasto
Page 140 top left Angelo Colombo/Archivio White Star
Page 140 top right Publifoto by kind permission of the Renzo Piano Building Workshop
Pages 140-141 Moreno Maggi by kind permission of the Renzo Piano Building Workshop
Page 141 center Gianni Berengo Gardin by kind permission of the Renzo Piano Building Workshop
Page 141 left by kind permission of the Renzo Piano Building Workshop
Page 141 right Gianni Berengo Gardin by kind permission of the Renzo Piano Building Workshop
Page 142 top Angelo Colombo/Archivio White Star
Page 142 center Grant Smith/VIEW
Page 142 bottom Grant Smith/VIEW
Page 143 Alamy Images
Pages 144-145 Alamy Images
Page 145 top Nick Guttridge/VIEW
Page 145 center Grant Smith/VIEW
Page 145 bottom Grant Smith/VIEW
Page 147 left Giulio Veggi/Archivio White Star
Page 147 center Marcello Bertinetti/Archivio White Star
Page 147 right by kind permission of the Santiago Calatrava S.A.
Page 148 Marcello Bertinetti/Archivio White Star
Page 149 top left Angelo Colombo/Archivio White Star
Page 149 top right Antonio Attini/Archivio White Star
Page 149 center left Araldo De Luca/Archivio White Star
Page 149 center right Marcello Bertinetti/Archivio White Star
Page 149 bottom Marcello Bertinetti/Archivio White Star
Page 150 top Marcello Bertinetti/Archivio White Star
Page 150 left Marcello Bertinetti/Archivio White Star
Pages 150-151 Antonio Attini/Archivio White Star
Page 151 left Marcello Bertinetti/Archivio White Star
Page 151 right Giulio Veggi/Archivio White Star
Page 152 Marcello Bertinetti/Archivio White Star
Pages 152-153 Marcello Bertinetti/Archivio White Star
Page 153 top left Angelo Colombo/Archivio White Star
Page 153 top right Antonio Attini/Archivio White Star

Page 153 center Giulio Veggi/Archivio White Star
Page 153 bottom Giulio Veggi/Archivio White Star
Page 154 top Alfio Garozzo/Archivio White Star
Page 154 center Antonio Attini/Archivio White Star
Page 154 bottom Antonio Attini/Archivio White Star
Page 155 Marcello Bertinetti/Archivio White Star
Page 156 top left Angelo Colombo/Archivio White Star
Page 156 top right Marcello Bertinetti/Archivio White Star
Page 156 left Giulio Veggi/Archivio White Star
Pages 156-157 Antonio Attini/Archivio White Star
Page 157 top Marcello Bertinetti/Archivio White Star
Page 157 center Araldo De Luca/Archivio White Star
Page 157 bottom Araldo De Luca/Archivio White Star
Page 158 Giulio Veggi/Archivio White Star
Page 159 top Farabolafoto
Page 159 bottom Farabolafoto
Page 160 top Araldo De Luca/Archivio White Star
Page 160 bottom Araldo De Luca/Archivio White Star
Pages 160-161 Araldo De Luca/Archivio White Star
Page 161 Araldo De Luca/Archivio White Star
Page 162 top left Angelo Colombo/Archivio White Star
Page 162 top right Araldo De Luca/Archivio White Star
Page 162 center Araldo De Luca/Archivio White Star
Page 162 bottom Araldo De Luca/Archivio White Star
Pages 162-163 Araldo De Luca/Archivio White Star
Page 163 left Araldo De Luca/Archivio White Star
Page 163 right Araldo De Luca/Archivio White Star
Page 164 top by kind permission of the Snøhetta A.S.
Page 164 center Angelo Colombo/Archivio White Star
Page 164 bottom by kind permission of the Snøhetta A.S.
Pages 164-165 by kind permission of the Snøhetta A.S.
Page 165 top by kind permission of the Snøhetta A.S.
Page 165 bottom by kind permission of the Snøhetta A.S.
Page 166 left by kind permission of the Snøhetta A.S.
Page 166 right Marcello Bertinetti/Archivio White Star
Pages 166-167 by kind permission of the Snøhetta A.S.
Page 167 top by kind permission of the Snøhetta A.S.
Page 167 center by kind permission of the Snøhetta A.S.
Page 167 bottom by kind permission of the Snøhetta A.S.
Page 169 left Antonio Attini/Archivio White Star
Page 169 center Marcello Bertinetti/Archivio White Star
Page 169 right per gentile concessione del Jumeirah International
Page 170 top left Angelo Colombo/Archivio White Star
Page 170 top right Keren Su/Corbis/Contrasto
Page 170 center Corbis/Contrasto
Pages 170-171 Charles et Josette Lenars/Corbis/Contrasto
Page 171 Giovanni Dagli Orti/Corbis/Contrasto
Page 172 Diego Lezama Orezzoli/Corbis/Contrasto
Page 173 top Paul Almasy/Corbis/Contrasto
Page 173 left Dave Bartruff/Corbis/Contrasto
Page 173 right Chris Lisle/Corbis/Contrasto
Page 174 left Paul Almasy/Corbis/Contrasto
Page 174 right Dave Bartruff/Corbis/Contrasto
Page 174 bottom Dave Bartruff/Corbis/Contrasto
Page 174 Henri et Anne Stierlin
Page 176 Keren Su/China Span
Pages 176-177 Liu Liqun/Corbis/Contrasto
Page 177 top left Dean Conger/Corbis/Contrasto
Page 177 top right Angelo Colombo/Archivio White Star
Page 177 bottom Keren Su/China Span
Page 178 top right Giulio Veggi/Archivio White Star
Page 178 top left Angelo Colombo/Archivio White Star
Page 178 center Massimo Borchi/Archivio White Star

Page 178 bottom Massimo Borchi/Archivio White Star
Page 179 Antonio Attini/Archivio White Star
Page 180 Yann Arthus-Bertrand/Corbis/Contrasto
Pages 180-181 Giulio Veggi/Archivio White Star
Page 181 top left Angelo Colombo/Archivio White Star
Page 181 top right Massimo Borchi/Archivio White Star
Page 181 center Yann Arthus-Bertrand/Corbis/Contrasto
Page 182 left David Samuel Robbins/Corbis/Contrasto
Page 182 right Massimo Borchi/Archivio White Star
Pages 182-183 Adam Woolfitt/Corbis/Contrasto
Page 183 top Paul H. Kuiper/Corbis/Contrasto
Page 183 bottom Massimo Borchi/Archivio White Star
Page 184 Marcello Bertinetti/Archivio White Star
Page 185 top left Marcello Bertinetti/Archivio White Star
Page 185 top right Angelo Colombo/Archivio White Star
Page 185 center Marcello Bertinetti/Archivio White Star
Page 185 bottom Marcello Bertinetti/Archivio White Star
Pages 186-187 Marcello Bertinetti/Archivio White Star
Page 187 Marcello Bertinetti/Archivio White Star
Page 188 Angelo Tondini/Focus Team
Pages 188-189 Wolfgang Kaehler/Corbis/Contrasto
Page 189 top left Angelo Colombo/Archivio White Star
Page 189 top right Marcello Bertinetti/Archivio White Star
Page 189 bottom Alamy Images
Page 190 Marcello Bertinetti/Archivio White Star
Page 191 top Marcello Bertinetti/Archivio White Star
Page 191 center Marcello Bertinetti/Archivio White Star
Page 191 bottom Marcello Bertinetti/Archivio White Star
Page 192 Dean Conger/Corbis/Contrasto
Pages 192-193 Panorama Stock
Page 193 top Liu Liqun/Corbis/Contrasto
Page 193 center Angelo Colombo/Archivio White Star
Page 193 bottom Panorama Stock
Page 194 top Marcello Bertinetti/Archivio White Star
Page 194 bottom Marcello Bertinetti/Archivio White Star
Pages 194-195 Marcello Bertinetti/Archivio White Star
Page 195 left Marcello Bertinetti/Archivio White Star
Page 195 right Marcello Bertinetti/Archivio White Star
Page 196 top Pierre Colombel/Corbis/Contrasto
Page 196 center Michael S. Yamashita/Corbis/Contrasto
Page 196 bottom Lee White/Corbis/Contrasto
Pages 196-197 Ric Ergenbright/Corbis/Contrasto
Page 197 right Marcello Bertinetti/Archivio White Star
Page 197 bottom Marcello Bertinetti/Archivio White Star
Pages 198-199 John Slater/Corbis/Contrasto
Page 199 top Dean Conger/Corbis/Contrasto
Page 199 center Pierre Colombel/Corbis/Contrasto
Page 199 bottom John T. Young/Corbis/Contrasto
Page 200 top left Alamy Images
Page 200 top right Angelo Colombo/Archivio White Star
Page 200 center AISA
Page 200 bottom Alamy Images
Page 201 David Samuel Robbins/Corbis/Contrasto
Page 202 Francesco Venturi/Corbis/Contrasto
Page 203 top AISA
Page 203 center Alamy Images
Page 203 bottom David Samuel Robbins/Corbis/Contrasto
Pages 204-205 Jeremy Horner/Corbis/Contrasto
Page 206 left Marcello Bertinetti/Archivio White Star
Page 206 right Marcello Bertinetti/Archivio White Star
Pages 206-207 Brian A. Vikander/Corbis/Contrasto
Page 208 left Marcello Bertinetti/Archivio White Star
Page 208 right Marcello Bertinetti/Archivio White Star
Pages 208-209 Marcello Bertinetti/Archivio White Star
Page 209 top Marcello Bertinetti/Archivio White Star

Page 209 bottom Marcello Bertinetti/Archivio White Star
Page 210 top left Marcello Bertinetti/Archivio White Star
Page 210 top center Marcello Bertinetti/Archivio White Star
Page 210 top right Angelo Colombo/Archivio White Star
Page 210 bottom AISA
Pages 210-211 AISA
Page 211 Michael S. Yamashita/Corbis/Contrasto
Page 212 Roger Wood/Corbis/Contrasto
Page 213 top left Angelo Colombo/Archivio White Star
Page 213 top right AISA
Page 213 center Corbis/Contrasto
Page 213 bottom Charles et Josette Lenars/Corbis/Contrasto
Page 214 top Roger Wood/Corbis/Contrasto
Page 214 bottom Arthur Thévenart/Corbis/Contrasto
Pages 214-215 Arthur Thévenart/Corbis/Contrasto
Page 215 Arthur Thévenart/Corbis/Contrasto
Page 216 Corbis/Contrasto
Page 217 top Corbis/Contrasto
Page 217 bottom Corbis/Contrasto
Page 218 Massimo Borchi/Archivio White Star
Pages 218-219 Galen Rowell/Corbis/Contrasto
Page 219 top left Angelo Colombo/Archivio White Star
Page 219 top right Massimo Borchi/Archivio White Star
Page 219 bottom Yann Arthus-Bertrand/Corbis/Contrasto
Page 220 top Elio Ciol/Corbis/Contrasto
Page 220 bottom Massimo Borchi/Archivio White Star
Pages 220-221 Robert Holmes/Corbis/Contrasto
Page 221 left Massimo Borchi/Archivio White Star
Page 221 right Massimo Borchi/Archivio White Star
Page 222 top Massimo Borchi/Archivio White Star
Page 222 center Massimo Borchi/Archivio White Star
Page 222 bottom Massimo Borchi/Archivio White Star
Pages 222-223 Massimo Borchi/Archivio White Star
Page 223 Massimo Borchi/Archivio White Star
Page 224 top left Livio Bourbon/Archivio White Star
Page 224 top right Angelo Colombo/Archivio White Star
Page 224 bottom Marcello Bertinetti/Archivio White Star
Pages 224-225 John Everingham/Art Asia Press
Page 225 left Corbis/Contrasto
Page 225 right Alamy Images
Page 226 Livio Bourbon/Archivio White Star
Page 227 left Alamy Images
Page 227 right Tiziana e Gianni Baldizzone/Corbis/Contrasto
Page 228 top Marcello Bertinetti/Archivio White Star
Page 228 center Robert Holmes/Corbis/Contrasto
Page 228 bottom Livio Bourbon/Archivio White Star
Page 229 AISA
Page 230 Alamy Images
Page 231 top left Ian Lambot
Page 231 top right Angelo Colombo/Archivio White Star
Page 231 bottom Ian Lambot
Page 232 top left Dennis Gilbert by kind permission of the Renzo Piano Building Workshop
Page 232 top right Angelo Colombo/Archivio White Star
Page 232 center by kind permission of the Renzo Piano Building Workshop
Page 232 bottom Noriaki Okabe by kind permission of the Renzo Piano Building Workshop
Pages 232-233 Yoshio Hata by kind permission of the Renzo Piano Building Workshop
Page 233 center by kind permission of the Renzo Piano Building Workshop
Page 233 bottom left Dennis Gilbert /VIEW
Page 233 bottom right by kind permission of the Renzo Piano Building Workshop
Page 234 left Gianni Berengo Gardin by kind permission of the Renzo Piano Building Workshop

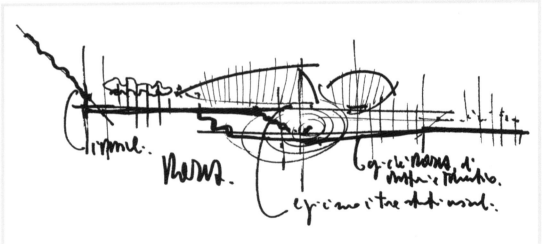

320 *Large sinuous 'shells' take shape in this sketch by Renzo Piano. For the ambitious project of the Music Park in Rome, the architect designed three independent pavilions based around musical instruments with the aim of creating suitably harmonic volumes inside a modern cathedral of music.*